THE FAILED PROMISE OF SENTENCING REFORM

THE FAILED PROMISE
OF SENTENCING
REFORM

MICHAEL O'HEAR

BLOOMSBURY ACADEMIC
NEW YORK • LONDON • OXFORD • NEW DELHI • SYDNEY

BLOOMSBURY ACADEMIC
Bloomsbury Publishing Inc
1385 Broadway, New York, NY 10018, USA
50 Bedford Square, London, WC1B 3DP, UK
29 Earlsfort Terrace, Dublin 2, Ireland

BLOOMSBURY, BLOOMSBURY ACADEMIC and the Diana logo
are trademarks of Bloomsbury Publishing Plc

First published in the United States of America by ABC-CLIO 2017
Paperback edition published by Bloomsbury Academic 2024

Cover photo: Incarceration. (Hélène Vallée/iStockphoto)
Cover design by Silverander Communications

Library of Congress Cataloging-in-Publication Data
Names: O'Hear, Michael, 1968– author.
Title: The failed promise of sentencing reform / Michael O'Hear.
Description: Santa Barbara, California: Praeger, 2017. |
Includes bibliographical references and index.
Identifiers: LCCN 2016050167 (print) | LCCN 2016050567 (ebook) |
ISBN 9781440840876 (hardcopy: alk. paper) | ISBN 9781440840883 (ebook)
Subjects: LCSH: Sentences (Criminal procedure)—United States. |
Law reform—United States.
Classification: LCC KF9685.O54 2017 (print) | LCC KF9685 (ebook) |
DDC 345.73/0772—dc23
LC record available at https://lccn.loc.gov/2016050167

ISBN: HB: 978-1-4408-4087-6
PB: 979-8-7651-2061-3
ePDF: 978-1-4408-4088-3
eBook: 979-8-2160-8290-3

To find out more about our authors and books visit www.bloomsbury.com
and sign up for our newsletters.

To my children, Lauren, Daniel, and Owen

Contents

Figures and Tables

Figures

Tables

Acknowledgments

This book would not have been possible without the generous support of Marquette Law School and its dean, Joseph Kearney. I am also grateful to James Ciment, Elisabeth Thompson, and Chad Oldfather for their helpful comments on earlier drafts, and to Carrie Kratochvil and Ben Hitchcock Cross for their help with the index. Finally, as always, I am deeply indebted to my wife, Jennifer Madden O'Hear, for her support and encouragement.

INTRODUCTION

An Era of Treading Water

Beginning in the early 1970s, the number of Americans behind bars grew with remarkable speed and consistency for about three decades—an unprecedented incarceration boom that put the U.S. imprisonment rate far above its historical norms. By the early 21st century, as indicated in Figure I.1, the imprisonment rate had quintupled from its previously stable, long-term level of about 100 prisoners per 100,000 residents.[1] By comparison to prior norms, the sharply elevated levels reached in the 1980s and 1990s pointed to a seemingly indiscriminate use of imprisonment that merited the label "mass incarceration."

The "boom" era, which might be roughly dated from 1973 to 2000, coincided with the widespread adoption of tough new sentencing laws. The Rockefeller Drug Laws in New York, passed in 1973 and prescribing a sentence of 15 years to life for various drug offenses, pointed the way to a quarter-century of mandatory minimums, "three strikes and you are out," "life means life," "truth in sentencing," and other enactments intended to put more offenders behind bars for longer periods of time. By and large, U.S. legislators seemed happy to encourage and support the national turn to mass incarceration.

Then, around the turn of the century, law-making trends underwent a surprising change. California's Proposition 36—adopted in 2000 and mandating treatment instead of incarceration for many drug offenders—makes for a stark contrast with the Rockefeller Laws and offers a neat symbolic start to the new era. A national economic

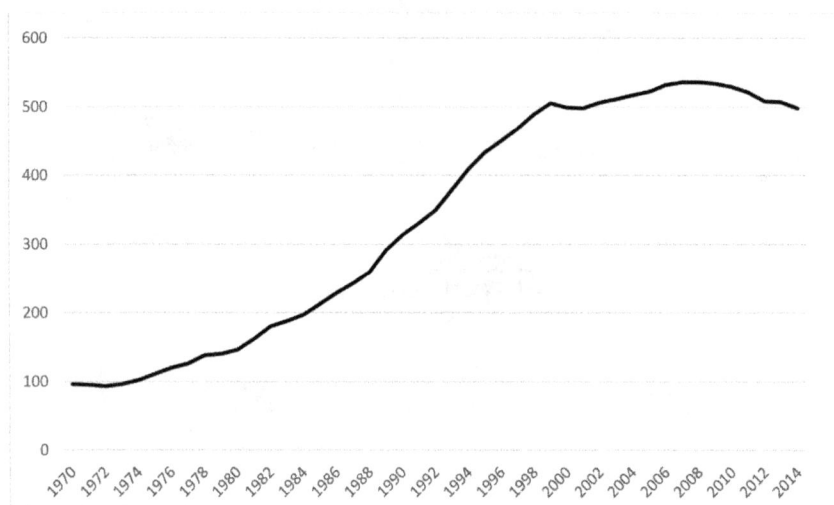

Figure I.1 American Imprisonment Rate, per 100,000 Residents, 1970–2014

recession the following year stressed state budgets and served as a wake-up call to legislators that perpetual growth in imprisonment—and hence in corrections spending—was unsustainable. By 2002, fiscal pressures had already led a handful of states to scale back mandatory minimums, which encouraged reformers across the country to press for additional measures to rein in or even reverse imprisonment growth.[2]

In the years since, state after state has adopted a dizzying array of reforms: repealing or softening minimum sentences, diverting drug-involved offenders from prison into treatment, liberalizing opportunities for parole release, creating more effective probation supervision to encourage sentencing judges to keep offenders in the community, granting early release to prisoners who were disabled or elderly, and on and on. Between 2000 and 2010 alone, at least 36 states adopted "back-end" sentencing reforms (that is, reforms providing prisoners with new opportunities for early release),[3] and a comparable number likely adopted reforms on the front end (that is, reforms affecting admissions to prison and the length of judge-imposed sentences). Further waves of reform have rolled across the national landscape since 2010 and remain very much in the news as I write this introduction in late 2016.[4]

Despite the extraordinary burst of reform activity—and the steady flow of critical commentary on mass incarceration from informed observers—remarkably little progress has been made in actually reducing the U.S. imprisonment rate. Beginning in 2000, there was a leveling off in the rate of growth, but growth did not really end until 2008. Even then, decarceration proceeded slowly. In 2014, the most recent year for which data are available, the imprisonment rate was only 7 percent below the 2008 peak, and essentially equal to what it had been at the start of the reform wave in 2000. For this reason, it seems appropriate to label the period since 2000—that is, the period following the imprisonment boom—as the treading water era. A great deal of effort has been going into reforms that are simply holding us in place. Mass incarceration is not getting worse, but it is not getting better, either.

Two additional considerations further demonstrate the fecklessness of reform in the new millennium. First, of the entire drop in imprisonment that has occurred in the United States since 2008, California alone accounts for more than 80 percent.[5] If California is taken out of the picture, then overall net decarceration in the United States has been almost nonexistent. And, as we will see in Chapter 7, California's decarceration resulted from a court order to address unconstitutional prison overcrowding. States not acting under such compulsion have demonstrated precious little ability to reduce imprisonment on their own.

Second, the treading water era has been one of persistently low crime rates, at least by comparison to late 20th-century norms. Figure I.2 provides a broad perspective on violent crime and imprisonment rates.[6] Violent crime has been falling sharply and consistently since 1992. Overall, violent crime has dropped more than 50 percent since its peak—a drop that dwarfs the paltry imprisonment decline. Even without any policy changes, such a big drop in violent crime should have yielded some significant decarceration; fewer criminals means fewer potential prisoners. The fact that imprisonment rates have instead basically remained constant since 2000, notwithstanding a big reduction in violent crime, indicates that reforms have had little on-the-ground impact in softening the tough-on-crime practices of the boom era.

This book is about sentencing reform in the treading water era, exploring what reforms were adopted and why they did not have more of an impact on the national imprisonment rate. As we will see, two common features of the 21st-century reforms have played particularly important roles in blunting their decarceration benefits. First, reforms have especially targeted nonviolent drug offenders for less punitive treatment. While there is no doubt that many such offenders received

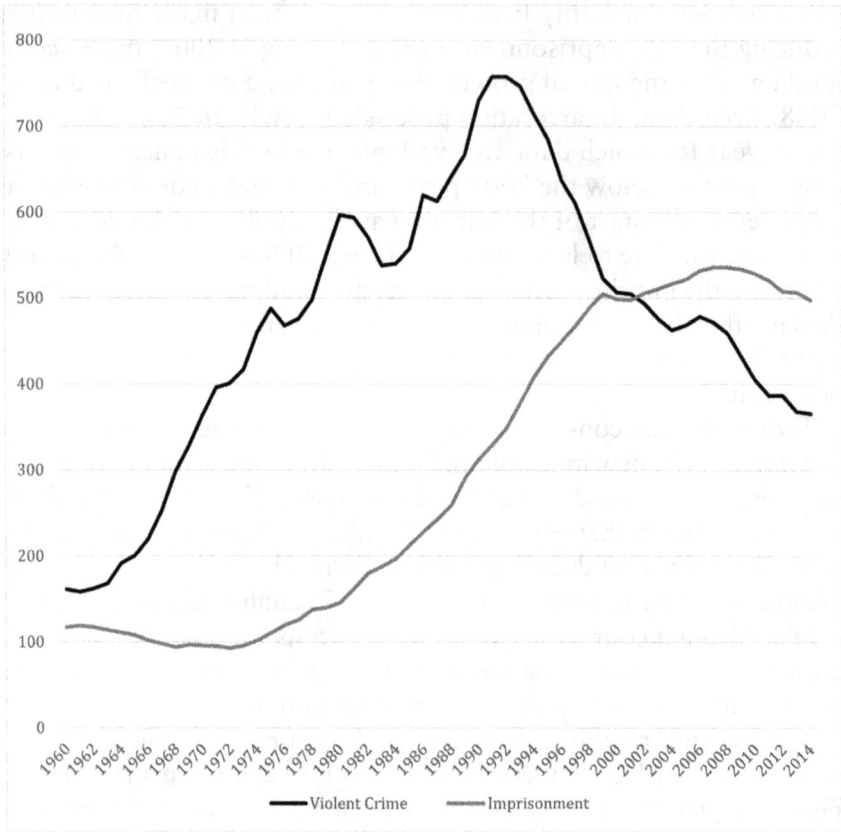

Figure I.2 Rates of Reported Violent Crime and Imprisonment, per 100,000 U.S. Residents, 1960–2014

excessive sentences during the boom era, these sentences were not actually a major driver of mass incarceration, so softening them now can only produce modest reductions in imprisonment. U.S. imprisonment rates will not return to anything close to their historic norms unless we also change how we deal with violent crime.

Second, reforms have relied on enhanced official discretion; that is, reforms have given judges, parole boards, and other criminal justice officials greater freedom to reduce prison terms or use alternatives to incarceration. For instance, as we have already noted, many legislatures adopted mandatory minimum sentences in the boom era; these laws took away the discretion of sentencing judges and required them to impose prison terms on certain groups of offenders. Since 2000, these mandatory minimums have been targeted by reformers, and

many of the tough-on-crime laws have indeed been softened or narrowed in a variety of ways, giving sentencing judges more freedom
to impose probationary sentences and keep offenders out of prison.
However, such reforms do not *require* judges to show greater lenience,
and often judges have continued to impose more or less the same sentences they had before reforms took effect. More generally, the problem with enhanced discretion—whether granted to judges,
corrections officials, or others—is that the underlying political dynamics that caused the imprisonment boom have in some important
respects remained unchanged, so politically accountable officials will
still tend to conform to the old tough-on-crime model even when they
have discretion to do otherwise.

The prevailing tone of this book is one of disappointment. My
view, to be clear, is that the United States can and should draw down
its imprisonment rate much more decisively than it has in the treading water era. Mass incarceration has imposed tremendous human
costs on offenders and their families, many of whom lived in circumstances of profound socioeconomic disadvantage even before their
run-ins with the law. There is little reason, moreover, to think that
public safety demands current levels of incarceration. To the contrary, there are quite good reasons to suppose that current imprisonment levels might be cut in half or more with little or no adverse
impact on crime rates. For instance, consider Figure I.2 again. No
consistent relationship is apparent between imprisonment and violent crime. In the 1960s, imprisonment remained constant, but violence rose sharply. Then, between the early 1970s and early 1990s,
imprisonment exploded, but violence did, too. In the mid- and late
1990s, imprisonment continued to grow rapidly, but violence now
dropped swiftly. Since 2000, imprisonment has once again basically
stabilized, but violence has continued to fall. On the whole, crime
seems to move independently of imprisonment, with changes driven
by distinct (and still mostly elusive) social dynamics. Indeed, as we
will see, in California and the few other states that managed to
achieve significant imprisonment reductions, crime rates fell right
along with imprisonment.[7]

Making the case against mass incarceration is not the principal purpose of this book—that case has already been made very effectively by
others[8]—but the reader may benefit at the outset by having some sense
of the key criticisms of current U.S. penal practices, which have, to
varying degrees, animated the post-2000 reform work that is this
book's subject. These criticisms include the following:

- Corrections spending has been one of the fastest growing components of state budgets since the 1970s, and now tops $50 billion annually.[9] These expenditures increase the pressure on budgets for education, health care, job training, substance abuse treatment, and other vital social services—budgets that have generally not kept pace with corrections spending. Spending on corrections at the local and federal government levels has also been rising rapidly and now exceeds $30 billion annually.
- Mass incarceration has been concentrated disproportionately in communities of color.[10] Blacks constitute about 38 percent of the nation's prison population, but only about 13 percent of the general population. Meanwhile, Hispanics constitute about 22 percent of the prison population, but only about 17 percent of the general population. Such disparities may exacerbate long-standing structural inequalities in U.S. society and contribute to distrust of legal institutions in minority communities.
- The U.S. incarceration rate far exceeds that of any other Western democracy.[11] It is more than four times higher than that of the United Kingdom, which itself has a relatively high incarceration rate by European standards. Indeed, the U.S. incarceration rate is about *ten times* higher than that of the Scandinavian countries. It is even nearly 50 percent higher than that of Russia—a nation that many Americans would consider to be a repressive police state.
- The deterrence and incapacitation benefits of long prison terms are much less than is commonly thought.[12] Research finds only modest deterrent effects from increased sentences, and suggests that the certainty of punishment may matter more than its severity if the goal is to scare potential offenders away from crime. Moreover, because of the natural tendency of most offenders to age out of their criminal behavior, little crime is avoided by continuing to hold offenders for decades after their convictions.
- The experience of imprisonment can cause short- and long-term damage to inmates in many respects, including their physical health, mental health, and employability.[13] In fact, the evidence suggests that imprisonment may *increase* the likelihood that some offenders will recidivate (that is, commit new crimes).[14] Imprisonment also imposes economic hardships on offenders' families, and increases the likelihood that their children will have behavioral problems.[15]

- Knowledge about what works in rehabilitative programming has advanced considerably since the beginning of the imprisonment boom in the 1970s; years of research have demonstrated the effectiveness of a variety of different interventions in reducing recidivism rates.[16] These successes suggest that many incarcerated offenders might be more effectively (and less expensively) managed through supervision and treatment in the community.

We will see many of these points recur in the narrative of later chapters.

Our story of the treading water era is organized as follows. Chapter 1 explores the causes of the imprisonment boom in more detail. Chapter 2 focuses on the War on Drugs and recent efforts to shift from enforcement-based to treatment-based responses to the nation's drug problems. This shift may be laudable in many respects, but, for reasons already suggested earlier, it has had only modest decarceration benefits.

Chapter 3 turns to back-end reforms, that is, the efforts to provide new opportunities for offenders to get out of prison early. While these opportunities have proliferated since 2000, they tend to be quite limited in their reach, either excluding most prisoners through unnecessarily restrictive eligibility criteria, or providing only small sentence reductions, or putting release decisions in the hands of highly risk-averse corrections officials.

Chapter 4 recounts the story of the Justice Reinvestment Initiative, a much-touted, federally supported reform effort that has led to notable legislative changes in about half of the states. These changes have brought greater effectiveness and efficiency to sentencing and corrections across the country, but they have not yet delivered on their initial promise to achieve large reductions in imprisonment and a reinvestment of the resulting savings into disadvantaged high-crime/high-incarceration neighborhoods. To the contrary, it seems that the justice reinvestment movement has been coopted by corrections officials and others to legitimize and preserve mass incarceration.

Chapter 5 shifts from state sentencing reform to federal. As state prison populations finally stabilized after 2000, the federal prison population continued its swift growth. Indeed, the federal prison system became the nation's largest during the treading water era. There was hope that reform would finally come to the federal system with President Barack Obama's election in 2008, but little changed during his first term in office. In his second term, President Obama tackled criminal justice reform more forcefully, and the federal prison population did begin to dip. However, few reforms have been embodied in legislation, and Obama's successor might easily reverse his administrative policies supporting decarceration.

Chapter 6 moves from legislative and administrative reform to judicial. In a much-heralded series of decisions beginning in 2000, the U.S. Supreme Court has become more active in the penal field. The Court's work effectively expanded the constitutional rights of defendants at sentencing. However, despite the controversial nature of the Court's decisions, their essentially cautious nature becomes clear upon closer inspection. Thus far, they have had little impact on the national mass incarceration problem.

The Supreme Court's most important decision was likely the 2011 ruling that required California to reduce the extraordinary overcrowding in its prisons. Chapter 7 discusses that case and the California story more broadly. In some respects, this story is the most hopeful in the book. California cut its prison population by a full quarter in just six years, and did so without experiencing any increase in violent crime. Yet, it is unclear whether anything like this could be achieved politically in other states not pressured into reform by the courts.

Finally, Chapter 8 synthesizes the lessons of the first seven chapters and suggests a path forward. The California experience highlights the sort of structural reforms that are probably necessary to achieve real decarceration in other states. Absent court orders to reduce imprisonment, though, such fundamental reforms are unlikely without changes in public beliefs and attitudes regarding crime and punishment. Among other things, reformers should move away from the cost–savings framework that has dominated recent debates about sentencing policy and emphasize the human dimension of mass incarceration. There are ethical, not merely economic, imperatives to end unnecessary imprisonment.

CHAPTER ONE

The Great U.S. Imprisonment
Boom, 1973–2000

To understand why recent reform efforts have not been more successful, we must first have a clear understanding of what drove
the great U.S. imprisonment boom. Reform efforts that do not target
the true causes of mass incarceration are unlikely to do much to draw
down the national imprisonment rate. Much discussion of the imprisonment boom in the academic literature centers on what we might call
"deep causes," that is, the long-term buildup of various social pressures
that created demands for more punitive crime policies. However, such
inchoate social demands had to be mediated through the institutions
that comprise the U.S. criminal justice system. These institutions include
the legislatures that create criminal laws, the police and prosecutors who
enforce the laws, the courts that interpret the laws and determine sentences, and the corrections officials who implement sentences. Changes in
the behavior of these institutions constitute *immediate* causes of the
imprisonment boom, and reform efforts will not be effective unless these
causes are also understood and addressed. In this chapter, we will first
consider immediate causes, and then work our way into the underlying
ideological premises of the institutional changes.

Crime and Imprisonment

Although the massive increase in the number of prisoners in the late
20th-century United States would seem strong evidence that the
nation's criminal justice institutions were behaving differently in
2000 than they had three decades earlier, we should pause to consider
another possibility—perhaps the boom in imprisonment was simply a
direct and inevitable result of a boom in crime. Imagine the criminal

justice system as a sort of industrial assembly line, with crime as the input and penal sanctions as the output. If inputs increase at a factory, we would naturally expect a corresponding increase in output; similarly, if serious crimes increase, there might be a corresponding increase in imprisonment but this would not necessarily indicate any real changes in the way the system was operating.

But though crime increases were surely an important immediate cause of the imprisonment boom, the crime–imprisonment relationship was far more complicated than my factory analogy suggests. As we saw in Figure I.2, reported violent crime in the United States did grow steadily in the years after 1961, eventually peaking in the early 1990s at a rate almost five times higher than it had been three decades earlier. However, the imprisonment boom did not begin until 1973—a full decade after the start of the crime wave. Why the delay? Why didn't the criminal justice factory just start churning out prisoners faster?

Upon reflection, it should be clear why imprisonment increases do not follow automatically from crime increases. At any given moment, a state has a particular, limited capacity to imprison. Most obviously, the state may be limited in its physical ability to house more prisoners, although this aspect of capacity may be more malleable than is commonly recognized. Single-bunk cells can be converted to doubles or triples, gyms and other common spaces can be converted to housing, and contracts can be entered into with private prisons. These were just a few of the strategies that were employed to accommodate growing numbers of prisoners without building new prisons.

Other capacity limits may be of even greater practical importance. There are only so many offenders that the police can investigate, prosecutors prosecute, and courts convict and sentence. If these law enforcement agencies are to keep up with increasing crime rates, they must be given assistance, which may come in one of two forms. First, they may be given larger budgets to permit the hiring of new personnel or the purchase of new, efficiency-enhancing technology. Second, laws may be changed in order to make it easier for these agencies to do their jobs. For instance, new laws that put more pressure on defendants to plea bargain may permit the courts to process many more cases in a given amount of time, and hence send many more defendants to prison.

Large-scale increases in imprisonment thus require certain policy choices; they do not simply happen as a matter of course when crimes increase. Indeed, increases in imprisonment can happen even without a rise in crime. Crime increases are neither a *sufficient* nor a *necessary* condition for imprisonment increases. As Figure I.2 indicates, violent crime in the United States dropped sharply and consistently for 20 years after the early 1990s, yet imprisonment continued to climb through most of that time period.

All of this demonstrates the importance of *policy* in driving imprisonment rates. While elevated levels of violent crime—levels that remain above pre-1970 norms to this day—have surely played a role in the imprisonment boom, it is just as clear that the system has changed in some fundamental ways, growing steadily tougher through a series of policy choices.

Toughness and Imprisonment

Criminal justice policies may be explicit or implicit. Explicit policies, as in a law adopted by the legislature, establish the framework within which criminal justice actors—police officers, prosecutors, judges, corrections officials, and others—do their jobs. These actors, in turn, establish implicit policies through their exercises of discretion on a case-by-case basis. Implicit policies, which may or may not reflect fully deliberate choices by the actors, become evident over time through a pattern of case outcomes.

For instance, the legislature might adopt an explicit policy that the sentence for armed robbery should be imprisonment for any period of time up to 10 years, which leaves judges with considerable discretion to determine actual punishment levels. Although we cannot expect absolute consistency in the exercise of this discretion, patterns inevitably emerge. For instance, the average sentence for first-time armed robbers might be two years, while the average sentence for repeat offenders might be eight years. Such a pattern would reflect an implicit policy choice to treat repetition of the crime as a highly aggravating sentencing factor.

Much writing on the imprisonment boom emphasizes the importance of explicit policy changes as drivers of increased toughness, especially new sentencing policies that reduced the discretion of sentencing judges and parole boards. However, implicit policy changes likely played a role that was at least as important.

Explicit Policy Change: Mandatory Sentencing Laws

In the early 1970s, on the eve of the imprisonment boom, broad official discretion was a pervasive feature of the U.S. criminal justice system. The police officer had discretion to arrest, the prosecutor to charge and plea bargain, the judge to select a sentence, and the parole board to set a release date. Against this historical backdrop, a striking theme in much of the nation's sentencing legislation from 1973 to 2000 was the constriction or elimination of discretion, particularly that of the sentencing judge and the parole board.

Adopted in 1973, New York's Rockefeller Drug Laws are often seen as the symbolic start of the tough-on-crime era. The legislation featured, among other provisions, a mandatory minimum 15-year prison term for distributing even small quantities (two ounces or more) of narcotics.[1] When sentencing an individual convicted of such an offense, the judge had no option to impose a lesser penalty, no matter how sympathetic the offender's circumstances or how unlikely he was to reoffend. Likewise, the parole board had no discretion to release the offender before the 15-year mark, no matter how well the offender was doing in prison or how clearly she had been rehabilitated. Other states soon followed suit with their own quantity-based drug minimums. The toughest of these was Michigan's so-called 650-Lifer law, which imposed a mandatory sentence of life without the possibility of parole (LWOP) for possession of 650 grams or more of heroin or cocaine (about 23 ounces).[2]

After 1973, the nation experienced recurrent waves of new mandatory minimums, with state after state jumping on the bandwagon for whatever happened to be the latest tough-on-crime fad. Mandatory prison terms were established for use of a firearm in the commission of serious felonies,[3] perpetration of a drug offense in a school zone,[4] repetition of violent or sexual offenses,[5] assaults in detention facilities,[6] and many other offenses.

The late 20th-century mania for mandatory minimums reached its climax in the "three strikes and you are out" laws of the 1990s. The state of Washington launched the fad when it adopted the nation's first three-strikes law through a ballot initiative in November 1993. Although many states already had habitual-felon laws on the books at that time, these laws "were not widely used, nor were they an important issue in the modern politics of law and order."[7] Washington's three-strikes law was the first to employ the baseball metaphor and to demonstrate the concept's extraordinary popular appeal; the initiative passed by a three-to-one margin.[8] This success unleashed a torrent of copycat laws, with 24 other states adopting their own three-strikes laws within three years.[9]

California's three-strikes law—the nation's most notorious—was adopted just months after Washington's in 1994. California required a life sentence for the commission of *any* felony after two prior convictions for a serious crime. Judges had no explicit discretion to impose a lesser sentence, even if the third conviction seemed quite minor. In highly publicized examples of the law's excessiveness, life sentences were imposed for such trivialities as stealing a slice of pizza and shoplifting five videotapes. Although offenders serving time on three-strikes sentences were eligible for parole, they had to spend at least 20 years in prison before they could be considered for release. In all, more than 9,000 offenders have received life sentences under the law, more than 4,000 of them for nonviolent third offenses.[10]

Judicial sentencing discretion has also been reduced in many states through the adoption of "presumptive" sentencing guidelines. Such guidelines specify a relatively narrow sentencing range (say, two to three years behind bars) for a given crime committed by a defendant with a given criminal history; the judge must normally select a sentence from within the range unless the case has some unusual features that justify a "departure." Although guidelines have some superficial similarity to mandatory minimums, they can be distinguished from minimums in a number of respects: guidelines are typically developed by expert commissions, they are more nuanced and take more variables into account in determining sentences, and they offer more flexibility in exceptional cases for the sentencing judge to impose a penalty below the recommended minimum.

First implemented in 1987 and employed only in federal court, the federal sentencing guidelines are the best-known example of this approach. The guidelines were associated with a dramatic increase in sentence severity, with the average prison time for federal inmates more than doubling from 26 to 59 months by 1992.[11] Although the federal guidelines developed a reputation for excessive harshness, especially in drug cases, state-level guidelines have generally been more moderate. Indeed, holding a number of other variables constant, states with guidelines have actually experienced a lower rate of imprisonment growth on average than states without guidelines.[12] Contrary to popular perceptions, restricting judicial discretion in this way does not *necessarily* lead to tougher sentences; it all depends on how exactly the restriction is designed and implemented.

State legislation has also targeted other forms of official discretion during the imprisonment boom, most notably the power of parole boards to release prisoners early. Parole-eligible sentences are often referred to as "indeterminate" sentences because one cannot know, at the time of imposition, exactly how long the offender will serve behind bars. Maine became the first modern "determinate" sentencing state in 1975 by abolishing discretionary parole.[13] Seven other states plus the federal government followed suit over the next 15 years.[14] By then, restrictions on parole had been rebranded as "truth in sentencing" (TIS). The 1990s witnessed an extraordinary flowering of TIS laws across the United States. By 2000, the number of parole-abolition states had grown to 15, with 20 additional states otherwise moving to reduce parole eligibility for at least some classes of offenders.

In the broader movement against parole discretion, perhaps the most dramatic development was the national embrace of the LWOP sentence. In 1970, only seven states authorized LWOP; since then, every state but Alaska has jumped on the LWOP bandwagon.[15] In 27 states, LWOP *must* be imposed as a mandatory minimum for conviction of some crimes.[16] Most of these states reserve mandatory LWOP for homicide, but many have also required LWOP for lesser offenses; recall, for instance, the Michigan 650-Lifer law for drug crimes. Reflecting these legal developments, the number of LWOP prisoners in the United States has grown sharply, quadrupling between 1992 and 2012, to nearly 50,000.[17] Although the number of new LWOP sentences each year tends to be small, they can have a large long-term effect on imprisonment since, once in, the LWOP prisoners will never leave. In Pennsylvania, for instance, LWOP now accounts for about 10 percent of the state's total prison population.

Implicit Policy Change: Tougher Exercises of Discretion

But are legislative restrictions on discretion the *dominant* driver of the imprisonment boom? That is certainly the common perception. Consider, for instance, a 2013 article on California's three-strikes law in *Rolling Stone* magazine.[18] The author, Matt Taibbi, opined, "This gets to the heart of what went wrong in America in the years following the mandatory-sentencing and Three Strikes crazes. We removed the human element from the justice process and turned our courts into giant, unthinking machines for sweeping our problem citizens under a rug. And it isn't just in California, but all over the country, where there are countless instances of outrageous and brutal mandatory sentences for relatively minor crimes."

Such assessments, however, overstate the importance of explicit policy changes, while missing the critical role of shifts in implicit policy (that is, general tendencies in the exercise of official discretion). There are good reasons to think that the U.S. criminal justice system would still have grown a lot tougher, and imprisonment still reached unprecedented highs, even without the widespread adoption of mandatory minimums, sentencing guidelines, TIS, and LWOP.

Consider mandatory minimums. Despite all of the media attention they receive, long mandatory minimums are not the norm in U.S. sentencing. California's infamous three-strikes law turned out to be the exception, not the rule. While two dozen other states adopted three strikes, no other state's version of the law had anything even close to the impact of California's. Designed in much more carefully targeted ways, the other three-strikes laws applied to many fewer cases. In the first few years following the three-strikes wave, only five of the laws had been applied more than 100 times, and only two (including California's) more than 300 times.[19] In some states that adopted three strikes, the numbers were almost laughably small, given all of the media hype surrounding the law —Alaska had just one three-striker; Colorado, two; Connecticut, one; Montana, zero; New Mexico, one; Pennsylvania, three; Utah, zero; Virginia, zero; and Wisconsin, three. Overall, based on data through 2005 and controlling for a variety of political, legal, and demographic variables, there is not a statistically significant relationship between a state's adoption of three strikes and the size of its prison population.[20]

To be sure, *some* mandatory minimums have had a sizable impact in *some* jurisdictions. There is the California three-strikes law, for instance. New York's drug minimums also played a prominent role in fueling imprisonment growth in that state. By 1997, New York prisons held nearly 9,000 inmates sentenced under the Rockefeller Drug Laws, which amounted to about 13 percent of the state's total prison population.[21] However, only a few hundred were serving the 15-to-life minimum that was the most notorious feature of the 1973 reforms.[22] Similarly, only 220 prisoners were serving LWOP sentences under Michigan's 650-Lifer law in 1998, when the law was substantially softened.[23] The federal system has likely been the nation's most aggressive in adopting long mandatory minimums, but even in that system, minimums are hardly the norm. In 2010, for instance, fewer than 15 percent of all federal offenders were subject to a mandatory minimum at sentencing.[24]

If mandatory minimums have had only a modest direct impact on national imprisonment growth, what about the other discretion-reducing innovations of the late 20th century? We have already seen that sentencing guidelines, if anything, may tend to *restrain* imprisonment growth. TIS, by contrast, typically does seem to contribute to increased imprisonment, but the effect does not seem consistently large.[25] Indeed, many states that abolished parole in the late 20th century experienced *below*-average imprisonment growth.[26] Conversely, eight of the ten states with the highest imprisonment rates in the nation retain discretionary parole release. Clearly, the mere existence of the possibility of parole in a state does not guarantee that the state will show restraint in its use of incarceration; everything depends on how generously parole discretion is exercised in practice.

As for the life without parole sentence, while the nation's number of LWOP inmates has grown quickly in recent years, it remains a small proportion—just a fraction of 1 percent—of the nation's overall prison population. Indeed, the number of inmates serving life *with* parole is more than double the number without.[27] While LWOP accounts for a sizable percentage of the prisoner population in some states, the numbers remain almost trivially small in others. Just five states (California, Florida, Louisiana, Michigan, and Pennsylvania) are home to nearly 60 percent of the nation's LWOP population.

Thus, while a state's explicit sentencing policies—like its crime rate —do matter in determining the size of the state's prison population, these are not the only things that matter. Consider this: since 1973, states have varied widely in what explicit policy changes they have adopted and when. Many passed three strikes, but about half did not. Many adopted drug minimums, but they did not follow any standard pattern in doing so; Michigan's 650-Lifer law always remained an outlier. About half adopted sentencing guidelines, but these differed considerably in their specifics, and many were abandoned within a few years. States adopted TIS laws in two distinct waves, with some states entirely eliminating parole and others retaining it in some more limited form. Nearly all of the states adopted LWOP, but they are divided over critical questions like whether LWOP should be limited to homicide offenses and whether LWOP should ever be mandatory. Yet, despite this notable diversity in sentencing laws, *all* states experienced sharp, consistent increases in imprisonment through most or all of the 1973–2000 time period. This fact alone is strongly suggestive of the influence of other factors besides explicit policy changes.

My own state of Wisconsin provides an illustration. Wisconsin's judges and parole officials retained their traditional discretion with few meaningful limitations through almost the entirety of the imprisonment boom. Mandatory minimums, like the state's three-strikes law, were narrowly targeted and infrequently applied. The most practically significant minimums were probably in the drug area, but Wisconsin's drug minimums were far less severe than those of New York or Michigan, topping out at 10 years for the highest volume distribution offenses. The 10-year minimum, moreover, was seldom applied in practice. For instance, one study found only 11 cases subject to the minimum over a two-and-a-half-year period in the early 1990s.[28] The most commonly applied minimum by far was merely a one-year term. Moreover, Wisconsin provided an unusually liberal "safety valve," permitting judges to disregard any of the drug minimums "in the best interests of the community"—a flexible power that judges frequently used in practice.

Wisconsin's parole commission did nearly as well as the judiciary in preserving its discretion. Wisconsin was one of the last states to adopt a TIS law, which did not start to affect prison terms in a significant way until after 2000, when the state's prison population was already essentially at its peak.

Discretion-reducing laws, in short, did very little to contribute to Wisconsin's imprisonment boom—and yet the Badger State experienced a sharper run-up in its prison population than the nation as a whole. So what caused the boom? The evidence points to *implicit* policy choices—to the increasingly tough ways in which officials were exercising the abundant discretion they retained.

In Wisconsin and elsewhere, there are five key discretionary actors in the system. First, the police determine who gets arrested and fed into the criminal justice system at the front end. Second, prosecutors determine which of the arrestees will get charged. Prosecutors also decide how serious the charges will be, what will be offered to the defendant in plea bargaining, and what sentence will be requested after conviction. Third, judges determine the sentence, which includes both *dispositional* (prison or probation) and *durational* (length of term) elements. Fourth, if the defendant is sent to prison, a parole board will often have discretion to determine the actual release date. Fifth, and finally, community corrections officials (probation and parole agents and their supervisors) will monitor the compliance of offenders with the conditions of their release. If an offender violates a condition of probation or parole, corrections officials typically have broad discretion to initiate revocation proceedings, which may lead to the imposition of a prison term.

The economist and law professor John Pfaff has attempted to determine more precisely how the system grew tougher in the mass-incarceration era.[29] He finds little evidence of longer average sentences. The real driver of imprisonment growth has been increased admissions to prison, not increased lengths of stay. What could cause such a massive increase in the number of individuals sent to prison? Pfaff's research, focusing particularly on the latter years of the imprisonment boom, highlights the prosecutorial role. He finds dramatic growth in felony filings in the United States after 1994 *even as arrests were falling*. In other words, police were sending *fewer* offenders to prosecutors, but prosecutors were feeding *more* offenders into the court system. This is powerful evidence that prosecutors were exercising their charging discretion in tougher ways in the mid- and late 1990s. Indeed, the rate of growth in felony filings corresponds almost exactly with the rate of growth in prison admissions, which suggests that the implicit policy choices of prosecutors may have been the leading driver of imprisonment growth in the final years of the boom.

Pfaff's research might seem to absolve legislators and their sentencing policy choices from any responsibility. However, there are at least two ways in which explicit policy choices likely contributed *indirectly* to greater prosecutorial toughness. First, tough mandatory sentencing laws significantly increase the prosecutor's leverage in plea bargaining. For instance, by manipulating the charges in a case, the prosecutor may be able to ensure that a defendant is protected from a minimum. (Usually, a minimum is only truly mandatory for the sentencing judge if the prosecutor chooses to pursue it.) By offering to take a minimum off the table, the prosecutor can often induce the defendant to take a plea deal even when the defendant has a viable defense and a real possibility of winning at trial. Trials are inherently unpredictable, and no defense lawyer can ever guarantee success—it is always a "roll of the dice." When taking this chance may result in the application of a long mandatory sentence, the defendant may find the prosecutor's offer of a minimum-free sentence to be irresistible. Such dynamics enhance prosecutorial efficiency—guilty-plea cases are much quicker and easier than trial cases—and make it feasible for prosecutors to initiate many more felony cases than otherwise would have been possible. Thus, absent the tougher sentencing laws of the late 20th century, prosecutors probably would not have been able to achieve the big increase in felony case filings that occurred in the 1990s.

Second, the much-hyped adoption of mandatory minimums, LWOP, three strikes, TIS, and so forth contributed to the tough-on-crime political zeitgeist of the imprisonment-boom era. Elected prosecutors were surely influenced by the way that the new sentencing laws demonstrated the political appeal of increasingly punitive responses to crime. Indeed, tough-on-crime legislative initiatives were not merely evidence of the public's punitive preferences, but may actually have partially caused or strengthened those public preferences. Through campaign ads, committee hearings, press events, and so forth, legislators are able to draw public attention to the threat posed by crime and to validate the knee-jerk, punitive emotional responses most people have when they hear of the victimization of innocent fellow citizens. Criminologist and law professor Michael Tonry summarizes the social science research this way:

> [P]ublic opinion findings showing that Americans regard crime or drugs as the nation's most pressing problem typically follow, not precede, media and political concentration on crime. Politicians who attempt to win favor by demonstrating their toughness nearly always say that they are honoring citizens' wishes. The evidence shows, however, that emphasis by politicians and the media on crime issues is what causes public anxiety to increase.[30]

This is not to say that public fear of crime lacked any rational basis; indeed, as we saw in Figure I.2, crime rates were relatively high throughout the era of the imprisonment boom. However, politicians were able to influence perceptions of how urgent the crime problem was compared to other threats to public safety and well-being, and to frame the policy responses that would dominate the public conversation. When increased imprisonment emerged as the leading policy response in the political sphere, electorally accountable prosecutors would have strong incentives to follow suit with more aggressive charging.

If Pfaff's data do not let legislators entirely off the hook, nor do they necessarily excuse judges and corrections officials from responsibility for the imprisonment boom, even during the final phase that is the focus of Pfaff's analysis. Although the average length of stay in prison may not have increased much in the 1990s, the context was such that even a standstill in the overall prison-term average could indicate real increases in the severity of the sentences being imposed for particular types of offenses. Recall that prosecutors were filing more felony charges even as crime and arrest rates were falling. These contrary trends strongly suggest that prosecutors were feeding more marginal cases into the felony system—cases in which the seriousness of the offense, or the dangerousness of the offender, was less clear. If judges and corrections officials were doing their jobs the same way as they had been before the 1990s, we would expect a *reduction* in length of stay as less serious cases flooded the system. Instead, length of stay remained relatively constant, suggesting that increased severity, at least with respect to some classes of cases, helped to boost the average.

Consider a comparison of two offenses, murder and assault. As a practical matter, murder is a low-discretion offense for police and prosecutors. Public attention is focused on this most serious of all crimes, and police and prosecutors are highly unlikely to ignore or undercharge an apparent murder except in very unusual circumstances. Happily, the number of murders dropped in the United States in the final years of the 20th century. Thus, in the nation's 75 largest urban counties, for which we have more complete court-processing data than are available for the nation as a whole, there was a 16 percent reduction in murder arrests between 1990 and 2000.[31] However, average sentence lengths for murder increased considerably over the decade, rising from 233 months in 1990 to 282 months in 2000. It seems unlikely that this change resulted from some general increase in the heinousness of murders, or of the dangerousness of murderers, in 2000.[32] Instead, through some combination of explicit and implicit policy choices, it appears that the system was handling murderers in a tougher way by the end of the boom era.

The crime of assault encompasses a much wider range of conduct than murder—everything from a slap or shove up to a nonfatal shooting. Assaults are far more common than murders and receive far less public attention, which effectively gives police and prosecutors more discretion in their arrest and charging decisions. A given barroom fight, for instance, might plausibly be charged as assault, aggravated assault, or disorderly conduct, or perhaps not charged at all. As with murder, the number of felony defendants *arrested* for assault in the 75 large counties *dropped* between 1990 and 2000, but, unlike with murder, the number of defendants *convicted* of felony assault *rose*. These trends are consistent with the hypothesis of more aggressive prosecution of marginal cases in the 1990s. So, too, is a reduction in sentence severity, with the average prison term dropping slightly from 80 months to 77 months.

Limitations in the data make it hard to draw firm conclusions about changes in average case severity over time, but the murder–assault comparison is at least suggestive that we should not make too much of consistency in overall average sentence lengths. As the averages are calculated, low sentences in the marginal assault cases—the ones that prosecutors might not have bothered with in 1990—may be masking sizable increases in sentences for murder and more serious assaults. To some extent, such increases would likely reflect greater severity on the part of sentencing judges.

Nor should we be the least bit surprised to learn that judges (and, for that matter, corrections officials) exercised their discretion in tougher ways during the imprisonment boom. After all, they were hardly immune from the same political dynamics that drove legislators to adopt mandatory minimums and prosecutors to charge more aggressively. U.S. state-court judges, like U.S. district attorneys, are normally elected, and therefore face much the same political pressures to appear tough on crime. Meanwhile, although corrections officials —parole board members, probation agents, and so forth—may not be elected themselves, they operate within government bureaucracies that are subject to political oversight and control. In this setting, per- ceived lenience—especially if it results in a high-profile crime commit- ted by an offender on parole or probation—can be just as much a career-killer for a corrections official as it can be for an elected judge or prosecutor.

The Premises of Tough-on-Crime Politics

Tough-on-crime political pressures drove increased penal severity in the United States through both explicit and implicit policy choices made by many actors throughout the criminal justice system. The political dynamics underlying the imprisonment boom reflected a widely shared set of beliefs about crime and its control.

The infamous Willie Horton ad offers a paradigmatic illustration of the logic of the late 20th-century tough-on-crime politics. The ad played a prominent role in George H. W. Bush's come-from-behind victory over Massachusetts governor Michael Dukakis in the 1988 presidential election. In the spring of that year, polls showed that Democrat Dukakis had a wide lead over Republican Bush, but, by midsummer, the Bush campaign and supporting groups were working hard to link Dukakis in the public mind to the Massachusetts prison furlough program. This program, which predated Dukakis's tenure as governor, granted short leaves for prisoners to spend time at home, an opportunity that was thought to help ease their path to eventual full-time reintegration into society. Although the vast majority of fur- loughs were completed successfully, there had been one catastrophic failure, that of an offender named Willie Horton.[33] As Republicans brought more attention to Horton, Dukakis's poll numbers fell. The governor's negative ratings nearly tripled between July and September, and surveys indicated that the furlough issue was the primary reason.[34]

Republican efforts to tie Dukakis to Horton reached their climax with "the ad," which ran on television in September. Funded and produced by a political action committee that was formally independent of the Bush campaign, the ad began with side-by-side images of the two candidates.[35] An announcer intoned, "Bush and Dukakis on crime. Bush supports the death penalty for first-degree murderers. Dukakis not only opposes the death penalty, he allowed first-degree murderers to have weekend passes from prison." Horton's mug shot then appeared on the screen. The announcer continued, "One was Willie Horton, who murdered a boy in a robbery, stabbing him nineteen times." An arrest photo flashed on the screen. "Despite a life sentence, Horton received ten weekend passes from prison. Horton fled, kidnapping a young couple, stabbing the man and repeatedly raping his girlfriend." Back to an image of Dukakis. "Weekend prison passes. Dukakis on crime."

From the time it first ran, the Horton ad drew sharp criticism, particularly for its racially inflammatory subtext—Horton was black and the "young couple" white. Yet, Bush's convincing victory in November seemed to validate the ad's effectiveness and confirm the emerging consensus that tough-on-crime had become a necessary survival strategy for politicians.

The ad's unstated premises merit close attention. First, the ad presupposes that the nation's crime policy problem can be reduced to the threat posed by a very particular category of crime: violent and/or sexual offenses perpetrated by a predatory stranger—a stranger who has committed such offenses in the past and who will continue to do so until forcibly stopped. Because fear of stranger assault and rape is so heavily inculcated by media and popular culture, we may not immediately appreciate how much is marginalized when the central challenge of crime policy is framed in these terms—white-collar crime, domestic violence, intoxicated driving, and child neglect, to name just a few examples. These and many other crimes are far more common than Willie Horton's, but effective responses to them are implicitly viewed as a matter of secondary importance at most.

If violent assaults are the paradigmatic crime in the world of the Willie Horton ad, then the paradigmatic criminal is the depraved brute—an offender beyond hope of rehabilitation, controllable only through force. The Willie Horton mug shot—the ad's visual centerpiece—drives the point home. Many commentators have noted how frightening Horton appears in the mug shot. Indeed, that was the very reason it was used. Larry McCarthy, the ad's producer, has recalled, "This guy looked like an animal. . . . [A]s an advertising guy, I should have been shot if I didn't use Horton's picture because the picture says it all. It says this is a bad guy and Dukakis let him out."[36] Even Horton himself agrees that he "looked like a zombie. . . . They chose the perfect picture for the ads. I looked incredibly wicked."[37]

Given the ad's characterization of the crime problem, the preferred solution seemed to follow in an intuitive fashion: simple incapacitation—that is, total physical control of the offender. The ad favorably highlighted candidate Bush's support of the death penalty, which is, of course, the ultimate form of incapacitation. If imprisonment is to be used instead, the ad seemed to say, then it must be rigorously maintained. Tied to Massachusetts's furlough program, candidate Dukakis was implicitly faulted for his lack of commitment to tough incapacitation.

And "fault" does seem the right word. The ad embraced a certain moral perspective in which the government official who might have stopped a crime becomes complicit in that crime. After all, the whole point of the ad was to hold Dukakis politically accountable for the misdeeds of Willie Horton, a man he had never met. The ad made no real effort to show that Bush's crime policies were more effective than Dukakis's. Instead, the ad was about emotion and blame. The frightening message for governors, legislators, prosecutors, judges, and corrections officials was that they, too, might be publicly shamed and perhaps lose their jobs over a random, outrageous act of violence.

How could that message not affect the way they made policy and exercised discretion? Wisconsin's parole chair in the 1990s, a thoughtful corrections official named John Husz, has described to me how he would scan the newspaper with trepidation every morning to check whether any of his parolees had committed a serious crime.[38] Eventually, he was driven from office, and his replacement predictably took a much more restrictive approach to granting parole. There are likely hundreds, perhaps thousands, of similar stories about the political costs of perceived lenience in the 1980s and 1990s that could be told.

From a policy standpoint, it is easy to dismiss the Horton ad, and the broader political trends that it exemplified, as simply irrational. How could any sensible person favor making policy by anecdote instead of by data? Prior to the Horton ad, furlough programs were in widespread use in the United States and generally well regarded by corrections experts. As terrible as Horton's crimes were, they were also highly unusual. And, of course, the death penalty also sometimes misfires, resulting in the execution of the wrongfully convicted. If we must pick between furloughs and the death penalty, how can we choose without a systematic comparison of the concrete results of each policy?

To view the Horton ad through this lens is to miss its real significance. The ad was not about the instrumental effectiveness of competing crime policies, but about their symbolic character. Policy makers and criminal justice officials must continuously choose between "them" and "us," the ad seems to say—between depraved, brutish predators and the innocent, vulnerable public. At bottom, the shaming of Michael Dukakis, John Husz, and so many other official victims of tough-on-crime politics was not because their policies did not "work," but because their policies were seen as a symbolic betrayal of the public they were supposed to represent: if you are not for us, then you are against us.

It is not entirely clear, one might add, that crime policy *should* be viewed in instrumental instead of symbolic terms. It is notoriously difficult to measure the concrete effects of competing policies. For instance, one of the most intensely researched questions in the field is whether the death penalty deters; yet, despite decades of data collection and analysis, sophisticated scholars still come to different conclusions.[39] Perhaps it is more sensible to think in terms of "doing justice," that is, treating offenders in ways that embody and express prevailing social views of right and wrong without regard to future crime-prevention effects.

However, even granting that moral-symbolic considerations must inevitably play a role in the making of crime policy, one need not necessarily accept the particular morality embodied by the Willie Horton ad, with its strict Manichean dualism of good guys and bad guys. A quite different perspective was embodied, for instance, in the famous 1967 report of President Lyndon Johnson's crime commission, *The Challenge of Crime in a Free Society.* Where the Horton ad reduced the fundamental nature of the crime problem to violent and sexual crime perpetrated by irredeemable predators, Johnson's commission depicted crime as varied and complex, including white-collar and many other types of nonviolent offenses, with root causes lying in several broad sociological phenomena, including the breakdown of parental authority, the swelling tide of baby boomers reaching their peak crime-committing years (teens and twenties), racial discrimination, and the concentration of poverty in urban slums.[40] The commission maintained that many criminals could be rehabilitated, and urged the development of more effective alternatives to criminal sanctions.[41] Where the Horton ad placed moral responsibility for crime squarely at the feet of the offender and the criminal justice system, Johnson's commission noted other sorts of causes, including provocation or carelessness by victims in some cases, the failure of citizens to report crime, and an "anything goes" attitude in U.S. culture toward making money.[42] The commission emphasized a broadly shared social responsibility to respond to crime and to address the underlying conditions that cause crime. The criminal justice system, the commission asserted in a striking passage,

> needs help. Warring on poverty, inadequate housing and unemployment, is warring on crime. A civil rights law is a law against crime. Money for schools is money against crime. Medical, psychiatric, and family-counseling services are services against crime. More broadly and most importantly, every effort to improve life in America's "inner cities" is an effort against crime. A community's most enduring protection against crime is to right the wrongs and cure the illnesses that tempt men to harm their neighbors.[43]

Clearly, the Johnson commission and the Horton ad inhabited two very different moral universes. In the one, the criminal is an outsider, an enemy whose well-being does not matter. Stopping crime is narrowly the responsibility of the criminal justice system, and tough physical control is the preferred strategy for carrying out that responsibility. In the other, the criminal is not so fundamentally different from others in society, but is largely a product of potentially changeable social conditions. Moreover, preventing crime is not just a matter for the criminal justice system alone, but is a matter of shared responsibility, with the preferred strategies including both services and support for offenders and a more broadly targeted antipoverty program.

In retrospect, *The Challenge of Crime in a Free Society* seems the last gasp of a progressive tradition that dominated U.S. criminal justice policy in the middle decades of the 20th century. The shift from this progressive tradition to the stark us-versus-them mentality of the Horton ad created a world in which it no longer seemed legitimate to take a chance on offenders; criminal justice officials would do so at their own risk. This was because (1) limitations on the offender's liberty were no longer seen as regrettable impositions on a fellow citizen that should be minimized, but as affirmatively desirable punishments that appropriately marked the offender as an outsider; and (2) the criminal justice official was no longer seen as sharing responsibility for the offender's avoidance of future crime with family, neighborhood, church, school, and other social service agencies—a shift that left the criminal justice official standing alone in the crosshairs of political condemnation if something went wrong.

There are many different theories as to why the politics of crime and punishment changed so much between the 1960s and the 1980s. To some extent, it was probably inevitable that the long run-up in violent crime would create public frustration and heighten demand for new ways of thinking about crime policy. It is also almost certainly the case that race played a role. At a time when overt racism was becoming socially unacceptable in the United States, support for harsher crime policies became a way of expressing racial hostility in ways that seemed superficially race-neutral.[44] The Willie Horton ad itself, with its frightening depiction of black criminality, is often seen as an illustration of these racial dynamics. Additionally, the new political dynamics also reflected the influence of a victims' rights movement, which emerged as an organized political force in the 1970s, drawing attention to, and building sympathy for, crime victims—a development whose necessary flipside seemed to be an increase in public fear and anger directed toward the victimizers.[45]

Deeper socioeconomic changes in U.S. society also probably played a role. The sociologist David Garland has developed a particularly rich and influential theory along these lines.[46] Garland describes a crisis of governance that faced the United States and other Western nations in the late 20th century as global competition, deindustrialization, de-unionization, and other socioeconomic forces threatened standards of living and fueled feelings of anxiety and instability. Unable to address these challenges effectively, political leaders resorted to increasingly punitive crime-control policies, both because criminals were a convenient scapegoat for society's ills and because the decisive, tough treatment of criminals might reassure the public of government's efficacy.

Whatever the underlying causes, political rhetoric in the late 20th century consistently reflected the conceptual premises that lay at the heart of the Willie Horton ad. To recap, these include the following:

- Predatory violent and sexual crime is the nation's preeminent crime problem;
- Many or most criminals are beyond rehabilitation and deserve only minimal care and support from society;
- Criminal justice officials should emphasize rigorous physical control of criminals;
- Officials who fail to incapacitate offenders to the maximum extent can be rightfully blamed for repeat offenses; and
- Any lenience or consideration shown to criminals presents not only a threat to the physical safety of others, but also a symbolic repudiation of crime victims.

Taken together, these premises predictably lead to the mandatory minimums, LWOP sentences, tougher prosecutorial charging practices, hair-trigger revocation policies, TIS laws, and similar explicit and implicit policy developments of the imprisonment-boom era.

CHAPTER TWO

War on Drugs: Escalation and (Equivocal) De-Escalation

President Richard Nixon famously declared a "war" on drugs in 1969, and U.S. political leaders continued to speak about drug enforcement in martial terms throughout the time of the imprisonment boom. We have already seen some notable intersections between the War on Drugs and the emergence of mass incarceration. For instance, the 1973 Rockefeller Drug Laws launched a new era of mandatory sentencing legislation. Not all of the mandatory minimums adopted over the next quarter century would target drug offenses, but many would. Such legislation helped to fuel a surge in the number of prisoners serving time for drug crime. Indeed, there seems a widespread belief that the War on Drugs was *the* major driver of mass incarceration. As we will see, however, drug imprisonment actually played only a secondary role in the imprisonment boom.

By 2000, it was becoming clear that public attitudes were shifting against the War on Drugs, partly because of the perception (not entirely true) that U.S. prisons were being filled with nonviolent addicts who could be handled more effectively through treatment than incarceration. Many reforms followed, amounting to a seeming de-escalation of the War on Drugs. Some reforms have contributed to a modest reduction in drug imprisonment rates since 2000, but the overall impact has fallen short of expectations. Indeed, the drug story ends up being a microcosm of the more general post-2000 sentencing reform story, illustrating many of the central limitations that have bedeviled other efforts to reduce imprisonment.

Drug Enforcement and the Imprisonment Boom

The War on Drugs was not just a matter of political rhetoric. The number of drug arrests in the United States nearly tripled between 1980 and 2000. By 2000, drug arrests outpaced arrests for serious violent crime by a ratio of nearly three to one. The number of prison admissions for drug offenses grew proportionately. Between 1985 and 2000, drug offenses accounted for about one-quarter of the total growth in the size of state prison populations.[1]

To some extent, all of this law enforcement activity on the drug front may seem to undercut my claim that fear of predatory violent and sexual offenses was the paradigmatic concern that underlay the imprisonment boom. Yet, upon closer inspection, it becomes clear that the War on Drugs drew much of its strength from the overriding fear of violence.

To be sure, other factors also played a role. For instance, the War on Drugs was animated, in part, by the broader cultural conflict between Richard Nixon's "silent majority" and the "me generation" that rose to prominence in the 1960s and 1970s, with its emphasis on personal fulfillment through individual expression, sexual freedom, and the exploration of altered states of consciousness. As a symbol of the younger generation's indiscipline and self-absorption, drug use became a natural target for those who feared that a complete breakdown in social order might be imminent.

In part, too, the War on Drugs reflected the efforts of inner-city residents to bring the criminal justice system to bear against the deteriorating conditions in their neighborhoods, much of which they attributed to drug trafficking and use. For instance, the social scientist Michael Javen Fortner has recently documented the role of black middle- and working-class activists in Harlem in pushing for adoption of the Rockefeller Drug Laws.[2] Fortner observes:

> By the late '60s, drug users were mugging residents and burglarizing homes, stores and churches. Loitering alcoholics, addicts and out-of-work young black males frightened the elderly and scared children.
>
> . . .
>
> In 1969, the Manhattan branch of the N.A.A.C.P. issued an anti-crime report that railed against the "reign of criminal terror" in Harlem. It warned that the "decent people of Harlem" had become the prey of "marauding hoodlums" and proposed

that criminals, including muggers, pushers, vagrants and murderers, be subjected to steep criminal sentences.[3]

Fortner notes that, by 1973, "nearly three-quarters of blacks and Puerto Ricans favored life sentences for drug pushers."

But, in addition to these and other dimensions, the War on Drugs was also, in part, an aspect of the national war on violence. For instance, the law professor William Stuntz has described how drug enforcement became a convenient tool for police and prosecutors to use against suspected violent criminals.[4] As Stuntz observes, the wave of violent crime that swept the United States in the late 20th century was not only quantitatively but also qualitatively different than earlier violence, as crimes committed by strangers became increasingly prominent. With stranger crime, it was harder to identify offenders and prove their guilt in court. Also, in many cases, criminal gangs made the work of police and prosecutors more difficult, as key witnesses were intimidated and silenced. In such an environment, drug prosecutions could be an appealing alternative to conventional prosecutions for violence. Drug cases are built on the work of undercover police officers and informants, and are thus able to avoid many of the witness issues that plague conventional violence cases. Likewise, there are few defenses in drug cases; in general, mere possession of drugs is in itself a crime. The fact that many violent offenders are involved in the drug trade, or at least use drugs themselves, means that drug charges are often a viable alternative to harder-to-prove allegations of violence. In short, many drug arrests and prosecutions are not really about the drugs at all, but instead result from suspicion of violent crime.

Such pretextual use of drug enforcement helps to explain why there is so much racial disparity in the War on Drugs. As many critics have observed, the racial demographics of drug *enforcement* are way out of line with the racial demographics of drug *use*. Given that blacks and whites use drugs at about equal rates, one might expect that the black share of drug arrests would correspond to the black share of the overall population. Yet, in 2000, blacks comprised about 35 percent of those arrested for drug crimes—nearly three times their proportion of the overall population. However, the racial demographics of drug arrests do match the racial demographics of violent crime much more closely; blacks accounted for 39 percent of the arrests for major violent crimes. These figures illuminate the implicit policy choices by police and prosecutors to use drug enforcement as part of an antiviolence strategy.

Of course, this tactical use of drug enforcement would have been far less appealing if drug penalties were insignificant compared to violence penalties. However, beginning with the Rockefeller Drug Laws in 1973, legislators around the United States steadily escalated drug penalties over the next two decades, especially for drug-distribution offenses. In effect, the law began to treat drug trafficking as a sort of violent offense in itself.

This legal treatment of drug crime not only accommodated the practical needs of police and prosecutors who were struggling to deal with the late 20th-century crime wave, but also reflected the pervasive drug-violence associations to which Americans were exposed in the media of that era. For instance, popular films of the time like *Scarface* (1983) and *New Jack City* (1991) depicted urban drug dealers as homicidal sociopaths. Nor were such depictions entirely fanciful. The arrival of crack cocaine in U.S. cities in the early and mid-1980s created lucrative new opportunities in the drug market and drew new gangs oriented to the crack trade into violent competition with one another. By 1985, the violence associated with crack distribution was becoming regular headline fodder in the newspapers.[5]

Drug distribution also seemed to have a violent character in another, more subtle sense. Even when dealers were not shooting at one another, they might still be seen as predators hooking young people on dangerous substances that were likely to cause serious harm to them in the long run. This perspective on drug trafficking was powerfully reinforced in 1986 through the cocaine-related death of college basketball star Len Bias. The ensuing media and political firestorm resulted in the adoption of many "Len Bias laws," which enhanced penalties for drug distribution resulting in death. The potentially lethal consequences of drug use also informed other new sentencing laws that increased penalties even when no particular fatality could be traced to the defendant, including the draconian federal mandatory minimums for crack distribution that were adopted just months after Bias's death. (As we will see in Chapter 5, these minimums were to have especially disproportionate and pernicious effects on black drug offenders.)

These various drug–violence links were obviously on the mind of the U.S. Supreme Court in 1991 when it upheld Michigan's 650-Lifer law (thought to be the nation's toughest drug sentencing statute) from a challenge based on the Cruel and Unusual Punishments Clause of the Eighth Amendment.[6] Writing the decisive opinion in the case, Justice Kennedy categorically rejected the defendant's characterization of his crime as "nonviolent and victimless." "To the contrary," Kennedy observed, the crime

> threatened to cause grave harm to society. Quite apart from the pernicious effects on the individual who consumes illegal drugs, such drugs relate to crime in at least three ways: (1) A drug user may commit crime because of drug-induced changes in physiological functions, cognitive ability, and mood; (2) A drug user may commit crime in order to obtain money to buy drugs; and (3) A violent crime may occur as part of the drug business or culture. Studies bear out these possibilities, and demonstrate a direct nexus between illegal drugs and crimes of violence.

Kennedy went so far as to analogize drug dealing to a type of murder.

The particular association between *distribution* and violence helps to explain why the penalties for distribution offenses escalated far more dramatically than those for simple possession or use. Although we now take this distribution–possession distinction for granted, drug sentencing has not always been handled that way. For instance, the infamous drug mandatory minimums adopted by Congress in the 1951 Boggs Act applied equally to distribution and possession.[7] If the drug war's basic thrust had been to strike a symbolic blow against the cultural revolution associated with the 1960s, then it might have made sense to revive the indiscriminate toughness of the Boggs Act. Instead, the drug sentencing laws of the late 20th century sharply distinguished distribution from possession, as did actual sentencing practices. Data from 2000, for instance, indicate that distribution defendants were more likely to be sent to prison than other drug defendants, and that the sentences of the former were more than twice as long on average as those of the latter.[8]

Although the War on Drugs drew much of its strength from the same fear of predatory crime that drove the imprisonment boom more generally, it is important to bear in mind that the war played only a relatively modest role as a direct cause of mass incarceration. Offenders convicted of drug crimes may have accounted for a quarter of the growth in state prison populations between 1985 and 2000, but that leaves three-quarters of the growth coming from elsewhere— mostly (conventional) violent and sexual offenses. Even without any drug imprisonment at all, the U.S. prison population would still have grown dramatically to unprecedented highs in the late 20th century.

Indeed, by 1999, there were more than twice as many violent offenders in state prisons as drug offenders, who accounted for only about one-fifth of the total.[9] Although drug enforcement often proved attractive as a way for police and prosecutors to deal with some violence, there remained plenty of conventional violence prosecutions, too. Moreover, despite the Supreme Court's easy equation of drug dealing with criminal homicide, lower-court judges tended not to sentence drug crimes quite that severely. Going back to the 2000 data, the average drug-distribution sentence (61 months) was roughly in line with that of lower-level violent crimes, but considerably shorter than the "big three" of robbery (97 months), rape (146 months), and murder (282 months).

To be sure, the War on Drugs contributed to the imprisonment boom in other, indirect ways that defy easy quantification. The extraordinary volume of arrests for low-level drug crimes in the 1990s—80 percent of drug arrests were for simple possession—may not have directly generated many lengthy prison sentences, but they did serve to mark the arrested as criminals. Drug arrests and convictions disqualified individuals from educational loans and other public benefits, established barriers to lawful employment, and generally contributed to a sense of alienation within the low-income communities of color that bore a disproportionate share of drug enforcement activities. It is not hard to imagine that drug arrests sent many initially low-level offenders down a path toward the commission of other crimes for which much longer sentences were eventually imposed.

Still, as the de-escalation movement slowly gathered steam—subtly in the 1990s, and then more visibly beginning in 2000—two key points should have been apparent. First, whatever other social benefits de-escalation might produce, it was unlikely to put more than a modest dent into mass incarceration. Second, drug crimes, especially those involving the distribution of crack and other "hard" drugs, had become deeply associated in the public mind with violence, and drug enforcement had become an integral part of official violence-control strategies. Absent fundamental changes in the sort of beliefs exemplified by the Willie Horton ad, drug–violence associations would severely limit what drug reformers could accomplish.

Treatment-Focused Reforms

Treatment over incarceration has been the mantra of most reformers. They have won a number of notable victories in recent years, especially in the widespread adoption of drug treatment courts. In practice, however, these specialized courts have often proven less an alternative to incarceration for drug-involved offenders than simply a different institutional context for the administration of incarceration. In that and other respects, drug treatment courts typify the limitations of most efforts to date to reduce mass incarceration in the United States.

Drug Treatment Courts

In the 1990s and early 2000s, drug treatment courts became the most widely embraced alternative to the conventional prosecution of drug cases. To many proponents, treatment courts contrasted sharply with the incarceration-first antidrug policies exemplified by the Rockefeller Drug Laws, offering more constructive responses to drug crime that would reduce recidivism and save money over the long run. To critics, treatment courts were the proverbial iron fist in a velvet glove, perpetuating rather than repudiating the punitive excesses of the War on Drugs.

There seems a measure of truth in both perspectives. In part, the uncertain character of treatment courts reflects the great diversity in the way that these locally administered programs are run from state to state and city to city. Whatever one might like to say about treatment courts, one can likely find supporting evidence from at least one of the thousands of such courts now in operation. In part, too, their uncertain character reflects the political realities facing treatment court supporters, who have felt the need to design and run programs so as to maintain an appearance of toughness and minimize the likelihood of Willie Horton–type catastrophes.

The nation's first drug treatment court was established in Miami in 1989. A city on the frontlines of the nation's struggle against cocaine trafficking, Miami had incarcerated a swelling number of drug offenders in the 1980s, but all of the law enforcement effort seemed to have little practical effect on the availability of drugs on the street.[10] Arrests for drug possession increased by 93 percent between 1985 and 1989 alone, and the court and correctional systems struggled to keep up. As criminologist John Goldkamp, the leading scholar of the Miami drug court, puts it,

As quickly as the State Attorney could prosecute, the cases kept coming, and the overcrowded jails and prisons had to release offenders at a rapid pace. As the judicial leaders, the State Attorney, and the Chief Public Defender sought to make the system work under the strain, it seemed that more cases were being processed faster, jail and prison cells were being filled, and probation and pretrial services were being overwhelmed, all with little apparent impact on the problem.[11]

In order to deal with the crisis, a senior Miami judge collaborated with prosecutors and public defenders to develop a new model for handling drug cases. The new model had two core components. First, participating offenders were diverted from incarceration and conventional case-processing into 12-month community-based, outpatient drug treatment programs. In and of itself, diversion into treatment was not a novel concept, although it did cut against the grain of the increasingly tough-minded drug war approaches of the 1980s. The second core component, however, was Miami's key innovation: the offender's treatment would be closely monitored by the judge through regular court proceedings featuring encouragement and rewards for progress and sanctions for backsliding, including short stints behind bars ("motivational jail"). The judge and lawyers would thus become partners with the treatment provider and engage in an unusually intensive way with the treatment process.

Early studies of the Miami drug court found some promising outcomes. Perhaps most notably, the drug court defendants had lower rearrest rates than did non-drug-court defendants facing similar charges.[12] Moreover, among those who were rearrested, the average time to rearrest was more than twice as long. To be sure, comparisons between drug-court defendants and others had to be evaluated cautiously because the drug-court participants were self-selected, not a random sample. (Dubious statistical comparisons have been a chronic problem plaguing research on drug courts and other diversionary initiatives.) Still, the numbers were sufficiently encouraging—and the drug caseload pressures in other cities sufficiently dire—so that the Miami model slowly began to spread to other jurisdictions.

Initially, the drug treatment court "movement" gathered steam as a grassroots phenomenon, pushed by local-level officials. The administration of President George H. W. Bush, and particularly Bush's hardline drug czar William Bennett, pointedly chose not to support Miami's initiative.[13] However, President Bill Clinton, Bush's successor, proved more receptive. (Perhaps not coincidentally, his attorney general, Janet Reno, had previously served as the state attorney in Miami.)

Most importantly, Clinton's signature crime policy legislation, the massive Violent Crime Control and Law Enforcement Act of 1994, included a new federal grant program to support the development of drug treatment courts. Over the next decade, the federal government would award tens of millions of dollars to local governments across the United States to support the creation of such courts.[14] By 2003, more than 1,000 drug treatment courts had been established, with the vast majority benefiting from federal funding. By 2015, the number had reached 3,400.[15] About half targeted adult offenders, with others focused on juveniles.

Because treatment courts have been developed at the initiative of tens of thousands of local officials spread across all 50 states, there is a tremendous amount of variation from court to court. However, because so many of the courts have been supported by federal money, there is some uniformity with respect to certain aspects of court operations. The federal grants, in other words, come with strings attached: local officials have to include a few standard features when they design their programs. Additionally, organizations like the federal Bureau of Justice Assistance and the National Association of Drug Court Professionals have developed influential best-practices recommendations.[16] It is thus possible to identify certain common, if still far from universal, characteristics of adult drug treatment courts:

- Restricted eligibility: many defendants are categorically excluded based on their current charges or prior convictions.
- Entrance is doubly discretionary: both the prosecutor and the defendant must agree to the defendant's assignment to a drug court.
- A guilty plea is the price of admission: drug court process is structured either as part of the sentence or as a presentencing diversion.
- Close supervision: court appearances and drug tests are much more frequent than in traditional probation.
- Mandatory participation in a drug treatment program: treatment providers are expected to collaborate with the judge in monitoring and enforcing compliance with the treatment plan.
- Graduated sanctions: failed drug tests and other program violations are met with sanctions, which are expected to start small (e.g., a verbal reprimand from the judge or a requirement for a written apology) and increase in severity (e.g., community service, a short jail term, or termination from the drug court).
- Indefinite duration: defendants move through distinct phases of treatment and supervision at their own pace, culminating

eventually either in successful graduation (which normally relieves the defendant from further incarceration on the underlying charges) or in a decision to terminate the defendant from the program for insufficient progress (which normally results in a traditional sentencing process on the underlying charges, to which the defendant has already pled guilty).[17]

Proponents argue that treatment courts have a proven ability to reduce rates of relapse and recidivism, which, in turn, may reduce criminal justice system costs over the long run, especially through reduced incarceration. The National Association of Drug Court Professionals, for instance, asserts that every $1 spent on treatment courts saves taxpayers $3.36 in system costs.[18]

Yet, there is a paradox at the heart of the treatment court story: despite the rapid proliferation of these courts, they have had, at most, only a modest impact on drug imprisonment. In 1990, when the Miami drug court was still in its infancy, U.S. prisons held about 179,000 inmates on drug charges.[19] Seventeen years later, the United States had added 2,146 drug treatment courts,[20] but the number of drug inmates had more than doubled to 369,000.[21] Simply put, the era of the drug treatment court in the United States has also been the era of mass drug incarceration. This is not to say that drug treatment courts caused the problem, but it is to suggest that drug treatment courts have hardly been the game changer that some proponents have envisioned.

Consider the experience of a specific state. In 2004, Wisconsin created a new Treatment Alternatives Diversion (TAD) program as a state-level analog to the federal grant program for treatment courts. TAD offered financial support for local officials to establish new diversion initiatives based on the drug treatment court model. For the first few years of TAD, seven counties shared an appropriation of $1 million per year. When researchers at the University of Wisconsin undertook a comprehensive assessment of TAD through 2013, they found that 90,318 days of imprisonment had been avoided as a result of successful diversions.[22] Although that may sound like a large number at first blush, some perspective is needed: over the same time period in which the TAD programs were in operation, close to 5,000 drug offenders entered Wisconsin prisons.[23] Even assuming, quite conservatively, that each inmate served only the bare minimum one year for a prison term, that would translate into more than 1.8 million days of imprisonment. Thus, despite millions of dollars of state spending,

TAD was only nibbling around the edges of drug imprisonment in Wisconsin.

Why have drug treatment courts not had more of an impact on drug imprisonment? The question has multiple, overlapping answers— answers that foreshadow the issues we will see with other reform efforts throughout this book.

First, large numbers of drug offenders are categorically excluded from participation in treatment court. Most importantly, there is the common exclusion of violent offenders. This key restriction is statutorily mandated for the many treatment courts receiving federal grants.[24] For purposes of the federal program, "violent offender" is defined broadly to include any defendant who possessed a dangerous weapon during his offense, regardless of whether the weapon was ever used or even openly displayed.[25] Thus, for instance, a defendant arrested after a traffic stop for having drugs in his car might be auto- matically excluded from drug court if he also happened to have a handgun in the glove compartment. Additionally, federal law excludes as "violent" any individual who has ever had a conviction in the past for a felony involving an intent to cause serious bodily harm to another, no matter how old or aberrational that crime was.[26] These exclusions are very important in light of William Stuntz's hypothesis that drug imprisonment is, in practice, largely a strategy for incapacitating people believed to have violent procliv- ities. The categorical exclusion for violent offenders thus tends to screen out the drug offenders who are precisely those most likely to be prison-bound, leaving the drug court with those offenders who are least likely to be sent to prison through the conventional criminal courts.

Other jurisdictions are even more restrictive than federal law requires. Some drug courts only accept misdemeanor defendants, who are, virtually by definition, not otherwise prison-bound.[27] Other drug courts exclude defendants who have any prior felony conviction of any sort, even for nonviolent crimes.[28] A different sort of categorical exclusion comes from the operation of mandatory minimum laws, which necessarily preclude drug-court participation to the extent they require imprisonment. One recent national study found that nearly one-third of drug-involved incarcerated offenders were prevented from participating in drug court by mandatory sen- tencing laws.[29]

These various upfront restrictions prevent many drug courts from serving in any significant way as a diversion from prison; these courts instead become a diversion from straight probation or, at best, from short terms of incarceration in the local jail. These categorical exclusions reflect a seemingly knee-jerk risk-aversion. No policymaker wants to have her name associated with a program that gives a break to the next Willie Horton. The restrictions have little to do with the actual relative risk posed by different offenders,[30] but are instead designed to avoid facile, politically perilous headlines like, "Felon Released to Drug Court Shoots Two."

Second, an otherwise prison-bound defendant who manages to slip through the categorical exclusions must still run the gauntlet of official discretion. Judges and prosecutors, responding to the same political concerns that drive restrictive *explicit* policies, are typically empowered to exclude defendants at their own discretion. In some jurisdictions, this discretion results in *implicit* policies that keep out defendants with any real criminal history, with little or no regard for the age or marginal nature of the defendant's prior legal entanglements.[31] Overall, recent federal grantees report that about 13 percent of the categorically eligible defendants who did not participate in drug court were excluded because of judge or lawyer objections.[32]

The combination of categorical and discretionary exclusions can lead to chronic underutilization. In recent years, for instance, drug courts receiving federal grants have served only half as many offenders as they had originally projected.[33] At the same time, in some jurisdictions, the drug court does operate at capacity; in many of these jurisdictions, the real problem is insufficient funding to meet demand[34]—a third major reason that drug courts have not had a large impact on imprisonment.

Underutilization in some jurisdictions and underfunding in others lead to small drug courts. Thus, while the total number of drug courts in the United States may sound impressive, it is important to bear in mind that many are quite small operations. For instance, in one recent six-month period, out of 82 federal grantees, 23 reported having fewer than 20 participants.[35] Most of the remainder had well under 100. The prevalence of small drug courts helps to explain their limited reach: one recent study estimated that out of about 1.5 million offenders arrested annually who are at risk of drug abuse or dependence, fewer than 4 percent enter drug court, as compared to more than 35 percent going to jail or prison.[36]

In addition to categorical and discretionary exclusions and resource constraints, drug-court numbers are also kept low by a fourth consideration: many eligible defendants simply choose not to participate.

Federal grantees report, for instance, that more than half of eligible defendants turn down offers of drug court.[37]

This may seem surprising: how could any rational person turn down a chance to avoid prison? But recall that many eligible defendants do not have the sort of record that would land them in prison; as they weigh the offer of drug court, they are more likely facing a short term of incarceration in the local jail as the worst-case alternative scenario. Moreover, some of the remaining defendants who *do* have a serious risk of prison will underestimate that risk, whether because of poor legal counsel or otherwise, and will base their drug-court decisions on mistaken beliefs about the likely alternatives. In either context, the costs and risks of drug court are apt to loom larger in the mind of the defendant. The costs and risks include the following:

- The defendant must typically plead guilty to gain entrance, which means that the defendant must surrender any potentially meritorious defenses and the possibility of an outright acquittal or dismissal of charges.
- The defendant must make frequent court appearances throughout the treatment period, which may present a serious hardship to poor defendants without convenient transportation options. Court appearances, moreover, may be humiliating and deeply intrusive into the defendant's personal life.[38]
- Treatment sessions themselves may also be time-consuming, inconvenient, and intrusive.
- The defendant must submit to regular urine tests, typically about twice per week in the first few months.[39]
- Failed drug tests, missed appointments, and other program violations result in sanctions, which may include a short term of "motivational jail." Judges vary widely in their reliance on jail sanctions, but some use jail so often that drug-court participants are apt to spend more time behind bars than they would have through conventional sentencing.[40]
- In contrast to a conventional criminal sentence, there is no definite time limit to these burdens and risks. Drug court lasts until the defendant successfully moves through all phases of the program or is terminated. Participants normally require at least a year or two to complete the program and sometimes even longer.[41] Many eligible defendants prefer the greater predictability of a conventional sentence, especially when that sentence would be measured in weeks or months instead of years.

Such considerations as these discourage drug-court participation and undercut its potential long-term benefits in reducing drug-related incarceration.

These aspects of the drug-court experience also point to a more generalized issue we will see with post-2000 sentencing reforms: efforts to reduce incarceration often involve enhanced new forms of supervision and surveillance in the community, which opens a backdoor to incarceration based on the failure to comply with challenging release conditions.

Fifth, even after a defendant has endured many months of drug court, there is no guarantee that she will avoid a return to conventional court and a regular sentence of incarceration. Failure rates vary quite a bit from drug court to drug court, but are typically in the neighborhood of 50 percent or more.[42] Failure in drug court, moreover, can result in an even longer sentence than would have been imposed if the defendant had gone straight to a conventional criminal court. Indeed, this seems to be the norm with at least some drug courts.[43]

The high failure rate results from the demanding conditions and close surveillance of drug court, the risk-aversion of officials who fear that today's relapsing addict may become tomorrow's Willie Horton, and another difficult reality that has also sometimes impaired other rehabilitation-minded sentencing reforms: no treatment program can guarantee success for any given offender. Human beings are not endlessly manipulable automatons. In other contexts, well-designed, well-run, well-funded programs have shown an ability to cut recidivism rates by as much as one half, but that still leaves plenty of repeat crime.[44]

Drug courts do not stand out as significantly more successful than other rehabilitative interventions. Recent studies of various drug courts have produced mixed results: some found statistically significant drops in recidivism for drug-court participants, while others found no significant differences, and at least one found that drug-court participants did *worse*.[45] Recent meta-analyses that combine the results of multiple studies of adult drug courts consistently find recidivism reductions that average between 7.5 and 14 percent.[46] This is not to say that drug courts should be viewed as a failure; even with modest crime reductions, most studies find that their benefits outweigh their costs.[47] It is to say, however, that the recidivism-reducing effects of drug courts, like those of other rehabilitative interventions, are unlikely to result in large reductions in imprisonment.

Sixth, and finally, drug courts have also been limited in their imprisonment-reducing effects by the phenomenon of "net-widening"—another important challenge facing diversion programs more generally. Net-widening occurs when a program that is intended to divert offenders from incarceration instead becomes filled with offenders who likely would have been sentenced to straight probation or perhaps not even prosecuted at all in the absence of the program. Net-widening results from a push and a pull. As we have already seen with drug courts, the officials who design and administer diversion programs will want to push out offenders who pose any real risk of failure. At the same time, they will want to pull in offenders who are likely to succeed, even if their offenses are minor. Police and prosecutors, seeing that the court system is now willing to devote time and resources to the previously ignored low-level cases, may respond by arresting and charging these cases more aggressively.

An illustration comes from Denver, where drug cases nearly tripled after the city's drug court completed its first full year of operation. Former Denver drug-court judge Morris Hoffman explains:

> It is clear that the very presence of drug court, with its significantly increased capacity to process cases, has caused police to make arrests in, and prosecutors to file, the kinds of ten-and twenty-dollar hand-to-hand drug cases that the system simply would not, and could not, have bothered with before. It is not just a matter of intensifying existing arrest and charging policies; since the adoption of the drug court the Denver Police Department has embarked on an extensive and unprecedented campaign of undercover "buy-bust" operations.[48]

Unfortunately, "likely to succeed" and "minor offense" do not *guarantee* success in drug court. Given the rigors of the program and the high failure rate, many low-level defendants caught in the "net" will get some motivational jail, and some will even fail out and face sentencing in conventional court. Importantly, the recidivism research indicates that giving intensive treatment to low-risk offenders can actually be criminogenic—that is, it can result in *higher* recidivism rates than would doing nothing at all.[49] In any event, once the low-level offender is returned to conventional court, the fact that the system would not have bothered with her at an earlier time will not necessarily save her from prison once she has been marked as a drug-court failure. In such ways, net-widening may actually produce a perverse outcome: *more* drug incarceration, not less, following the implementation of a drug court. In Denver, for instance, the number of prison sentences for drug offenses more than doubled over the first four years that the city had its drug court.[50]

In sum, the combination of small size (due to categorical and discretionary exclusions, defendant refusals, and resource constraints), high failure rates, and net-widening has undercut the ability of drug courts to achieve large net decreases in the number of prisoners serving time for drug offenses. A well-run drug court may still be worthwhile from an overall cost–benefit perspective. However, from the standpoint of reducing imprisonment, the drug-court story seems simply one of treading water.

California's Proposition 36

The prevailing drug-court model took shape in the late 1980s and early 1990s, when the War on Drugs was still at its height. The model remains deeply marked by the punitive attitudes that prevailed in its formative years. Punitive components include the reliance on motivational jail, the intensive regimen of drug testing, the use of public shaming in court proceedings, and the threat of prison sentences as an inducement for defendants to enter and remain in drug court. By 2000, however, it was evident that public enthusiasm for the War on Drugs was on the wane. For instance, the number of Americans who classified drugs as the nation's top problem peaked at 37 percent in 1990 and then fell precipitously to 6 percent by the end of the decade.[51] Moreover, several national surveys in 2001 and 2002 indicated that large majorities of Americans favored treatment over incarceration for nonviolent drug offenders.[52] This created space for new policies that represented a somewhat sharper break from the ideology of the War on Drugs than drug courts had been.

Adopted by an overwhelming 61 percent of the California electorate in November 2000, Proposition 36 was the first demonstration of the new political environment to gain widespread national attention. In essence, this ballot initiative aimed at providing court-supervised treatment for drug offenders, but without the threats of incarceration that lay at the heart of the drug-court model. Under Proposition 36, defendants convicted of nonviolent drug possession offenses are— with a few categorical exclusions—entitled to be sentenced to probation instead of incarceration, subject to the completion of mandatory drug treatment.[53] Once in treatment, the defendant cannot readily be incarcerated for failed drug tests or other violations of the treatment regimen. A sort of "three strikes" system controls: for the defendant's first two drug possession arrests after being placed on probation, the court cannot revoke probation without making certain special findings about the defendant's dangerousness or unamenability to treatment.[54] It is only a third arrest that can lead to revocation and the potential for incarceration. On the other hand, if the treatment program is successfully completed, the defendant's conviction is set aside and the arrest expunged—the defendant is thus excused from having to disclose the arrest on most employment applications.

Although Proposition 36 gained far more national attention, Arizona's Proposition 200 was actually the nation's first victorious mandatory-treatment ballot initiative and a model for the California law. Adopted by a whopping 65 percent of Arizona's voters in 1996, Proposition 200 similarly required probation and treatment for drug possession offenses.[55] Like the subsequent California initiative campaign, Arizona's was bankrolled by three wealthy businessmen, investor George Soros, educational entrepreneur John Sperling, and insurance executive Peter Lewis. Unlike the California law, however, Proposition 200 also included a provision legalizing medical marijuana, a politically popular measure that may have buoyed the mandatory-treatment provisions.

In seeking to duplicate their Arizona success in California, Soros, Sperling, and Lewis benefited from early analyses of Proposition 200, which found significant money-savings from the diversion of drug offenders to treatment.[56] These promising results were amplified by California's Legislative Analyst's Office, which provides official estimates of the fiscal impact of proposed ballot initiatives. In the case of Proposition 36, the office projected annual savings of $100 million or more.[57] On the other hand, since the Golden State had already approved medical marijuana in 1996, mandatory treatment would have to stand on its own in California. Additionally, the state's judiciary and law enforcement establishment mounted a stiff opposition to Proposition 36, arguing that the threat of incarceration was necessary to make addicts take treatment seriously.[58] In essence, they claimed that the drug-court model was preferable to the Proposition 36 approach. However, they had a hard time getting their message through to the voters: they were outspent six to one by Soros and his allies, who emphasized the projected cost-savings, the potential for expanded use of treatment to reduce recidivism, and the need to ensure adequate prison space for violent offenders.[59]

Emboldened by their successes in Arizona and California, the supporters of Proposition 36 attempted similar campaigns in 2002 in Ohio, Michigan, Missouri, Florida, and the District of Columbia.[60] However, only the D.C. initiative won approval, and even that victory was overturned by courts.[61] With the losses of 2002, the mandatory-treatment movement petered out, at least as a matter of ballot-initiative campaigns. To be sure, about a dozen states did adopt new diversion laws for drug offenders through regular legislative processes.[62] These laws replicated various aspects of Proposition 36, but none included the key prohibition on motivational jail that particularly marked the California law and its Arizona predecessor.[63] Nationally, it thus seems that the drug-court model has prevailed over the rival Proposition 36 model for court-supervised treatment.

Even within California, Proposition 36 has remained controversial. In 2006, the legislature attempted to amend Proposition 36 so as to give judges greater power to incarcerate participating offenders, but the amendment was declared unconstitutional.[64] Meanwhile, treatment for Proposition 36 defendants has been chronically underfunded. In 2008, yet another ballot initiative attempted to enhance the treatment budget, but this effort came up short at the polls.[65] The latest research now indicates that Proposition 36 treatment does seem to reduce recidivism, but probably not by quite as much over the long run as drug-court treatment.[66]

It is difficult to assess precisely, but Proposition 36 has probably not had a large effect on imprisonment. The initiative took effect on July 1, 2001. Over the next four years, the number of California prisoners held on drug-possession charges dropped by about 4,000.[67] However, this still left in prison about 14,000 drug-possession offenders and 35,000 drug offenders overall. Furthermore, the 4,000-prisoner reduction must be viewed from the perspective of California's gargantuan prison population, which stood at about 160,000 when Proposition 36 went into effect and experienced a net *increase* of about 4,000 over the next four years—easily offsetting whatever gains were achieved by the ballot initiative. Even assuming that Proposition 36 gets all of the credit for the 4,000 drug prisoner drop, this was hardly a high-impact reform in the context of California corrections in the early 2000s. Moreover, it is not clear how much credit Proposition 36 should get. The number of drug-possession prisoners in California actually began to fall before Proposition 36 passed and continued to fall in the months between its passage and effective date. This suggests that some additional forces beyond the legal change may have contributed to the continued decline after the effective date.

If we revisit the reasons why drug courts have not had more of an impact, it quickly becomes apparent why Proposition 36 has also had a limited effect on imprisonment. First, Proposition 36 is subject to important categorical exclusions that parallel those typically found in drug courts, such as prohibitions on certain defendants with prior violent convictions or who face concurrent nondrug charges.[68] Proposition 36 does provide a five-year "wash out" period for older convictions, which is more generous than many drug courts. On the other hand, Proposition 36 is strictly limited to defendants convicted of simple drug possession or use. Trafficking defendants, as well as defendants facing nondrug charges relating to drug use (e.g., retail theft to support a drug habit), are excluded, even though many drug courts would take such defendants. Thus, Proposition 36 excludes a large percentage of drug-involved defendants, including those whose prior records create the greatest risk of a significant prison term through conventional sentencing. Those defendants who do ultimately get diverted to treatment under Proposition 36 would not have faced long prison terms anyway: some research indicates that the pre–Proposition 36 sentencing norm for those covered by the law would have been only 30 to 90 days in jail.[69]

Second, although Proposition 36 does not formally provide for discretionary exclusion of otherwise-eligible defendants, police and prosecutors often are able to exclude defendants through strategic charging.[70] This de facto discretion comes from the prohibition on defendants who face a concurrent charge for a nondrug misdemeanor or felony count, an exclusion that has been interpreted broadly by the courts. Thus, for instance, a drugged driver charged with both driving under the influence of drug and drug use would be excluded from Proposition 36.[71] Similarly, defendants might be excluded based on charges of cultivation of marijuana (even if the cultivation was for personal use), possession of a controlled substance while armed, or forging a prescription in order to obtain drugs for personal use.[72] Such restrictive interpretations of Proposition 36 effectively give law enforcement officials considerable discretion to keep defendants who are perceived to be dangerous in the conventional system and on track for incarceration.

Third, Proposition 36, like many drug courts, has been plagued by chronic underfunding. However, unlike the situation with drug courts, the judges operating under Proposition 36 cannot turn defendants away when treatment slots are full. Instead, underfunding results in delays in treatment and uneven service quality.[73]

Fourth, as with drug courts, Proposition 36 permits defendants to opt out of treatment and remain within the conventional system. Predictably, however, opting out does seem less common under Proposition 36. Not only does the California law spare participants the threat of motivational jail, but it also establishes a more definite, 12-month limit on treatment. Additionally, Proposition 36, unlike most drug courts, permits defendants to go to trial prior to treatment. Thus, potentially meritorious legal defenses need not be waived as the price of admission. Nonetheless, while most eligible defendants accept Proposition 36 probation, not all do. In a few counties, the refusal rate may approach 50 percent, although in most the rate is probably far lower.[74] Public defenders report that the primary reason for refusals is that some defendants still prefer simply to do their incarceration and avoid the burdens of mandatory treatment even in the softer Proposition 36 system.[75]

Fifth, the failure rates for Proposition 36 defendants are even higher than the norms for drug courts.[76] Only about one-third of those sentenced under Proposition 36 actually show up for treatment and successfully complete the program.[77] The elevated failure rates likely reflect underfunding and associated delays in treatment, the difficulty of excluding or kicking out hardcore addicts and others who seem unresponsive to the program, and possibly the absence of jail sanctions for backsliding. Whatever the chief cause, high failure rates mean that many Proposition 36 diversions from prison will prove only temporary.

Finally, as with some drug courts, there is evidence of net-widening under Proposition 36: in the five years following the initiative's adoption, drug arrests in California increased consistently and more rapidly than the national average.[78] Interview research with police officers also indicates that some may be increasing drug arrests now in the hope that more arrestees will be getting treatment.[79]

In sum, Proposition 36's modest effect on imprisonment reflects much the same considerations that have similarly limited the impact of drug courts. Most prominently, these considerations include risk-aversion in the design and administration of these diversion programs, inadequate resources, and a high failure rate.

Reform of Mandatory Minimums

Even as the Proposition 36 movement died out as a national phenomenon in the early 2000s, states increasingly turned to a different strategy for reducing drug imprisonment. Back in 1973, it had been the Rockefeller drug minimums in New York that heralded the arrival of the War on Drugs, as well as the imprisonment-boom era more generally. Many other states followed suit, including Michigan with its 650-Lifer law, the nation's toughest. Such mandatory minimums then became a natural target for reformers as public attitudes toward drug enforcement finally began to shift.

National Overview

Since 2000, at least 14 states have softened drug-specific mandatory minimums.[80] Additional states have softened habitual-offender minimums in the hope of reducing drug imprisonment. The drug-specific reforms fall into five categories. First, some states, including Connecticut, New Jersey, Georgia, and Hawaii, have created new "safety valves" that give judges discretion to impose a below-minimum sentence in some cases. Second, other states have narrowed the reach of their school-zone laws. (Such laws impose mandatory minimums for drug distribution within a certain distance of a school.) For instance, Kentucky reduced the reach of its school zones by 2,000 feet. Indiana has adopted a similar reform. Third, some states, including North Dakota, South Carolina, and Delaware, have exempted first-time offenders from minimums. Fourth, other states, including Ohio and Massachusetts, have increased the volume of drugs required to trigger some minimums. Fifth, and finally, a few states, including Rhode Island, New York, and Michigan, have entirely repealed some mandatory minimums.

Symbolically, such reforms mark a striking departure from the pre-2000 time period, when it seemed that drug minimums were only capable of moving in the direction of greater severity. Nonetheless, their imprisonment-reduction potential is limited in some important respects. For one thing, most reforms soften, but do not repeal, minimums. Additionally, several merely provide judges with discretion to disregard a minimum; such reforms will only be effective to the extent that judges are willing to employ the discretion. Moreover, many leave high *maximum* sentences in place, which permit judges to continue imposing the same sentences they had been imposing prereform. Furthermore, many reforms have been adopted without retroactive effect, meaning that many prisoners sentenced under the old, discredited minimums will continue to languish behind bars without any benefit from the legal changes. In such states, reforms may not produce any measurable reduction in drug imprisonment for many years. Finally, some reductions in drug minimums were only obtained at the cost of *increased* minimums for violent or sexual offenses.[81]

The End of Drug Minimums in Michigan

Since Michigan and New York led the way with tough drug minimums in the 1970s, their subsequent turn against minimums merits some closer attention. Consider Michigan first. Opposition to 650-Lifer grew over the 1990s, fueled by press coverage of individual cases of unjust sentences. For instance, the case of Gary Fannon, Jr., reached national attention through a 1992 article in *Rolling Stone* magazine.[82] Fannon, an unexceptional kid from the Detroit suburbs, became involved in cocaine dealing at the instigation of an undercover cop. Although he was a first-time offender and only 18 years of age, Fannon received a mandatory sentence of life without the possibility of parole (LWOP) under 650-Lifer. As he was led away to prison at the end of his sentencing, his mother Linda fainted. She soon became a leading advocate for reform.[83]

After nearly a decade behind bars, Fannon's conviction was overturned in 1996,[84] but that decision did nothing for the others serving LWOP sentences under 650-Lifer. Continuing coverage of their cases in the *Detroit Free Press* helped to keep public attention focused on the law's excesses.

In 1997, the Michigan reform effort received a major boost from the involvement of a national sentencing reform organization, Families against Mandatory Minimums (FAMM). FAMM had been founded in 1991 by Julie Stewart, then a staffer at the libertarian Cato Institute, whose brother had received a five-year sentence in federal court for growing marijuana.[85] In seeking reform of 650-Lifer, Stewart and her colleagues drew on sympathetic stories like Fannon's, as well as research showing that treatment was often a more cost-effective response to drug offenses than incarceration.[86] In 1998, they achieved their first legislative victory in Michigan when the mandatory minimum for "650" trafficking offenses was reduced from LWOP to 20 years in prison.

In contrast to many other mandatory minimum reforms, Michigan's 1998 amendment was made retroactive: those prisoners already sentenced under 650-Lifer could apply for parole after serving 20 years, or in some circumstances even a little earlier.

However, while the reform was able to correct a few cases of clear injustice, it could not have much of an impact on Michigan's swollen, 42,000-person prison population. Despite all of the national press attention given to 650-Lifer, few offenders had actually been sentenced under the law. Thus, a mere 169 prisoners became eligible for parole based on the 1998 reform, and many of them would still have to wait many years before their cases could be considered by the parole board.[87] The small number of 650-Lifers in 1998 reflected both the high threshold quantity for mandatory LWOP (650 grams) and the many decisions by prosecutors not to seek LWOP, often in exchange for assistance by the defendant in apprehending and prosecuting other offenders. The case of actor and comedian Tim Allen provides a well-known example. Although Allen had been arrested in Michigan for delivery of more than 650 grams of cocaine, he struck a deal with prosecutors and ended up serving only two and a half years in prison.[88]

Moreover, even as they reached the minimum-time-in-prison requirements, the 650-Lifers faced another major hurdle: a politicized, increasingly restrictive parole board. In yet another echo of the Willie Horton story, the Michigan legislature redesigned the parole board in 1992 after a parolee committed a much-publicized series of rape-murders.[89] After the parole restructuring, corrections professionals with civil service protections were replaced by nonprofessionals who could more easily be removed by the Director of Corrections for release decisions that backfired. Not surprisingly, the rate at which parole applications were granted fell from 66 percent in 1988–1991 to 56 percent in 1994–1997.[90] Lifers were especially hard hit—their grant rate was a miniscule 0.2 percent.[91]

FAMM recognized how limited the 1998 reform was and continued to advocate for broader changes to drug sentencing in Michigan. Not only did a 20-year mandatory minimum remain on the books for offenses involving 650 grams of cocaine or heroin, but so, too, did a number of additional minimums triggered by lower quantities. More extensive reforms came in 2002, supported by a diverse coalition of politicians from both parties, faith-based and civil-rights organizations, and even the state prosecuting attorneys' association.[92]

Reformers most heavily emphasized the potential cost-savings from eliminating minimums.[93] For instance, FAMM touted an analysis by the *Detroit News* indicating that reforms might save Michigan $41 million in 2003 alone, assuming the reforms were made retroactive.[94] Such promises of reduced corrections costs resonated with the public at a time when Michigan, like many other states, was still reeling from the fiscal aftershocks of the 2001 Recession. Additionally, the reform effort may have been bolstered by the well-financed, contemporaneous push to put a Proposition 36–type diversion initiative on the ballot in Michigan. Although that push ultimately came up short, for a time it made the FAMM proposal on mandatory minimums appear to be a middle-of-the-road alternative to more radical reforms. As the Michigan House's legislative analyst put it, "the [FAMM] bills represent a compromise between law enforcement and advocates for sentencing reform."[95]

Consistent with that spirit of compromise, the bills were marked by some of the same limitations that have generally blunted the imprisonment-reducing effects of mandatory minimum reform. To be sure, Michigan's 2002 law was considerably more ambitious than the 1998 law. The legislature eliminated *all* quantity-based minimums and eased drug sentencing in a number of other respects. Still, the legislature retained high *maximum* sentences, including the possibility of life for the highest-quantity drug offenses, and essentially left judges with the discretion to continue imposing the same sentences they had been before the reforms. This was important because, in a great many drug cases, judges were choosing to impose sentences *higher* than the mandatory minimums. For instance, in trafficking cases involving less than 50 grams—which accounted for the great majority of cases subject to minimums—the average judge-imposed sentence was 2.4 years, more than twice as long as the minimum.[96] It was far from clear that elimination of the minimum would have any discernible effect on this important category of cases.

Moreover, as has often been the case with reforms purporting to reduce imprisonment, the legislature took with one hand even as it was giving with the other. Although minimums were eliminated, the legislature simultaneously made the state sentencing guidelines tougher in some drug cases. Taking the crude, quantity-based minimums out of the picture and giving greater force to the guidelines promised a more nuanced approach to drug sentencing, but guaranteed no overall reduction in severity. Some defendants would be better off in the new system; others would be worse off. It was hard to predict what the net effect would be on imprisonment, but the Department of Corrections indicated that the guidelines changes might actually increase its need for prison beds over the long run.[97]

Michigan did make the 2002 reforms partially retroactive, which meant that the new law would almost certainly be imprisonment-reducing in the short run as a small flood of inmates became eligible for parole early. Of course, the scale of the imprisonment reduction would ultimately depend on the generosity of the politicized parole board.

In the end, Michigan did achieve a quick, sizable reduction in its number of offenders imprisoned on drug charges, which dropped from 5,485 in 2002, the year the reforms were adopted, to 4,517 a year later.[98] After that, further progress stalled; three years later, Michigan still held 4,427 drug prisoners. Yet, the fact that the new equilibrium proved durable underscored that some real changes had been made in the way the system was handling drug cases. For instance, the proportion of convicted drug offenders sentenced to prison dropped from 18 percent in 2002 to 11 percent in 2008.[99]

While Michigan's abandonment of drug minimums did make a difference in some cases, the continuing presence of thousands of drug offenders in Michigan's prisons attested to the persistence of drug war punitiveness. Moreover, the gains achieved through reduced drug imprisonment were swamped by increases in imprisonment for other offenses, as the state's overall prison population rose to an all-time high of 51,554 in March 2007.[100]

New York Drops the "Rock"

In contrast to Michigan, New York achieved much more impressive reductions in drug imprisonment after 2000, and those reductions, in turn, played a key role in the state's overall efforts to cut imprisonment. New York's drug war de-escalation proved more consequential in large part because New York's earlier drug war *escalation* had been more dramatic. Drug prisoners contributed much more to New York's imprisonment boom than they had to the nation's as a whole, which meant that the Empire State could get more imprisonment-reduction benefits from de-escalation than most other states.

As with Michigan, New York's marquee drug minimum from the 1970s—an indeterminate term of 15 years to life for sale of 1 ounce or possession of 2 ounces—actually ensnared relatively few defendants. In 2004, on the eve of significant reforms to the Rockefeller

Drug Laws, New York imprisoned only 481 offenders under the 15-to-life provision—or only about 0.7 percent of the state's massive prison population.[101] In part, this small number resulted from various reforms adopted 25 years earlier, including a doubling of the quantity of drugs required to trigger the minimum. Additionally, as with 650-Lifer in Michigan, prosecutors had developed strategies to avoid application of the minimum.

Although few New Yorkers were serving 15-to-life under the Rockefeller Laws, more than 16,000 were otherwise imprisoned on drug charges in 2004. Indeed, this number had already fallen sharply from its peak. In 1997, New York held nearly 23,000 drug prisoners, amounting to one-third of the entire state prison population.[102] By contrast, Michigan's proportion was only about 13 percent in that time period.[103] Nationally, the number for all states was about 20 percent.[104] New York's extraordinary run-up in drug imprisonment resulted in part from the application of other mandatory minimums besides the infamous 15-to-life. Like Michigan, New York had an array of lesser minimums for lower quantities of drugs. Additionally, sentences of most imprisoned drug offenders were enhanced under the Second Felony Offender Law, which had been adopted at the same time as the Rockefeller Drug Laws.[105]

The Rockefeller Laws had been controversial from the start, but criticism mounted throughout the 1990s. The basic arguments for reducing drug imprisonment echoed what we have already seen in California and Michigan: treatment would produce better results for drug offenders at much lower cost. As with FAMM in Michigan, the "Drop the Rock" coalition in New York successfully generated publicity around the minimums issue and coordinated the efforts of activists.[106] Its campaign was aided by a widely reported 1999 poll of New York voters, showing strong support for reducing sentences and increasing judicial discretion in drug cases.[107]

Even before any formal amendment to the Rockefeller Drug Laws, criminal justice officials in New York began to respond to the turning tide of public opinion. Beginning in 2000, felony drug arrests in New York fell sharply and consistently for five consecutive years, dropping by about 40 percent overall in that time period.[108] The proportion of convicted drug offenders sent to prison also plummeted, falling from 21 percent in 1997 to 10.5 percent in 2008.[109] In other words, fewer felony drug cases were being pushed into the court system by the police, and those that did make it to court were being treated more leniently there. Notably, these important trends were already established before the state legislature undertook any fresh reform of mandatory minimums.

In 2003, motivated in part by fiscal pressures, Republican governor George Pataki inserted a few narrowly targeted provisions into the state budget bill to facilitate earlier parole release for some New York inmates, including those serving time under the drug minimums.[110] The next year, Pataki reached agreement with legislative leaders on a bipartisan reform package that more directly took on the Rockefeller Drug Laws.[111] The triggering weights for the most severe sentencing categories were doubled, and the infamous 15-to-life was entirely eliminated; henceforth, the highest-volume drug offenders would be given a determinate term of between 8 and 20 years. (With a determinate sentence, recall that the judge decides on a specific prison term within the range. By contrast, with an indeterminate sentence, the judge imposes a range, and the parole board later selects a release date within the range.) Moreover, those already serving 15-to-life terms were given the benefit of retroactivity. Over the next two years, nearly 200 prisoners were resentenced under the reforms and then released. In 2005, the legislature extended the right to request resentencing to a broader set of imprisoned drug offenders.[112]

Although the most extreme mandatory sentences had been repealed, the Rockefeller Drug Laws remained controversial, with judges still obligated to impose prison terms in lieu of community-based treatment in many cases. A Democratic takeover of state government in 2009 helped to ensure the adoption of more sweeping reforms. The 2009 law eliminated all of the drug mandatory minimums in New York except for the highest-level drug offenses.[113] Also excluded were offenders with a violent felony conviction in the past 10 years. In addition to eliminating the minimums, the 2009 reforms also made it easier for judges to send offenders to treatment and provided resentencing opportunities for hundreds of prisoners.[114]

In the time period of these reforms, New York achieved dramatic reductions in drug imprisonment. Between 1996 and 2013, the state's number of imprisoned drug offenders plummeted from 23,511 to 6,422—an astonishing 73 percent drop.[115] As a result, New York has become increasingly well-known nationally as one of the few real imprisonment-reduction success stories in the new millennium. What is less well-known is that reduced drug imprisonment accounts for nearly the entirety of New York's overall imprisonment drop. Indeed, as indicated in Figure 2.1, if drug offenders are excluded, New York's prison population has barely budged at all since its 1999 peak.[116]

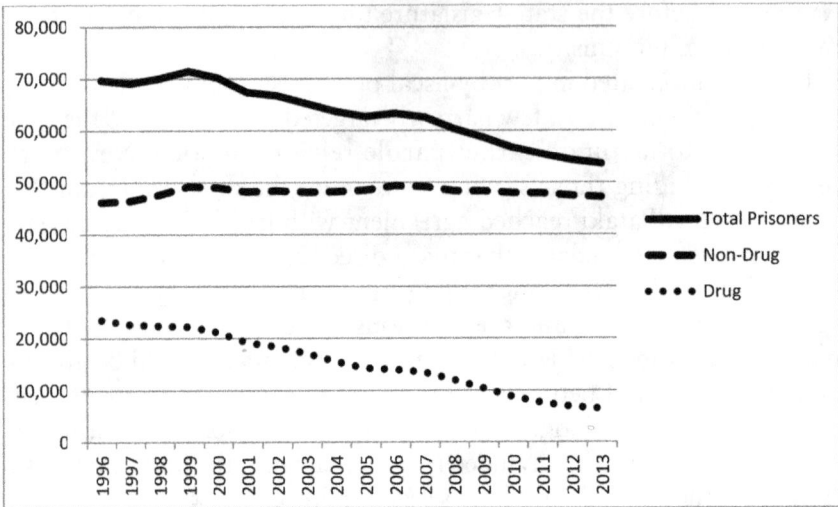

Figure 2.1   New York Prisoners, 1996–2013

It is not clear, though, how much of New York's remarkable drug-imprisonment reduction has been due to mandatory minimum reforms or other explicit state policy changes. The drop began in the late 1990s, well before the most-touted law reform, and Figure 2.1 reveals no particular acceleration in the drop after either the 2004 or 2009 changes. Shifts in policing practices, which began a few years before mandatory minimum reforms, likely played a role that was at least as important. Between 1999 and 2012, felony drug arrests in New York fell by half.[117] Additionally, drug offenders benefited from the development of drug courts and other local diversion initiatives, as well as from the implementation of "merit time" and other early release measures that will be discussed in more detail in the next chapter.

The mandatory minimum reforms, moreover, were limited in various ways that we have already considered in other jurisdictions: the reforms were focused particularly on defendants without prior convictions for violent crime, and they kept high maximum sentences in place, which enabled judges to continue imposing tough sentences if they wished. The reforms also included the creation of two new drug felonies.[118] One study comparing the outcome of felony drug arrests in New York before and after the 2009 reforms found only a slight decrease in the proportion of cases resulting in prison terms, which fell from 10 percent in 2008 to 9 percent in 2010.[119] Although there was a slight uptick in the percentage of diversion (treatment) cases, the number of incarceration (prison or jail) cases remained more than five times greater than the number of diversion cases. Another study of cases from New York City found that the average prison term in drug cases actually *increased* between 2008 and 2010.[120]

In sum, New York offers a very encouraging story about the ability of a state to achieve dramatic reductions in its use of imprisonment, but the *how* part of the story seems complicated and uncertain. One lesson that emerges from a closer look at the New York experience is that mandatory minimum reforms seem neither necessary nor sufficient in themselves to bring about sharp reductions in imprisonment.

Marijuana Reform

Beginning with the first drug treatment court in Miami in 1989 through Proposition 36 and the more recent elimination of mandatory minimums, the central focus of the drug reforms we have considered has been the diversion of drug offenders from costly incarceration into more effective treatment. However, reformers have seemingly accepted certain key premises of the War on Drugs: that the law may properly prohibit the recreational use of controlled substances, that the criminal justice system should play a lead role in the suppression of drug use and trafficking, and that at least some drug offenders— the higher-level dealers, the hardcore addicts who will not accept treatment—do belong behind bars. A different, slower-developing reform movement has more directly challenged these premises, at least with respect to one particular drug. The movement to legalize marijuana struggled to gain traction for a decade, but since 2012, legalization advocates have racked up victories in Colorado, Washington, Oregon, Alaska, California, Nevada, Massachusetts, and the District of Columbia. These developments mark the nation's clearest break to date from the War on Drugs. It remains to be seen, however, whether the legalization movement will spread beyond the libertarian West and a few of the liberal enclaves of the Northeast, and, if so, whether it will have any discernible effect on mass incarceration.

The legalization movement followed on the heels of an earlier wave of marijuana reforms. In 1996, California became the first state to legalize the use of marijuana for medical purposes.[121] As with Proposition 36 four years later, California adopted medical marijuana through a well-funded ballot-initiative campaign, with a similar cast of characters supporting both measures.[122] For instance, George

Soros, the billionaire investor who played a key role in financing the Proposition 36 effort, kicked in $350,000 for medical marijuana.[123] The campaign rested on claims that marijuana effectively alleviates various chronic medical conditions, particularly certain conditions related to AIDS and cancer. Television ads focused on sympathetic cases, like that of a cancer patient who used marijuana to ease nausea.[124] Thus, the beneficiaries of the law were not depicted as recreational users, but as the unfortunate victims of dread diseases. However, the broadly worded California law extended beyond the worst hard-luck cases and practically invited a blurring of the lines between medicinal and recreational uses. Critics charged, not altogether unfairly, that the medical-marijuana law amounted to a de facto decriminalization of marijuana.

Despite such criticism, the 1996 California initiative proved the first of many medical-marijuana laws. By the end of 2014, 23 states and the District of Columbia had approved medical marijuana.[125] However, not all states adopted such broadly worded laws as had California. One recent study summarized the current state of medical marijuana this way:

> California and Colorado receive a lot of attention in the medical-marijuana debates, but they represent one end of a broad spectrum. They allow brick-and-mortar medical-marijuana stores (called dispensaries) and have very expansive definitions of what conditions justify obtaining a medical recommendation. In some other states, including Vermont, the medical-marijuana system is more controlled, serving more as an adjunct to the health system than as a loophole for recreational users. Indeed, 11 (mostly southern) states in 2014 passed even more-restrictive medical marijuana laws.[126]

To whatever extent some medical-marijuana laws functioned as a sort of quasi-decriminalization, they had a precursor in the decriminalization movement of the 1970s, which led to substantial reductions in criminal penalties for marijuana offenses in 12 states.[127] However, such decriminalization is distinct from legalization, which removes the threat of even fines from adult users of marijuana and permits the development of legal distribution systems. There are several different models for legalization, but many advocates for legalization contemplate that marijuana would be treated like alcohol—that is, be readily available to adult consumers, but subject to considerable regulation and relatively high taxes.

Encouraged by the success of Proposition 36 and the first handful of medical-marijuana initiatives, reformers put legalization on the ballot in Alaska in 2000 and Nevada in 2002. Both efforts failed badly; neither managed to win even 41 percent of the vote.[128] However, national public opinion surveys showed steadily rising support for legalization. From just 16 percent in 1990, support had crossed the 50 percent threshold by 2013.[129] In part, this reflected a process of generational turnover; for decades, surveys have shown greater support for legalization among those born after 1945 than those born earlier.[130] Among other implications, generational turnover means that more Americans have had personal experience with marijuana; nearly half (49 percent) now say they have tried the drug.[131] Not surprisingly, prior use correlates with legalization support.[132] Additionally, it is possible that widespread acceptance of medical marijuana has contributed to a growing perception that marijuana is a relatively benign drug.[133] More than two-thirds of Americans now believe that marijuana is less harmful than alcohol.[134]

Whatever the cause for the shift in public opinion, 2012 proved the breakthrough year, with Colorado and Washington adopting legalization ballot initiatives. Proponents argued that marijuana was a relatively safe substance, law enforcement resources would be better used to address other issues, and taxation of marijuana would generate millions of dollars in new state revenues. Notably, the very first argument in favor of the initiative in Washington's official voter pamphlet was that it "frees law enforcement resources to focus on violent crime."[135] If the War on Drugs was fueled in the 1980s and 1990s by the perceived connection between drugs and violence, then it seems a natural strategy for reformers to turn the tables and depict the two offense categories as being in competition with one another for limited police, court, and corrections attention.

Still, to whatever extent the movement spreads, marijuana legalization is not likely to produce sizable direct reductions in imprisonment. For one thing, there are relatively few prisoners serving time for marijuana offenses. One recent study put the national number at about 40,000[136]—a very small fraction of the 1.6 million total. But even that number may overstate the impact of national legalization since about half of the 40,000 are also serving time for other offenses. Moreover, some uncertain—but likely substantial—percentage of the marijuana-only prisoners pled down to the marijuana conviction as part of a deal, or were at least suspected of more serious offenses but only charged with marijuana because that was the most convenient strategy for police and prosecutors. If such options were not available, many of the defendants would simply be prosecuted, convicted, and imprisoned for other crimes. To be sure, there are additional prisoners convicted of non-marijuana offenses who are serving time as a result of probation or parole violations relating to marijuana use, but the terms of incarceration following such low-level violations tend to be short; even taking these marijuana violators into account, full national legalization would hardly make a discernible dent in mass incarceration.

Further to this point, about three-quarters of marijuana prisoners have been convicted of *trafficking* offenses, not simple possession.[137] Many of these offenders are enmeshed in black market networks that involve other drugs and, in some cases, violence. And even the true marijuana-only distributors would not necessarily stay out of trouble in a world of legalized weed. For instance, some would turn to the distribution of other drugs, or would continue to distribute marijuana illegally in circumvention of new taxes and regulations. (The availability of legal tobacco has not prevented the development of a robust black market in tax-free cigarettes.) One way or another, it seems unrealistic to think that all or even most of the offenders currently serving time on marijuana offenses would have managed to stay out of prison if the drug had been legalized.

The Post-2007 Drop in Drug Imprisonment

None of the explicit policy changes we have considered in this chapter has had, or is likely to have, a big impact on drug imprisonment by itself. Yet, as indicated in Figure 2.2, there was finally a sizable drop in drug imprisonment in the United States beginning in 2007.[138] Over the next six years, the overall number of drug prisoners fell by nearly 17 percent.

Figure 2.3 puts the drug-imprisonment trends in broader perspective, making clear that recent reductions are not much more than a drop in the proverbial bucket of U.S. mass incarceration. Still, the drug-imprisonment trends are notable, and more than fully account for the recent modest reductions in overall imprisonment. In other words, if drug imprisonment were taken out of the picture, overall imprisonment in the United States would have continued its steady, four-decade upward climb.

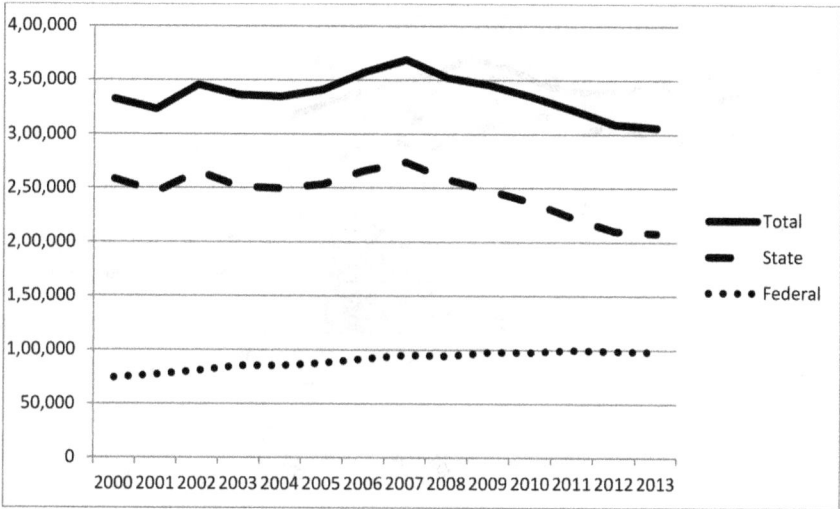

Figure 2.2   Drug Offenders in U.S. Prisons, 2000–2013

What brought about the post-2007 drop in drug imprisonment? In part, the recent trend must reflect the accumulated effects of all of the explicit policy changes discussed in this chapter. Yet, even more fundamental may be implicit changes in policing policies, much as we saw in the New York data. Figure 2.4 depicts drug imprisonment and adult arrests for drug distribution, which account for the vast

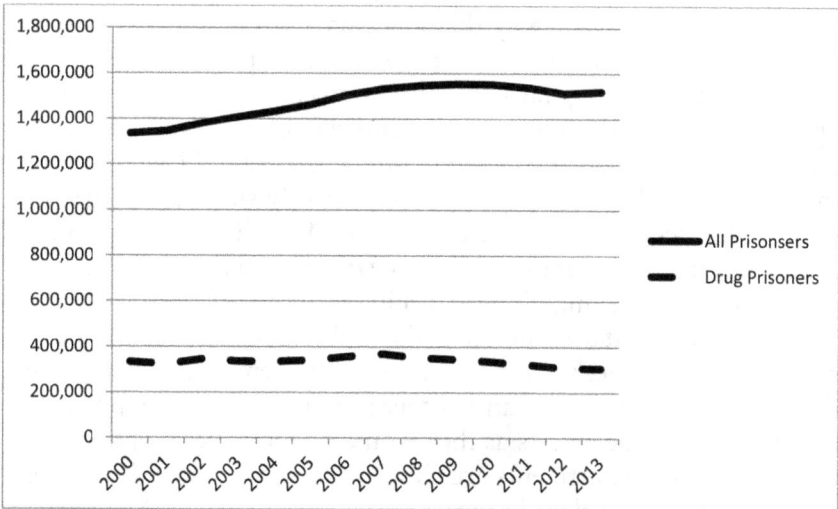

Figure 2.3   U.S. Imprisonment Trends, 2000–2013

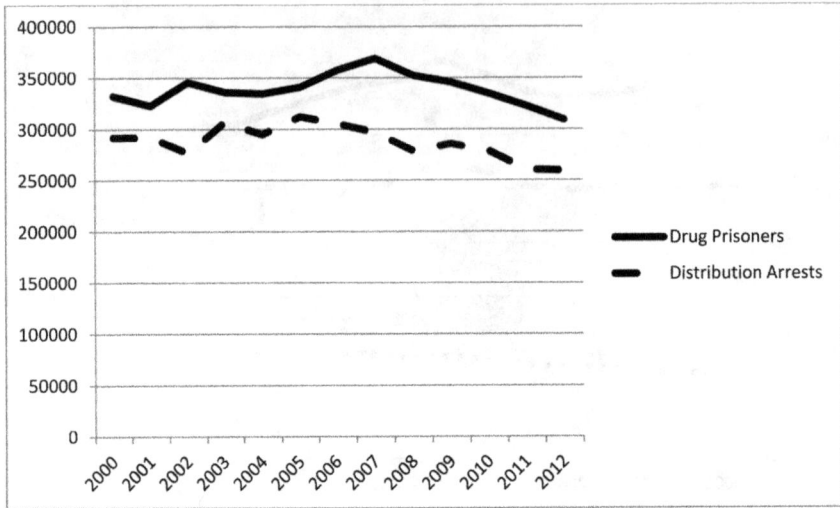

Figure 2.4 Drug Imprisonment and Distribution Arrests, 2000–2012

majority of drug prisoners. Distribution arrests peaked in 2005 and then fell 17 percent over the next seven years—precisely the size of the drop in drug imprisonment. Although the drop in drug arrests started two years before the drop in drug imprisonment, this lag is not surprising given the length of time required to convert drug arrests into prison sentences; one would not expect new arrest trends to translate into new imprisonment trends immediately.

It is not entirely clear why the police have been arresting so many fewer drug offenders, but the trend is not limited to traffickers; possession arrests have also gone down by 14 percent since 2005. It does not appear that reduced drug *usage* explains the drop in drug arrests. For instance, the number of American adults reporting illicit drug use in the past month has actually increased steadily since 2005, growing from 7.9 percent to 10.3 percent in 2014.[139] Tens of millions of Americans thus commit drug offenses each year, but the annual arrest totals are only reaching about 1.5 million. Drug offenses are like the dust "bunnies" that accumulate in the dark corners and under the furniture in your home: the more you look for them, the more you will find. It is not too much of an exaggeration to say that the police can make as many drug arrests as they would like to make. For some reason, U.S. police departments are choosing to make fewer drug arrests now than they did a decade ago.

Although definitive explanations are not available, it is not hard to imagine some of the factors that have likely contributed to the trend. For instance, if the War on Drugs was, at least in part, a desperate response to unusually high levels of violence in the United States beginning in the 1960s, then the steady, sustained decline in violence that began in the early 1990s would relieve some of the pressure that caused police departments to enforce drug laws so vigorously. Additionally, if the War on Drugs resulted in part from the frustration of black Americans with deteriorating safety and quality of life in the inner city, police enforcement activities engendered their own back-lash, as exemplified by the Black Lives Matter movement that achieved national prominence in 2015. Evolving public attitudes have altered the political context in which urban police departments estab-lish their priorities and strategies, discouraging aggressive stop-and-frisk practices, for instance, as well as arrests for crimes that are not clearly victimizing. Explicit policy changes such as the elimination of drug mandatory minimums may have also played an indirect role in the implicit policy changes, serving as confirmation of the shift in political sentiment against the War on Drugs.

Some of the dynamics seem to be illustrated by the New York City experience, albeit on a somewhat earlier time frame than the nation as a whole. In the 1990s, the NYPD's narcotics unit was the depart-ment's fastest growing, more than doubling in size by 1999.[140] After 1999, however, narcotics staffing fell sharply. By 2006, the unit's size had fallen below where it had been even in 1990, reflecting a dramatic realignment of department resources. Predictably, felony drug arrests in the city dropped in tandem with the reduction in dedicated narcot-ics officers.[141]

What motivated this shift in Big Apple policing? In part, the NYPD may have been reacting to growing public opposition to the War on Drugs; recall that the Drop the Rock movement was gathering steam in New York in the late 1990s and early 2000s, resulting in significant reforms to the Rockefeller Drug Laws in 2004. But even more impor-tant, suggests law professor and criminologist Franklin Zimring, were the changing demographics of drug use and the replacement of open-air drug markets with more private means of distribution, both of which contributed to a large drop in drug-related violent crime in the city.[142] Against that backdrop, the drawdown of the narcotics unit seems to indicate that the earlier 1990s buildup had little to do with suppressing drug use per se. Zimring puts it this way:

One very likely explanation [for the drawdown] is that the police had succeeded in achieving the two major strategic objectives that animated the narcotic unit's expansion—driving drug markets off the streets and reducing drug traffic-related violence. . . . Indeed, the almost 60 percent drop in narcotics unit strength is strong circumstantial evidence that the open air market and lethal violence aspects of drug traffic were the department's chief priorities all along.[143]

Whatever its underlying causes, though, it is important to keep the national drop in drug arrests in perspective: drug arrests in the United States today remain 50 percent higher than they were in the early 1990s. It is apparent that drug war de-escalation remains an uneven, equivocal phenomenon.

Drug War De-Escalation as Microcosm

Drug enforcement in the United States took a sharply punitive turn in the late 20th century as drug-control policy became swept up in the broader backlash against violent crime. The War on Drugs represented a blurring of the distinction between violent crime and drug crime, which were increasingly seen as interconnected in a variety of important ways. By 2000, however, it was clear that many Americans were uncomfortable with the extent to which drug crime and violent crime were being equated in both explicit and implicit policies. Not all drug offenders presented a serious risk of armed violence, and not all drug distribution had an inherently violent or predatory character.

As we have seen, states responded to growing public skepticism of the War on Drugs by adopting a variety of de-escalating reforms. The basic thrust of these reforms has been to put the tools of drug enforcement to work in a more discriminating fashion—distinguishing the nonviolent drug offenders more sharply from the violent, the treatable offenders from the nontreatable, and the offenses involving marijuana from those involving the "harder" drugs. The reforms have been highly beneficial for some offenders. However, for dealers in cocaine or other hard drugs who have prior convictions or seemingly violent tendencies, sentencing in 2017 may be little different in practice from sentencing in 1997.

Treatment courts, repeal of drug mandatory minimums, and marijuana legalization—all of these may be good reform policies for many important reasons, but they are unlikely in and of themselves to return

U.S. imprisonment rates to anything approaching their historical norms. Most fundamentally, this is because the War on Drugs did not really drive the imprisonment boom to begin with. Although drug imprisonment constituted a steadily larger share of overall imprisonment in the late 20th century, it never moved much above the one-fifth mark. Even if every single prisoner primarily serving time for drug offenses was immediately released, the national imprisonment rate would remain several times higher than it was prior to the imprisonment boom.

In this regard, New York is the outlier. Because it stepped up drug imprisonment much more aggressively than most other states, New York had more low-hanging fruit to reap when it decided to de-escalate. As a result, New York did achieve a remarkable imprisonment drop through reductions in drug imprisonment. However, reformers in other states should not assume that they can duplicate New York's success.

Beyond the fundamental problem that drug imprisonment constitutes only a quite limited share of overall imprisonment, there are other reasons to doubt that recent drug war reforms could really change the mass incarceration picture even if they were more widely adopted. In this chapter, I have identified certain recurring themes in the recent reform efforts that limit their imprisonment-reducing potential. First, they tend to exclude offenders with a record of violence, even when that record is relatively old or minor. Second, they typically leave judges with discretion to continue imposing the same prison sentences they had in the past, and do little in themselves to alter the political pressures that push judges, prosecutors, and corrections officials toward excessive toughness. Third, many rely on new systems of treatment and supervision with high failure rates. These reforms may divert offenders from incarceration on the front end, but leave many offenders serving as much or even more time behind bars on the back end. This problem may be exacerbated by stinginess in funding treatment services, which can significantly impair their effectiveness. Fourth, and finally, proponents typically frame the reforms as a way to shift law enforcement resources, including prison beds, away from low-level drug offenders to more serious criminals. Perhaps inadvertently, their rhetoric reinforces the popular view that there are many dangerous predators among us who ought to be locked away for as long as possible. Indeed, the reformers' implicit trade-off—less imprisonment for the low-level drug offenders, but more imprisonment for others—becomes quite explicit in some of the reforms, such as the 2002 Michigan measure that eliminated mandatory minimums but also simultaneously toughened some of the drug sentencing guidelines.

We will see these four themes sound repeatedly outside the drug context in the chapters to come.

CHAPTER THREE

The Early Release "Revolution"

As we saw in Chapter 1, dozens of states adopted determinate sentencing (aka "truth in sentencing") reforms between 1975 and 2000. These reforms aimed at increasing the certainty *at the moment of sentencing* about how much time the offender would actually spend in prison. Reformers particularly sought to reduce or eliminate the power of parole boards, which traditionally had vast discretion to release offenders before the end of their terms. In part, determinate sentencing reflected a growing mistrust of parole boards, which typically lacked any real transparency in their decision making and seemed prone to racial bias and other forms of arbitrariness. But determinate sentencing also reflected a desire to ensure longer real terms of imprisonment, especially for violent and sexual offenders. Consistent with that end, determinate sentencing did tend to escalate rates of imprisonment growth, although the effects varied quite a bit from state to state.[1]

Once the 2001 Recession hit, cash-strapped states did not take long to begin chipping away at their determinate sentencing reforms. Soon, dozens of states were expanding or adopting "compassionate" release for elderly and seriously ill inmates, "good time" credits toward early release for good behavior, and even old-fashioned parole release. Scholars soon began to suggest that there was an early release "revolution" afoot.[2]

Upon closer inspection, however, it became clear that the revolution was half-hearted at best. Indeed, many early release measures were repealed within a handful of years. Furthermore, those that proved more durable tended to have quite modest effects on imprisonment levels. In general, the early release programs were narrowly targeted by legislatures and conservatively implemented by criminal justice officials.

Compassionate Release

Compassionate release programs offer early release to inmates for whom continued imprisonment represents a particular hardship, including those who are terminally ill, physically or mentally disabled, or simply very old. There is a great variety in these programs, and they go by different names in different states, including medical parole, medical furlough, and geriatric release. Programs of this sort date back at least to the 1970s,[3] but have been expanded in many states since 2000 as a way to deal with burgeoning prison populations and the unusually high expenses associated with ill and disabled inmates. Forty-six states currently offer some version of compassionate release, but the procedures have generally proven slow, cumbersome, overly cautious, and ineffective at providing much relief to the targeted inmate populations.[4]

On the face of it, there does seem to be a compelling fiscal case for compassionate release. Reflecting the increased use of life sentences and other multi-decade terms of imprisonment, America's elderly inmate population has grown even more explosively since the 1970s than has the national prison population as a whole. One recent report determined that nearly a quarter million inmates are now aged 50 or older.[5] This population is unusually expensive to incarcerate. While the average cost per inmate nationally is about $34,000 per year, the average cost of an older inmate (50 plus) is $68,000—fully twice as much.[6] This extra cost results largely from the disabilities and chronic illnesses that tend to afflict the elderly. About half of older prisoners suffer from medical problems like diabetes, hypertension, arthritis, dementia, or asthma.[7] Moreover, the particular circumstances of incarceration complicate the treatment of older prisoners and often make their medical conditions even more expensive to manage than they would be for seniors in free society. For instance, specialized treatment is apt to require a trip out of the prison to a hospital, with staff members needed to provide transportation and then guard the inmate while he is receiving care—frequently paid on an overtime scale. Consider one elderly female prisoner's experience in California:

> The shrunken 82-year-old wakes up every morning to change
> into her prison uniform. Then guards must outfit her with ankle

chains, belly chains, and handcuffs. Next, she is transported 40 minutes for dialysis. She suffers from chronic renal failure, a condition that she figures costs the state $436,000 a year, not counting the two $24.75-an-hour armed corrections officers who guard her, all five feet and 90 pounds, for up to 8 hours a day three times a week.[8]

Even back in the prison, elderly inmates may consume a disproportionate share of staff time to the extent that they require extra assistance with daily activities or special accommodations in their housing.

While the costs of imprisoning the elderly may be unusually high, the public safety benefits tend to be unusually low. Recidivism rates fall as offenders age. One national study found that, among inmates released at age 45 or older, only about 17 percent were returned to prison for a new crime within three years.[9] (The corresponding rate for those in the 18–24 age range was about 30 percent.) State-specific studies find even lower recidivism rates for even older classes of inmate. In New York, for instance, only 4 percent of prisoners aged 65 or older were returned to prison for a new crime, while in Virginia the rate for prisoners aged 55 or older was an even more miniscule 1.3 percent.[10]

In light of such numbers, many states instituted or liberalized compassionate release programs as they dealt with the fiscal aftermath of the 2001 Recession. Wisconsin's experience illustrates both how such programs are designed and why they have proven such a disappointment. The Wisconsin legislature first authorized compassionate release as part of a 2002 law intended to close a budgetary shortfall.[11] Inmates could petition for early release based either on terminal illness (six months or less to live) or age. For age-based release, 60 would suffice if the inmate had served at least 10 years in prison; otherwise, petitioners had to be at least 65. Class A and B felons, the highest-level offenders, were excluded. Even more important than this limitation, though, was the process, which seemed markedly tilted against the petitioning inmate. The inmate first had to get approval from officials at his prison, with no right to appeal an adverse decision.[12] Then, the inmate had to present his petition to his original sentencing court, which had wide discretion to approve or deny the petition based on whether the release would serve the "public interest." Of course, a risk-averse elected judge had little reason to give any benefit of the doubt to a petitioning inmate.

With few inmates released under the original legislation and another budget crisis looming, Wisconsin lawmakers tried again in 2009.

Compassionate release was liberalized in several respects. Class A and B felons were made eligible. Health-based release no longer required a terminal illness, but could be ordered as a result of any "extraordinary health condition," defined to include a condition for which treatment was not available in prison. Perhaps even more promising were changes to the process. Petitions would no longer go to prison officials and then back to the sentencing court, but would instead be decided by a new Earned Release Review Commission comprising gubernatorial appointees.

Pushed through a Democratic legislature by a Democratic governor, the 2009 reforms quickly became a partisan lightning rod.[13] Republicans accused Democrats of endangering public safety. Even if the released inmates were sufficiently disabled so as to require nursing home care, this seemed to provide no reassurance to Republicans, who argued that other nursing home residents might be victimized.[14] Critics became particularly hyperbolic when a Class B felon was granted compassionate release for the first time: Paula Harris, the petitioner, was a "convicted murderer" and "dangerous criminal," in the words of one leading Republican.[15] Never mind that she suffered from congestive heart failure and had trouble walking. She died two years after her release.

Harris proved to be not only the first but also the last Class B felon to gain compassionate release in Wisconsin. Following a Republican sweep of state elections in 2010, the ban on Class B felons was reinstated, the Earned Release Review Commission eliminated, and the original compassionate-release procedures restored. In truth, however, the commission had been hardly any more receptive to compassionate release than had the judges. Over the two years that the 2009 reforms were in place, the commission approved only eight compassionate releases.[16] Not one was based on age alone. Moreover, five of the eight released inmates died within four months, indicating that the standards for a qualifying health condition remained very dire, despite a theoretical relaxation of the terminal-illness requirement. Meanwhile, as against this paltry number of releases, 73 Wisconsin prisoners died in custody in 2010 and 2011, and more than 300 prisoners were aged 65 or older, which would have qualified them for age-based release assuming they had served at least five years of their sentence.

The Wisconsin story brings together all of the key challenges that have plagued compassionate release initiatives across the United States. In the original 2002 legislation, risk-averse lawmakers built in high standards and categorical exclusions that left out many inmates who were not terminally ill, but who posed no threat to public safety and suffered disabilities that were difficult to manage in prison in a humane, cost-effective way. Even beyond that, lawmakers gave effectively unlimited discretion to deny petitions to corrections officials and judges—decision makers who had every reason to be just as risk-averse as the lawmakers themselves. Then, when standards were relaxed in 2009, compassionate release drew partisan fire as a threat to public safety. Doubtless reflecting the overheated environment of partisan attack, the new system proved no more generous in practice than the old.

Other states have had similar experiences. New York released only 371 inmates on medical parole between 1992 and 2014, an average of fewer than 17 per year.[17] By comparison, the New York prison system averages about 100 inmate deaths from natural causes each year. In 2014, only 30 inmates even bothered to file applications for medical release; 6 of these died before their review. Pennsylvania is even more restrictive, granting only nine compassionate releases from 2010 to mid-2015.[18] The Pennsylvania law requires inmates to prove to a judge that they are terminally ill and could receive better care outside of prison. Critics charge that inmates are effectively required to obtain a lawyer in order to navigate the system. Virginia has more flexible criteria in its geriatric parole program, but the results are hardly more impressive: only 46 releases between 2002 and 2013.[19] In one year, researchers found that not even 1 percent of about 800 eligible inmates were granted geriatric release by the state parole board, even as 84 inmates died in prison over the same time period.

A recent national survey of state compassionate release laws found several critical recurring features limiting their effectiveness.[20] Seventeen states specified a maximum expected life expectancy for an inmate to be eligible for early release, typically either 6 or 12 months left to live, but in one state (Kansas) just 30 days. Twenty-seven states required an inmate to be incapacitated. Only 17 states specifically indicated that mental or psychological impairments could be considered as a basis for early release. Only 17 states had what the researchers considered to be clearly defined processes and rules for early release. Twenty-five states categorically excluded inmates sentenced to life without parole, while 11 categorically excluded those convicted of sexual offenses. Finally, the researchers observed, there was "little consistency, or even clarity" concerning whether and how to take into account "the well being of the incarcerated person and his/her family."

The latter point highlights the grounding of "compassionate" release laws in fiscal, not genuinely humanitarian, considerations. These fiscal considerations, however, have not been sufficiently compelling to induce lawmakers to define eligibility broadly to include anywhere close to the full population of older inmates who no longer pose a significant threat to public safety. Nor have these considerations induced the discretionary decision makers—judges, prison officials, parole boards—to grant compassionate release in a prompt, reliable way even to the truncated class of inmates who are legally eligible.

Good Conduct Time

As early as the 1850s, inmates in some states could earn credit toward early release by following prison rules and staying out of trouble.[21] "Good conduct time"—or, as it is more commonly known, simply "good time"—provided positive incentives for *good* behavior to complement the brutal corporal punishment that was used to discourage *bad* behavior. By 1910, every state had a good-time system in place.[22] However, in the imprisonment-boom era of the late 20th century, good time lost ground as part of the general movement toward determinate prison terms (i.e., truth in sentencing). By making the prison term partially depend on behavior in prison, good time left some uncertainty at the moment of sentencing over when exactly the defendant would get out.

However, at the same time that many states were restricting or eliminating good time, a few others were *expanding* good time as part of a desperate effort to manage prison overcrowding. As a result, by 2000, American good-time law was a crazy quilt of state-to-state variation. In some states, no inmates could qualify for any good time; at the other extreme, some states provided day-for-day credit, effectively cutting sentences in half for inmates who stayed out of serious trouble. Between the extremes, states typically permitted sentence reductions of one-quarter to one-third for good behavior. In the 1990s, however, even some of the more generous states reduced the good-time credits that could be earned by violent and sexual offenders.

Since 2000, at least 19 states have adopted or liberalized good-time programs.[23] As with the contemporaneous reforms to compassionate release, these good-time reforms had a lot to do with the need to rein in imprisonment growth in an era of extraordinary fiscal pressure.

At the same time, much research indicates that good time can do more than just save money; it can also make prisons safer and more orderly, and even reduce the recidivism rates of inmates after they are released.[24] Particularly promising is a variation on good time called "earned time." Earned-time credits depend not only on staying out of trouble, but also on participating in education, employment, vocational training, or other constructive activities in prison.

New York provided an early and influential exemplar of successful reform using the earned-time model. In 1997, New York's legislature authorized a new "Merit Time Program," which allowed some nonviolent inmates to earn up to a one-sixth reduction in their minimum term of confinement based on the successful completion of GED, vocational training, or substance-abuse programming, or the completion of 400 hours of service as part of a community work crew.[25] The legislature then expanded the program to make more drug offenders eligible in 2003. By the end of its first decade, New York had released about 24,000 inmates under the program, saving taxpayers an estimated $372 million in operating costs and $15 million in capital construction.[26] These inmates, moreover, seemed to have somewhat lower recidivism rates than otherwise comparable offenders.[27]

Despite these promising numbers in the assessment report on the program's first decade, a few cautionary notes might also have been sounded. First, more than three-quarters of the inmates released early were serving time for drug offenses. Merit time was thus part of the network of reforms that helped New York to achieve dramatic reductions in drug imprisonment after the mid-1990s. Yet, as we saw in Chapter 2, New York had previously experienced a much faster *increase* in drug imprisonment than had the nation as a whole. In other words, New York had a lot more low-hanging fruit—nonviolent drug offenders serving lengthy prison terms—to clear out of its system than did most other states. Outside of New York, barring violent offenders from good-time reforms would more seriously curtail their impact. Second, a one-sixth reduction in prison terms was relatively modest for good time, and meant in New York that inmates were getting out on average only about six months earlier than they would have anyway.[28] The fact that these marginally earlier releases added up to so much savings was a reflection of the immense size of the New York prison population; other states would have much less to gain from shaving a few months off prison terms. Finally, while recidivism rates seemed to be somewhat lower for merit time inmates, they were still substantial, with 31 percent returned to prison within three years[29]—a sobering reminder that no amount of good conduct in prison can guarantee good conduct in the community.

The modest scope of New York's reforms may have helped to protect them politically. Other states experienced difficulties in keeping good-time reforms going. Consider the Illinois experience. With day-for-day credit going back to the 1970s, Illinois long had one of the nation's most generous good-time programs.[30] Developments in the 1990s cut both directions. On the one hand, the system grew tougher on violent and sexual offenders, reducing their maximum credit to 4.5 days per month. On the other hand, in 1990, in order to deal with overcrowding, the legislature authorized the Department of Corrections to award up to an additional 180 days of credit per inmate.[31] Throughout the 1990s, the department maintained a policy of withholding any of the extra 180 days until after an inmate had served at least 60 days in a state institution. In 2009, however, the department dropped the 60-day rule, thereby significantly accelerating the release of many short-term prisoners.

The 2009 reform provoked considerable opposition. News reports drew public attention to the potential for some offenders who were sentenced to prison to avoid any real prison time. For instance, a one-year term would be cut to six months through day-for-day credit, and most of those six months would be covered by the 180-day credit.[32] The press reported on offenders sentenced even to two- and three-year prison terms getting out only a few days or weeks after sentencing. This was possible in some cases due to the interplay between day-for-day credit, the 180-day credit, and credit for time served in local jails while awaiting trial or sentencing. Critics also claimed, with little apparent basis in fact, that the 2009 reform resulted in the early release of dangerous offenders who went on to commit murders and other serious crimes that would not have occurred without the reform.[33] Finally, in December 2009, Illinois governor Pat Quinn suspended the entire 180-day credit program, even for inmates who had served more than 60 days. Eventually, facing a sudden, sharp increase in the prison population—Illinois added more prisoners to its system than any other state in 2010[34]—the legislature restored the pre-2009 system, with the 180-day credit once again available to inmates *after* they served 60 days.[35]

Washington State also had a short-lived good-time liberalization. Before 2003, Washington generally offered a one-third reduction in prison terms, with a smaller, 10 percent reduction for serious violent or sexual offenders.[36] However, in 2003, the state legislature upped the potential reduction to one-half for certain nonviolent offenders. The reform reflected some skittishness on the part of lawmakers, who specified that the 50 percent rule would expire in 2010 unless first renewed by the legislature. In the interim, the legislature directed the nationally well-regarded Washington State Institute for Public Policy to study the reform's impact.

Issued in 2009, the institute's final report offered a positive review.[37] About 20 percent of released prisoners were benefiting from the good-time liberalization, although the average benefit was only about 63 days. Still, even that modest reduction translated to an average savings of $5,501 in imprisonment costs per prisoner. The effect on crime rates was mostly a wash. The institute found a small but statistically significant 3.5 percent reduction in felony recidivism rates under the 2003 reform, but this benefit was almost exactly offset by having more offenders out of prison and in the community. Overall, taking into account reduced imprisonment costs and other factors, the institute calculated net benefits of more than $7,000 per offender.

Despite this evaluation, Washington's lawmakers quietly allowed the 50 percent initiative to expire in 2010. Even without a public scandal like Illinois's, it proved too difficult to maintain political support over the long run for a liberalizing reform of good time.

The collapse of the Illinois and Washington reforms seems all the more remarkable in light of their modest scope. Like the earlier New York reform, these measures aimed merely to shave a few weeks off the prison terms of a narrow class of relatively low-level offenders. Similar reforms adopted in Wisconsin at the same time proved no longer-lived.[38] Public fear and resentment of prisoners seem sufficiently strong that good-time expansion remains a politically tenuous proposition.

As with compassionate release, proponents of expanding good time have tended to emphasize potential cost-savings. Perhaps reforms would prove more significant and durable if better grounded in ethical considerations. If the offender who commits bad acts deserves imprisonment, it does not seem much of a stretch to say that the offender who then commits *good* acts deserves reduced imprisonment.[39] Properly structured, good time should hold more than just fiscal appeal.

Parole Reform

Although most states curtailed parole during the imprisonment boom, few states eliminated it entirely. One 2002 study found that

33 states still retained indeterminate sentencing for most offenses.[40] Facing budget pressures, many such states were drawn to the potential for parole reforms to move low-risk offenders out of prison more quickly. In 2001, for instance, Mississippi partly rolled back its truth in sentencing legislation, restoring parole eligibility for first-time, non-violent offenders at the one-quarter mark of the prison term.[41] In all, at least seven states liberalized their parole systems between 2000 and 2010, albeit mostly in the same sorts of narrowly targeted ways as Mississippi had.[42]

For generations, American parole has been bedeviled by the sad limitations of parole boards: a lack of genuine correctional expertise, little or no training for members chosen all too often on the basis of political connections, and inadequate time and resources to give each eligible applicant for parole a timely, thorough review. Reforms in some states have targeted these aspects of the parole process.

New Jersey supplies a well-known example. A 1979 law established presumptive parole dates for each offender, but release depended on a hearing to determine whether the offender posed too great a risk for immediate return to the community.[43] By the late 1990s, the hearing process had become badly backlogged. Close to 6,000 inmates awaited overdue hearings, amounting to nearly 20 percent of New Jersey's prison population.[44] Inmates filed a class action lawsuit against the state in 2000, resulting in a settlement agreement by the end of the year.[45] Under the agreement, the parole board consented to resolve the backlog within two years and became subject to financial penalties for not providing timely hearings in the future. The board then adopted streamlined procedures, including greater use of video teleconferencing for hearings, which helped parole officials to eliminate the backlog even before the court-approved deadline.[46] The state legislature also helped by increasing the size of the board from 11 to 15 members; since most parole decisions are made by two-member panels, more board members means that more hearings can be conducted.[47] As a result of these changes, New Jersey experienced a sharp increase in the number of parole releases approved by board panels, which jumped from 2,579 in 1998 to 9,297 in 2001.[48] The board's improved efficiency thus contributed to a notable 3,000-inmate decline in the state's prison population over the same three-year time period.

Louisiana provides another example of helpful reform to a parole board's operations.[49] In 2011, the state legislature required for the first time that parole board members undergo training and orientation—an important development in a state in which members often lack any criminal justice experience. Louisiana's new training program includes prison visits, meetings with inmates, and ride-alongs with parole officers. The program's implementation seemed to have a positive effect on grant rates, which rose from 33 percent in 2011 to 47 percent in 2012. As parole board chair Sheryl Ranatza puts it, the training gave "board members the tools in their toolbox to be confident in their decisions."[50]

Even with more efficient, better-informed procedures, however, parole boards remain subject to persistent political pressure, and tend to err on the side of denying early release. The specter of Willie Horton still looms. For the same reason, pushing up eligibility dates, as Mississippi and other states have done, may not have much of an effect on the actual number of releases. In the words of a former member of New York's parole board, "It's always safer to deny than to parole; it takes no courage and is the safest route to job security. One doesn't want to find oneself in the headlines."[51]

In order to counter these pressures, some states are revisiting the concept of presumptive parole. As we have seen, New Jersey adopted a version of this strategy back in 1979. South Dakota, Colorado, and New Hampshire exemplify the more recent iteration of this reform trend.[52] In South Dakota, for instance, presumptive release dates may be anywhere from 25 percent to 75 percent of the sentence, based on the inmate's criminal history and current offense. Inmates who substantially comply with certain goals set for their education and treatment in prison are released on the presumptive date without even having to appear before a parole board, thereby entirely bypassing the harsh political dynamics that may affect board decisions. (Of course, this approach to presumptive parole would have saved New Jersey from its late 1990s backlog crisis.)

A system of largely automatic early releases can curtail the implicit policy-making power of parole boards and other discretionary actors. However, such a system will not necessarily avoid the harsh political dynamics that affect *legislative* decisions. Thus, presumptive parole was repealed in New Hampshire,[53] and failed to gain passage in Michigan in 2015 despite gubernatorial support.[54] In the latter state, reform faced stiff opposition from the attorney general and other law enforcement officials. Echoing the fear-mongering that was so prevalent in the 1990s, Oakland County's sheriff confidently asserted, "In society, we're going to see more victims [with presumptive parole]; I can guarantee that."[55]

Conclusion

Prisoners remain a deeply stigmatized group in U.S. society. Informed commentators frequently remark on the vast differences in the treatment of prisoners in the United States and Europe.[56] The controlling principle behind European corrections is that the offender should be prepared for reintegration into free society.[57] In the United States, by contrast, prisoners are presumed depraved and dangerous, and the controlling principle is simply to keep them behind bars as long as possible. In general, the costs of paying for a burgeoning prison system have seemed tolerable if doing so prevents a few Willie Hortons from getting out early.

These views help to explain why the post-2000 early release reforms seem so half-hearted. We have seen time and again hasty repeals, narrow eligibility requirements, and unnecessarily conservative implementation by judges and corrections officials. If policy makers seem skittish about early release, they have good reason—we have seen reforms repeatedly castigated as a threat to community safety by politicians and the media. Whether or not grounded in reality, these criticisms resonate with a public that is predisposed to see prisoners in a harsh light. New Jersey is the exception that proves the rule; the Garden State achieved some meaningful decarceration through parole reform, but only as a result of litigation pressures. The New Jersey decarceration story thus foreshadows the California decarceration story.

Elsewhere, more robust early release reforms may require a fundamental reorientation of U.S. attitudes toward prisoners. The European approach is premised on the assumption that prisoners can and should be reintegrated into free society, and this assumption in turn reflects an ethical imperative to respect the equal dignity of all people, including those behind bars. Despite occasional use of the "compassionate release" label, U.S. reformers have generally shied away from the ethical in favor of the fiscal. Yet, cost–benefit analysis may not get far with a public so strongly inclined to view early release as a pathway to horrific victimization.

Given the particular stigma borne by prisoners, reformers disappointed with the performance of early release programs have placed greater hope in other sorts of initiatives, especially reforms intended to keep *nonimprisoned* offenders on the right side of penitentiary walls. These "front-end" reforms will be the focus of the next chapter.

CHAPTER FOUR

Justice Reinvestment: Dominant Reform Model of the Treading Water Era

The early release reforms we considered in Chapter 3 had a fragmentary, ad hoc quality. At least initially, states proceeded in isolation from one another, grasping at straws for ways to reduce their burgeoning prison populations. After a few years, though, imprisonment-reducing reforms in many states grew more philosophically coherent and coordinated with one another, coalescing around the idea that by reducing prison populations, states would save money, which could be redirected to initiatives that would prevent recidivism. This so-called justice reinvestment (JR) movement achieved initial successes in five states between 2004 and 2008. From there, JR spread with remarkable speed. By 2015, at least 34 states had attempted to develop reform proposals using the JR process, and at least 28 had enacted JR legislation.[1]

The JR movement can point to significant imprisonment reductions in a few participating states, but the overall JR picture is more mixed. Critics, including some of those who first developed the JR concept, charge that the movement has lost sight of its original social justice mission. With the endorsement and financial support of the federal government, however, the JR movement continues to serve as the nation's leading driver of sentencing reform. Until the JR model evolves or is supplanted by a new approach, U.S. imprisonment rates are unlikely to drop to anything approaching the nation's historical norms.

Development and Dissemination of the JR Model

JR emerged from the pioneering criminal justice mapping work of Eric Cadora. In 1998, while he was working for the Center for

Alternative Sentencing and Employment Services in New York City, Cadora hit upon the idea of using a law enforcement tool—the precise mapping of crime "hot spots" in order to direct policing resources more efficiently—to study the allocation of corrections resources.[2] Cadora taught himself how to use mapping software and focused first on his own borough, Brooklyn. He discovered the existence of many "million-dollar blocks"—city blocks in which so many residents were being sent to prison for such a long time that they would ultimately cost taxpayers at least $1 million. These million-dollar blocks were almost invariably located in some of the most impoverished sections of Brooklyn.

Cadora wondered if some of that money could be spent in ways that would produce greater benefits for the disadvantaged neighborhoods in which crime and incarceration were so concentrated. He thought his maps might help people to see more clearly how criminal justice decisions were also effectively fiscal decisions about spending priorities. Within a year, Cadora began sharing his maps with criminal justice agencies and policy makers. Word of his innovative approach spread, and soon officials in other states were asking him to find their own million-dollar blocks.

Cadora's initial work was supported by a grant from the Open Society Institute, a think tank and reform advocacy organization funded by the billionaire financier George Soros. (Soros, as we saw in Chapter 2, also played a lead role in funding the campaign for California's Proposition 36 and other drug-reform measures.) In 2001, Cadora moved to Open Society on a full-time basis and continued to develop the ideas that would become JR.[3]

Cadora and his Open Society colleague Susan Tucker are credited with coining the term "justice reinvestment" in a 2003 paper.[4] "There is no logic," Cadora and Tucker asserted, "to spending a million dollars a year to incarcerate people from one block in Brooklyn—over half for non-violent drug offenses—and return them, on average, in less than three years stigmatized, unskilled, and untrained to the same unchanged block." Citing research showing that high levels of incarceration tend to make a neighborhood less safe, not more, Cadora and Tucker characterized society's investments in prison, probation, and parole as a "business failure." Money should be reallocated, they argued, to more productive uses. Thus, they said, "[t]he goal of justice reinvestment is to redirect some portion of the $54 billion America now spends on prisons to rebuilding the human resources and physical infrastructure—the schools, healthcare facilities, parks, and public spaces—of neighborhoods devastated by high levels of incarceration."

Cadora and Tucker seemed to envision a sort of "virtuous" circle in which higher levels of public safety would be achieved at lower cost. Unnecessary incarceration would be systematically identified and reduced, savings would be reallocated to social services delivering higher crime-reduction benefits than simple incarceration, the resulting drop in crime would generate more justice-system savings, these savings would also be reallocated to yet more social services, and on and on.

Yet, in a passage that would often seem forgotten in the later history of JR, Cadora and Tucker also insisted that JR was "more than simply rethinking and redirecting public funds. It [was] also about devolving accountability and responsibility to the local level. Justice reinvestment seeks community level solutions to community level problems. ... The solution to public safety must be locally tailored and locally determined."

Even as Cadora and Tucker were introducing the terminology of "justice reinvestment," their approach was already gaining traction with legislators in one state, Connecticut.[5] Leading the way was Democratic representative Mike Lawlor, a lawyer and criminal justice professor representing suburban East Haven. Lawlor introduced the nation's first JR bill in 2003, calling for cuts in imprisonment and the redirection of savings into social programs that were expected to reduce recidivism, including drug treatment and mental health services. Recognizing the power of Cadora's maps, Lawlor invited him to present his research in Connecticut. Lawlor observed, "I think Eric is able to graphically depict the insanity of our current system for preventing crimes in certain neighborhoods. We're spending all of this money and not getting very good results. I think when you look at it the way Eric is able to depict it in those neighborhood graphs, you can see how crazy this all is."[6] Lawlor's bill passed the following spring.

JR gained important validation when Connecticut's prison population, previously among the nation's fastest growing, began to fall without any corresponding increase in crime.[7] Indeed, Connecticut's recidivism rate dropped in the aftermath of JR, as did the state's crime rate more generally. Seeing Connecticut's success, other states soon adopted JR-inspired reforms of their own. Kansas and Texas acted in 2007, while Rhode Island and Arizona followed closely on their heels in 2008.[8]

The Texas legislation was probably the most important in stimulating further growth of the budding JR movement. After all, Texas was a proud red state with a long history of being among the nation's toughest on crime. Texas's adoption of JR gave cover to politicians across the country who feared that support of JR would be castigated as thinly disguised lenience. (A national public opinion study in 2010 tested the effectiveness of various ways of framing sentencing reform. The researchers concluded, "[T]he fact that Texas is shifting its emphasis from prisons was the strongest and most memorable message."[9]) Moreover, the size of the Texas's prison population allowed the state to claim some eye-popping savings from JR—$684 million in averted prison construction and operating expenses in 2007.[10]

By then, other agencies and organizations had replaced Open Society as JR's lead national sponsors: the federal government's Bureau of Justice Assistance, the Pew Charitable Trusts, and the Council of State Governments Justice Center.[11] Together, these groups would systematize and formalize an off-the-shelf JR process for other states to adopt, extending—and perhaps subtly revising—the original vision of Eric Cadora and Susan Tucker.

Why did JR grow so quickly from a short conceptual paper in 2003 to a well-funded, sophisticated reform movement that, just a decade later, had been embraced to varying extents by a majority of states? The criminologist Todd Clear, an early collaborator with Eric Cadora, has identified four reasons for JR's stunning political success.[12] First, the sustained drop in crime rates after the early 1990s reduced fear levels and established an opening for new policy ideas. Second, the increasingly widespread realization that the prison population was reaching unprecedented highs fueled public interest in imprisonment-reducing strategies. Third, much new research, some covered in the media, intensified questions about the fairness and efficacy of mass incarceration. Fourth, and finally, state fiscal crises created an urgent need to reduce corrections budgets. Clear characterized this as "[b]y far, the most proximate catalyst for the emergence of justice reinvestment."

JR also received an important boost from Congress. Hearings in 2009 highlighted the apparent successes of the first handful of adopters.[13] Then, in 2010, congressional leaders organized a national JR summit and appropriated funding to support state-level initiatives. Importantly, the funding was to be channeled through the Bureau of Justice Assistance, which had already been collaborating on JR with Pew and the Council of State Governments Justice Center. Much of the federal money would pay for technical assistance (TA) for participating states from Pew, the Justice Center, and a third organization, the Vera Institute of Justice. The key role of these organizations in future JR efforts would help to ensure some state-to-state uniformity in the reform process. The organizations labeled their collaborative effort the Justice Reinvestment Initiative, or JRI. (I will use this label to differentiate the second wave of reform, beginning in 2010, from the first; the term "JR" will be used to refer to both waves collectively.)

As formalized by the lead organizations, the JRI process encompassed seven parts.[14] First, a participating state was to convene a bipartisan, interbranch working group of criminal justice officials and policy makers to oversee the reform effort. Second, one of the TA providers would collect and analyze a great quantity of data from the state, identifying its key criminal justice cost drivers. Third, the TA provider and the working group would develop policy options. Fourth, after a reform approach was selected, it would have to be embodied in legislation and formally adopted. Fifth, the TA provider would help with the development of an implementation plan, identifying the critical state agencies, budgetary needs, and performance measures. Sixth, savings were to be reinvested in "evidence-based" public safety strategies and programs. Finally, states were to measure outcomes, particularly in the areas of crime and incarceration rates, recidivism, parole and probation revocations, and criminal justice costs. Additionally, throughout the process, states were to engage stakeholders, including businesses, service providers, law enforcement, and victim groups.

As indicated in Table 4.1, 34 states had at least initiated the process by 2015, with 28 reaching the point of enacting JR legislation.[15] JR has even become an international phenomenon, with JR reforms adopted in Australia and the United Kingdom.[16]

In 2014, the Urban Institute and the Bureau of Justice Assistance published a much-anticipated assessment of the JRI's effectiveness. As of that time, eight of the second-wave states had JRI policies in place for at least a year, and all eight had experienced reductions in imprisonment.[17] Total projected savings from the JRI were calculated to be as much as $4.6 billion. The JRI was also lauded for promoting the adoption of evidence-based practices, cross-agency collaboration, and enhanced data collection. Reinvestment of savings into new, evidence-based criminal justice programs totaled $165.8 million. The report concluded, "The Justice Reinvestment Initiative has successfully promoted interest in justice system reform and the use of [evidence-based practices]

Table 4.1 JR States, 2003–2015

JR Participants	Legislation Adopted?
Alabama	N
Alaska	N
Arizona	Y
Arkansas	Y
Connecticut	Y
Delaware	Y
Georgia	Y
Hawaii	Y
Idaho	Y
Indiana	N
Kansas	Y
Kentucky	Y
Louisiana	Y
Maryland	N
Michigan	N
Mississippi	Y
Missouri	Y
Nebraska	Y
Nevada	Y
New Hampshire	Y
North Carolina	Y
Ohio	Y
Oklahoma	Y
Oregon	Y
Pennsylvania	Y
Rhode Island	Y
South Carolina	Y
South Dakota	Y
Texas	Y
Utah	Y
Vermont	Y
Washington	N
West Virginia	Y
Wisconsin	Y

across the 17 JR states [covered in the study]. The preliminary results indicate that enacted reforms have the potential to reduce or limit the growth of justice system populations and, thus, produce savings."[18]

At about the same time, however, a more critical assessment appeared, authored by Eric Cadora, Susan Tucker, Todd Clear, and others who had been involved in the initial development and first-wave implementation of JR. They credited JR with "softening the ground" for mass-incarceration reform, but argued that the JR efforts to date were "aim[ing] too low" and even risked "institutionalizing mass incarceration at current levels."[19] They observed, "Justice Reinvestment was developed as a public safety mechanism to downsize prison populations and budgets and re-allocate savings to leverage other public and private resources for reinvestment in minority communities disproportionately harmed by the system and culture of harsh punishment."[20] However, they charged, JR had made little progress in reducing corrections budgets or in directing what savings had been achieved to the communities most adversely affected by mass incarceration. The basic problem, as the authors saw it, was the overriding emphasis on developing coalitions of *state*-level policy makers, resulting in reforms that served their interests, but paid little heed to the perspectives of local communities.

In order to better appreciate these competing perspectives on JR, it may help to consider one state's experience in more detail.

North Carolina: A JR Case Study

North Carolina offered the nation's leading sentencing success story in the 1990s, as the state adopted a well-regarded guidelines system that stabilized what had been an explosively growing prison population.[21] By 2009, however, policy makers were again becoming alarmed about the direction of corrections spending in the state. Although arrests had held steady since 2000, the prison population continued to increase.[22] The corrections budget climbed by about two-thirds over the decade and was projected to continue growing through 2020. Newly elected Democratic governor Beverly Perdue thus joined with a bipartisan group of other state leaders in requesting assistance from the Council of State Governments Justice Center, which formally initiated the JRI process. Funding and TA came from the usual suspects: the Justice Center, Pew, and the federal Bureau of Justice Assistance.

Justice Center staffers gathered reams of data from state agencies, conducted meetings with a wide range of stakeholders, and attempted to identify priorities for reform. Their findings focused attention on problems with North Carolina's system of community supervision, that is, the supervision of offenders sentenced to probation or serving a period of continued supervision after release from prison.

First, many offenders initially sentenced to probation were being revoked and incarcerated for violating the terms of their release, even though the violations were usually only technical in character.[23] In other words, the violations were not new crimes in themselves, but were lesser infractions, such as missing appointments with probation officers (POs) or associating with the wrong people. Probation was typically imposed with a suspended sentence of incarceration; if violations led to revocation, then that suspended sentence would have to be served in full. In FY 2009, the Justice Center discovered that revocations accounted for more than half of all admissions to prison in North Carolina, but fewer than one-quarter of these revocations involved the commission of a new crime. The Justice Center estimated that North Carolina was spending more than $100 million annually to incarcerate revoked probationers.

Second, no supervision at all was being provided for the vast majority (85 percent) of North Carolina's newly released prisoners, who had a higher recidivism rate than the probationers who were consuming most the of the state's community supervision resources. And finally, the Justice Center determined that North Carolina provided insufficient resources for mental health and drug treatment for those on community supervision, and allocated what resources were available without regard to risk or need.

When it came time to translate these findings into a framework for legislative reform, the Justice Center emphasized three overarching priorities for the Tar Heel State: "strengthen probation supervision, hold offenders accountable in more meaningful ways, and reduce the risk of reoffending."[24] Notably absent was any explicit goal of reducing the size of the state prison population or even reducing the size of the corrections budget, let alone shifting funds from prisons to community-based, community-controlled social services—Cadora and Tucker's original vision for JR. Instead, the JR agenda in North Carolina was subtly marked by tough-on-crime rhetoric ("strengthen supervision," "hold offenders accountable"), and plainly quite friendly to the state corrections bureaucracy.

The Justice Center's eight specific recommended reforms were much in the same spirit.[25]

- POs were to be given new authority to employ "swift and certain responses" to violations. POs might send an offender to jail for up to three days without the need for a court hearing—what practitioners would refer to as a "quick dip"—thus providing a new alternative to full-blown revocation and giving POs the ability to spend less time in court and more time supervising the people under their charge.

- Low-risk probationers were to be given a minimal-supervision status, thereby permitting POs to devote more of their time to higher-risk offenders.
- All felony offenders returning from prison would become subject to at least nine months of postrelease community supervision, with sex offenders subject to five years. Technical violations of the terms of release would result in revocation and a flat three months return to prison, except for sex offenders, who might be returned for longer. Although this reform would add many new offenders to the community supervision program, it was hoped that the existing POs could handle the influx of postrelease offenders, thanks to the new rules reducing the supervision of low-risk probationers.
- A new sentencing option would increase the penalties for repeat breaking-and-entering offenders, with some offsetting reductions in severity for other nonviolent offenders sentenced under North Carolina's habitual felon law.
- Inmates would no longer be required to find a spot in the prison system's limited work or educational programs in order to get "earned time" reductions in their sentences, but corrections officials would also receive new authority to extend the sentences of inmates for bad behavior.
- More low-level drug offenders would become eligible for the state's existing diversion and treatment program.
- Judges would be given the authority at the time of sentencing to make offenders eligible for reduced prison terms based on the completion of rehabilitative programs recommended by the Department of Corrections (DOC). (Called "Advanced Supervised Release" [ASR] in North Carolina, this option is called a "risk-reduction sentence" elsewhere.)
- Responsibility for existing state-funded, community-based treatment programs would be shifted from the counties to the DOC, with a mandate to concentrate resources on high-risk offenders and improve the quality of services provided.

Additional policy options noted by the Justice Center included a 90-day cap on incarceration for technical violations of probation, increased postrelease supervision for higher-level offenders, and the diversion of misdemeanants from prison to local jails. (North Carolina was unusual among states in using its state prisons to house misdemeanants sentenced to as few as 91 days behind bars; the general rule elsewhere is that sentences of less than a year are served in a local jail.)

There was little trace of Cadora and Tucker's vision in the North Carolina proposal. On its face, each imprisonment-reducing reform seemed more or less counterbalanced with an offsetting imprisonment-increasing reform. Returns to prison for technical violations of postrelease supervision would be capped at three months, but many more reentering offenders would become subject to supervision (and hence revocation). The habitual felon law was softened for some offenders, but repeat breaking and entering would result in longer sentences. More inmates would qualify for earned time reductions, but corrections officials would also have more authority to extend prison terms for misconduct.

Additionally, the proposed reforms suffered from the same basic limitations that we have seen repeatedly in the reforms discussed in earlier chapters. North Carolina's JRI package provided new tools to criminal justice officials, but, at the same time, it left officials with ample discretion to disregard or undermine the new tools. It also carefully declined to extend certain incarceration-reducing provisions to violent and sexual offenders, focusing instead on lower-level offenders—who tended not to constitute a large share of the prison population to begin with. As a result, the Justice Center's own projections showed an almost trivial reduction in imprisonment of just 2 percent between 2011 and 2017. Factoring in the three additional "policy options" brought the projected decrease to a healthier, but still modest, 9 percent, with much of that decrease simply representing a shift of inmates from prisons to jails as a result of the new approach to incarcerating misdemeanants.

The Justice Center proposal's "reinvestment" projections were similarly modest. Even including the three optional reforms, the proposal called for a mere $10 million annually in reinvestment—a miniscule sum when compared to the $1.51 billion DOC budget.[26] Moreover, it appeared that all of the reinvestment would remain under the control of the DOC, in the form of increased prison-based programming, increased treatment for offenders on community supervision, and additional POs.

Given the DOC's recapture of savings and the expansion of its discretionary powers—for example, the new ability to bypass the courts in penalizing probation violations—it seems that the whole JRI process in North Carolina was coopted by corrections officials (a charge that has been leveled against JRI reforms elsewhere, too). Even new directives for the DOC to refocus community supervision resources only ratified a reform track that the DOC was already on.[27] Of course, corrections-led reforms, whatever other benefits they may deliver, are unlikely to result in real reductions in corrections budgets, let alone a massive reinvestment in, as Cadora and Tucker put it, "rebuilding the human resources and physical infrastructure—the schools, healthcare facilities, parks, and public spaces—of neighborhoods devastated by high levels of incarceration." In North Carolina and across the country, JRI proposals have been "insider" reform—technocratic change that may rationalize the system in some respects, but that also predictably safeguards the prerogatives of key officials and agencies.

JRI reforms are also structured and marketed in ways that make them a difficult target for tough-on-crime politicians. The technical complexity of the reforms alone creates a daunting challenge for outsiders to decipher what is going on. Rhetoric and presentation may also feature a certain degree of misdirection. For instance, in the Justice Center's main policy proposal document in North Carolina, a recommended softening of the habitual felon law appeared as an add-on bullet point under the heading, "Accelerate incarceration of people convicted on multiple occasions of breaking and entering."[28] The rhetorical gestures toward toughness, the promise of enhanced supervision of the most dangerous offenders, and the careful efforts to obtain the buy-in of insiders—the Justice Center's North Carolina document repeatedly cited focus group sessions with district attorneys and other law enforcement personnel—help to ensure a quiet, smooth passage of JRI reforms, as does the requirement of bipartisan support at the outset of the JRI process.

Such proved to be the experience in North Carolina. Legislators unveiled their JRI bill in April 2011, embodying the Justice Center's proposed reforms, including the optional recommendations. Politicians from both sides of the aisles voiced enthusiastic support from the start.[29] The state's county leaders provided the only discordant response, objecting to the added cost of having to house misdemeanants in local jails. They were mollified, however, by reassurances that the state would pay to house the influx of new inmates and that local participation would be voluntary.[30] In the end, the JRI bill passed swiftly and easily, with only one "no" vote.[31]

By 2014, there were many indications that JR had proven a success in North Carolina. The Justice Center issued a three-year report trumpeting the good news.[32] Most notably, since 2011, North Carolina's prison population had dropped by 3,400, or about 8 percent, and the state had closed 10 institutions. Probation revocations—a major driver of prison admissions in the years leading up to the JRI reforms—had been cut in half. Overall, the Justice Center calculated that North Carolina was on track to save $560 million by 2017. Part of the savings was being reinvested in new POs, with 175 hires expected by the end of 2015. Moreover, all of this was being achieved without any apparent negative effects on public safety. Indeed, reported crime *dropped* in North Carolina by 11 percent between 2011 and 2014.

Beneath these promising numbers, though, there were causes for concern. For one thing, almost all of the imprisonment drop occurred in the first year or so of the reforms; thereafter, North Carolina was back to treading water. Between December 31, 2011, and December 31, 2012, the Tar Heel State shed 2,304 prisoners,[33] accounting for more than two-thirds of the total reduction claimed by the Justice Center. Indeed, in 2014, the prison population actually grew slightly.

Digging deeper, it is clear what drove the immediate, short-term drop. As indicated in Figure 4.1, North Carolina's prisons held nearly 2,200 fewer short-term (one year or less inmates) at the end of 2012 than they had at the end of 2011—almost exactly equal to the total reduction in prisoners in that time period. This drop in short-termers—and hence the overall drop in imprisonment—largely resulted from just two aspects of the complex JRI package.[34] First, the 90-day cap on incarceration for technical violations of probation replaced a system in which many technical violators would have been revoked and sent to prison for two or three times that length of time—an important source of pre-JRI short-termers.[35] This was a solid improvement, but one whose benefits were mostly achieved in the first year or so; there was little reason to expect sizable ongoing gains from shaving a few months from the average imprisonment imposed for technical violations. Second, JRI shifted many misdemeanants—short-termers, by definition —from prisons to local jails.[36] As a result, North Carolina's JRI initiative did not reduce *incarceration* so much as it reduced *imprisonment*. In early 2015, for instance, North Carolina jails were holding an average of 705 diverted misdemeanants per day.[37]

To be sure, the prison–jail shift was hardly meaningless. Taking advantage of existing, underutilized jail capacity may have helped North Carolina to avoid the new prison construction that had been projected

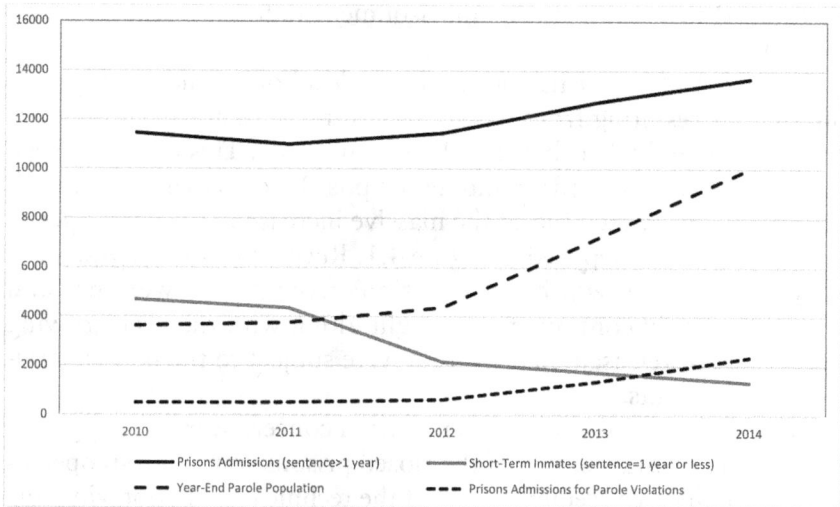

Figure 4.1   North Carolina Prison and Parole Trends, 2010–2014

as necessary by 2020. However, excess jail capacity was not unlimited, and North Carolina would not be able to continue drawing on that resource indefinitely to further reduce the demands on state institutions. Moreover, from the inmate's perspective, the prison–jail shift was more of a mixed bag. While jail incarceration normally meant that the inmate would be closer to home and family, jails offered fewer programs to help inmates use their time constructively.[38]

Figure 4.1 reveals other areas of concern about the ability of North Carolina's JRI reforms to deliver significant, sustainable further reductions in imprisonment. For instance, the number of new inmates being sent to prison for sentences of longer than one year grew steadily after the reforms were adopted. Strikingly, over the same time period, North Carolina experienced steady *decreases* in arrests for major violent crime[39] and felony convictions,[40] suggesting that the surge in longer sentences may have reflected enhanced toughness in the handling of felony defendants. Among other things, prosecutors were seeking habitual-felon enhancements more frequently, as well as taking advantage of the new habitual breaking and entering law.[41] It seems that many of the prison beds left vacant by short-term inmates were later filled by long-term inmates—a trade-off that might deliver reduced imprisonment in the short run, but that risked *increased* imprisonment over the long run. The failure to deal in a serious way with prosecutorial and judicial discretion in North Carolina threatened to undermine the imprisonment-reduction benefits of the reforms.

Figure 4.1 also reveals another dark cloud on the horizon: prison admissions resulting from parole violations were up sharply—more than four times higher than they had been before. This trend followed predictably from the JRI mandate for postprison supervision for all released felons, which fueled the massive increase in the parole population that is also depicted in Figure 4.1. Revocations from *probation* may have been down, but revocations from *parole* were up, and would probably continue to rise right along with the ever-growing percentage of released inmates who were subject to the new supervision requirements.

Even apart from the data, other areas of concern were also apparent by 2014. For instance, two of the closed prisons were set to reopen as special confinement centers for all of the technical probation violators subject to the 90-day sanction, thus undercutting some of the fiscal benefit of the reforms.[42] Additionally, funding for the state reimbursement plan was proving inadequate to cover further projected increases in the local jail population.[43] Also, prosecutors were opposing use of the new ASR sentencing option (offering early release based on the completion of rehabilitative programs in prison).[44] As a result, judges imposed ASR sentences in only about 1 percent of eligible cases. Advances in rehabilitation outside of prison also seemed tenuous: court and corrections personnel across the state continued to voice concerns about excessive caseloads for POs and the inadequacy of treatment resources.[45] The "reinvestment" dimension of JR also provoked concern. As one evaluating agency observed, North Carolina had closed prisons as a result of the 2011 reforms, "but if, to what extent, and for what purpose those savings have been reinvested is unclear."[46]

Perhaps most troubling of all was the legislature's seeming disinterest in building on the JRI law to achieve more significant and durable reductions in imprisonment. Quite the contrary, with the fiscal pressures of a growing prison population at least temporarily removed, legislators embraced a host of new, anecdote-driven, punishment-enhancing measures that were reminiscent of the crime du jour lawmaking of earlier decades.[47] For instance, the legislature made it a crime for a prisoner to possess a cellphone after one inmate used his phone to orchestrate a plot against the family of the official who prosecuted him.[48] Similarly, after a tragic accident at the North Carolina State Fair, the legislature created a new felony for illegal operation of an amusement ride resulting in a serious injury.[49] These and other new crimes suggested a disquieting possibility: perhaps, like a gas expanding to fit whatever size container it is in, a state's penal laws grow in severity to fill whatever extra capacity develops in its prison system.

JRI Reforms Elsewhere

North Carolina's reforms resulted from an off-the-shelf deliberative process and relied on the usual JRI TA providers. Not surprisingly, what North Carolina did generally tracked the changes adopted in other JR states. Each participating state was unique in some respects, but certain recurring themes stand out.

First, like North Carolina, most JRI states sought to reduce the amount of prison resources being used to respond to technical violations of probation and parole.[50] Most commonly, this meant establishing new systems of graduated sanctions, with additional options short of full-blown revocation, like North Carolina's "quick dips" of one or two days in jail. Some states sought to facilitate the use of intermediate sanctions by giving POs the authority to impose them administratively, that is, without a return trip to court. As in North Carolina, the articulated ideal was often "swift, certain sanctions"— trading off severity along the way. A popular model was the Hawaii Opportunity Probation with Enforcement (HOPE) program. Established in 2004 by a charismatic Honolulu judge, Steve Alm, HOPE streamlined the sanctioning of probation violations and used short stints in jail as an alternative to revocation.[51] A randomized control trial found that, after one year, HOPE probationers had fewer missed appointments, failed drug tests, new arrests, revocations, and incarceration days than non-HOPE probationers.[52] In the wake of this research, at least three of the JRI states explicitly adopted pilot programs on the HOPE model.[53] Whether or not HOPE was so explicitly invoked, however, its influence was obvious and pervasive across nearly all of the JRI reform packages.

Some states, such as Pennsylvania and South Carolina, sought to push the graduated sanctions approach through formalized new guidelines for responding to violations. Some, including Ohio and South Carolina, held out financial incentives for community supervision agencies to reduce revocation rates. Others established caps on incarceration terms for technical violations, similar to North Carolina's 90-day limit. Finally, at least a handful of states established positive incentives for offenders on community supervision by offering credits toward early discharge—analogous to the good-time programs through which prisoners earn early release by staying out of trouble.

A second major recurring theme has been the refocusing of community supervision and treatment resources on offenders with the highest levels of objectively assessed risks and needs. Criminologists now recognize that lavishing criminal justice attention on offenders with low risks and needs not only wastes limited resources, but can actually be criminogenic, that is, risk-*increasing*.[54] Community corrections officials now have a number of nationally well-regarded risk-needs assessment (RNA) instruments available, but many jurisdictions have been slow to adopt them. Almost without exception, though, JRI reform proposals have included an emphasis on RNA. Most commonly, states have incorporated RNA into probation planning, for instance, by adopting different levels of supervision for different levels of risk. Thus, while high-risk offenders might be required to check in frequently with POs, low-risk offenders might have minimal contact with their POs. In some states, JRI plans have also called for RNA to be used in sentencing, parole, and pretrial release decisions.

Third, most JRI reform packages sought to enhance the quality, availability, and diversity of community-based sentencing and treatment options. Ideally, these improvements would make judges and prosecutors more amenable to keeping offenders out of prison, and would also help offenders to succeed on community supervision and avoid revocation. Thus, for instance, several reform proposals included additional funding for community-based treatment. Others included new or expanded options for the electronic monitoring of offenders. Some states particularly singled out drug courts and other specialized "problem-solving courts" for expansion or improvement. At least one state, Georgia, aimed to establish more day-reporting centers (a hybrid sort of incarceration holding inmates for a limited period of time each day). Another state, Arkansas, created a new community service sentencing option that was available even for some felonies.[55] Several state plans included training for corrections and court personnel in "evidence-based" practices in community supervision. (This was one the JRI movement's most common catchphrases, connoting practices whose usefulness had been established through research.) Other states looked to tighten up the standards for, and the monitoring of, contractors providing treatment services for community corrections.

A fourth theme, apparent in about half of the JRI states, was the reduction of sentencing ranges for low-level drug or property offenses.

In Arkansas, for instance, first-time marijuana possession was reduced from a felony to a misdemeanor as long as the quantity was less than 4 ounces, while the monetary loss triggering the most severe theft penalties was raised from just $2,500 to $25,000.[56] Utah likewise reduced penalties for marijuana possession, and also sharply reduced the reach of its sentence enhancement for drug offenses in school zones, the radius of which shrank from 1,000 to just 100 feet.[57] Sometimes, though, sentence reductions for some offenses were offset by sentence increases for others, as we have already seen in North Carolina. Similarly, South Carolina reduced maximum sentences for some burglaries and made all property offenses involving losses of less than $2,000 misdemeanors, but also increased maximum penalties for several other offenses and established a new 30-year mandatory minimum for arson resulting in death.[58]

A fifth theme, also apparent in about half the states, was the adoption of reforms to ease the path for prisoners to obtain parole or otherwise to return earlier to the community. Parole processes were streamlined in Pennsylvania, West Virginia, and elsewhere. Louisiana moved up parole eligibility dates for first- and second-time offenders. Idaho authorized guidelines for parole release that were intended to reduce time served for property and drug offenders.[59] Arkansas adopted compassionate release. Delaware and Oregon expanded their earned time programs. South Carolina made some prisoners eligible for work release during the last three years of their sentences.[60]

Sixth, like North Carolina, several states sought to reduce the number of released inmates returned to the community without any ongoing criminal justice supervision. Because a certain number of these offenders would inevitably fail on supervision, the reforms would likely result in some increased incarceration (as was the case in North Carolina), and thereby offset gains achieved through other reforms.

Seventh, and finally, several states partially counterbalanced the general focus of the JRI on offenders and corrections by including reforms to help victims or law enforcement. For instance, a few states enhanced the ability of victims to collect restitution from offenders. Idaho was one, adopting a new requirement that 20 percent of any deposits made into a prisoner's account be captured to satisfy restitution obligations.[61] South Carolina was another, providing for extended periods of community supervision for offenders who failed to pay off their restitution.[62] Meanwhile, Oregon and Pennsylvania increased funding for victim services. Also, Kansas, Oklahoma, and

Pennsylvania included law enforcement funding in their JRI reforms. Indeed, in Pennsylvania, most of the expected JRI savings were committed to the police—twice as much as was allocated to local probation offices.[63]

Evaluation: From Fixing Communities to Fixing Correctional Systems

Through all of the technical details and state-to-state variations, there does seem a grand, unifying vision behind the past decade of JR reforms, and that vision is not the same as Eric Cadora and Susan Tucker's. JR first developed from the discovery of "million-dollar blocks," those microcommunities consuming a vastly disproportionate share of state correctional resources. In its original form, JR presented a fundamental challenge to business as usual in the criminal justice system—it was a call for correctional dollars to be moved out of bureaucratic, centralized state agencies and into the neighborhoods that were most affected by mass incarceration. Those communities would be empowered to address their own problems through improvements in education, public health, and infrastructure, among other areas.

By contrast, JR in practice, especially in its now-dominant JRI form, implicitly embodies the following key premises: (1) there is nothing problematic about the front-end decisions of police and prosecutors that push individuals into the criminal justice system; (2) the basic scale of correctional populations—that is, the number of individuals behind bars or on community supervision—should be accepted as a given; (3) the basic scale of correctional budgets should also be accepted as a given; (4) the overriding purpose of sentencing reform is to achieve better outcomes from applying a given correctional budget to a given correctional population; (5) the only outcome that really matters is improved public safety, most importantly in the form of reduced recidivism rates; and (6) the job of reducing recidivism is most fundamentally the responsibility of existing correctional agencies, which can accomplish that goal by reducing expenditures on low-risk offenders and increasing the intensity of supervision and the quality and availability of behavioral-health treatment for high-risk offenders. In short, the JR vision has morphed from empowering and improving *communities* to empowering and improving *correctional systems*.

There seems nothing inherently objectionable about the ideal of greater correctional efficiency, but this ideal should be recognized as one that is only tangentially related to the ideal of drawing down U.S. incarceration rates. As the old saying goes, when all you have is a hammer, every problem looks like a nail. Incarceration is the familiar, basic tool of U.S. corrections officials, and the nation's four-decade imprisonment boom built up a vast and unprecedented capacity to utilize that tool. JR-empowered corrections officials are unlikely to surrender much of that capacity, and as long as the capacity continues to exist, officials will continue to use it as the ultimate response to the chronic antisocial behavior of the poor, the addicted, and the mentally ill individuals who are thrust daily into their charge. True, the efficiency ideal may impose some restraint when it comes to building new prisons. However, once facilities are in place, the marginal cost of putting one more offender behind bars tends to be quite low. If correctional efficiency, not the well-being of disadvantaged communities, has become our pole star, then significant, durable imprisonment reductions will almost certainly prove elusive.

Various recurring features of recent reforms make clear the inherent limitations of JR, at least as it has come to be practiced. First, JR tends to focus on the diversion from prison of low-level offenders who do not typically get long sentences anyway. While such diversions may achieve seemingly impressive reductions in the number of offenders admitted to prison, the impact on the overall size of the prison population tends to be much more modest. Express carve-outs for violent and sexual offenders reinforce the tendency of JR reforms to leave the core, long-term prison population largely untouched.

Second, JR may provide prosecutors, judges, and POs with new diversionary options, but these officials often retain wide discretion about their use. (Discretion is also preserved with new "risk-reduction" options for prison terms.) Without any real changes to the political dynamics and incentive structures that caused discretion to be exercised more severely during the imprisonment boom, new options are likely to be underutilized. They are also subject to the constant threat of sharp constriction in the wake of a high-profile failure. In the JR state of Arkansas, for instance, efforts to enhance parole release in 2011 were undermined two years later when a parolee fell under suspicion of murder; after new parole policy changes, state jail bed use jumped from 400 to 1,000 in just two months.[64]

Third, the extension of community supervision to previously unsupervised classes of offenders, and the sharpening of supervision intensity for classes who were only lightly supervised before, inevitably leads to more sanctions for violations of supervision. Even in a system of graduated sanctions that start small, the violations will eventually add up for a number of offenders to significant incarceration—incarceration that for some would not have been imposed in the pre-JR system.

Fourth, while many JR reforms include reductions in statutory sentencing ranges for certain offenses, those reductions are commonly offset to some extent by increases in the ranges for other offenses. Additionally, as we saw in North Carolina, even if the official JR legislation includes few or no increases, quick reductions in imprisonment may result in a relaxation of legislative restraint and the adoption of many new crimes and sentence enhancements in short order.

Fifth, reinvestment commitments tend to be weak. Given the other limitations discussed before, the only plausible path offered by JR to sizable, long-term reductions in imprisonment would be through a large drop in recidivism rates. Such a drop seems unlikely in the absence of a massive infusion of new funds into high-quality programs that would help offenders to address mental illness, addiction, educational deficits, and the like. In theory, such funds could come from savings in imprisonment costs; although initial drops in imprisonment may be modest under JR, one might imagine that virtuous circle, in which more treatment begets lower crime, lower crime begets reduced imprisonment, and reduced imprisonment begets an ever-growing pot of funds for even more treatment.

However, JR states have not adopted strong reinvestment mechanisms. Indeed, some states have no formal reinvestment plans at all.[65] Others committed only small percentages of projected savings. As we have seen, North Carolina's plan called for $10 million in annual reinvestment, out of $269 million in savings over the first five years.[66] Even the commitments that were made were hardly firm and reliable. In New Hampshire, for instance, savings promised for mental health treatment were instead applied to balance the state's budget.[67] Nor were JR savings necessarily even planned to go predominantly to offender treatment. Pennsylvania, as we have seen, allocated most of its savings to police agencies. In addition to law enforcement, victim services also figured prominently in the reinvestment plans in some states. Moreover, for the money staying within correctional systems, treatment had to compete with growing needs for surveillance and other basic supervision activities. For instance, a full quarter of the spending in North Carolina's reinvestment plan was set aside simply for hiring more POs.[68]

Sixth, and finally, the rhetoric surrounding JR may also be counterproductive. We noted the tough talk in North Carolina. JR plans and their political patrons tend to emphasize a need to maintain adequate prison space for violent and sexual offenders, reinforcing public fear of these potential Willie Hortons. More generally, JR rhetoric treats offenders in depersonalized terms, largely reducing them to a risk category. The well-being of offenders and their families seems of little interest, except to the extent that addressing their mental illnesses might reduce recidivism risk. JR does not truly challenge the dominant mode of public discourse over crime and punishment—that "othering" rhetoric that treats offenders in objectified terms as mere threats to be controlled. Indeed, if anything, JR works to legitimize the discourse through its quasi-scientific veneer and pretensions to apolitical expertise. In the world of JR rhetoric, there seems no higher praise for a reform than to label it "evidence-based." One looks in vain, though, to find reforms that are framed as "ethics-based."

In light of all of these limitations, it should not be surprising that JR states have failed, on the whole, to achieve particularly large reductions in imprisonment. Table 4.2 sets forth changes in imprisonment rates for those states enacting JR reforms by 2013.[69] Just 4 of the 24 managed double-digit reductions, and 10 actually experienced increases. The overall average change was a rather modest 2.2-percent reduction. By contrast, the remaining, non-JR states actually achieved a slightly *higher* average reduction of 2.9 percent, as also indicated in Table 4.2. These rough comparisons should be evaluated with caution, of course, since they do not correct for differences in crime rates and other structural factors that might conceivably be favoring the non-JR states. (They also do not take into account gains achieved before 2010 in the first-wave JR states and potential long-term gains in the second-wave JR states.) Still, based on the available data, it would be hard to conclude that the JR process reliably offers sizable reductions in imprisonment. One might well question whether JR itself is evidence-based.

A final blind spot of JR merits attention. Perhaps no reform is more fundamentally characteristic of JR than RNA—widening the use of, and intensifying the reliance on, RNA at all steps of the criminal justice process. However, standard approaches to risk assessment produce results that systematically disfavor traditionally disadvantaged groups.[70] Race is a particular concern. A leading critic, the political scientist and law professor Bernard Harcourt, observes, "The fact is, risk today has collapsed into prior criminal history, and prior criminal history has become a proxy for race. The combination of these two trends means that using risk-assessment tools is going to significantly

Table 4.2   Imprisonment Rate Changes, 2010–2014

States Enacting JRI Reforms by 2013	Change in Imprisonment Rate	Other States	Change in Imprisonment Rate
Arizona	0.2%	Alabama	−1.4%
Arkansas	8.6%	Alaska	−6.2%
Connecticut	−14.3%	California	−20.6%
Delaware	1.1%	Colorado	−14.8%
Georgia	−9.8%	Florida	−6.7%
Hawaii	−4.8%	Idaho	5.1%
Kansas	5.0%	Illinois	−0.5%
Kentucky	3.8%	Indiana	2.8%
Louisiana	−5.8%	Iowa	−8.4%
Missouri	3.1%	Maine	4.3%
Nevada	−5.6%	Maryland	−10.0%
New Hampshire	6.2%	Massachusetts	−8.1%
North Carolina	−11.6%	Michigan	−2.0%
Ohio	−0.9%	Minnesota	6.0%
Oklahoma	2.1%	Mississippi	−11.4%
Oregon	−2.1%	Montana	−3.7%
Pennsylvania	−1.7%	Nebraska	15.1%
Rhode Island	−0.3%	New Jersey	−14.8%
South Carolina	−12.8%	New Mexico	3.1%
South Dakota	0.5%	New York	−8.9%
Texas	−10.5%	North Dakota	5.5%
Vermont	−4.8%	Tennessee	1.6%
West Virginia	3.6%	Utah	−2.4%
Wisconsin	−1.8%	Virginia	−3.8%
		Washington	−4.8%
		Wyoming	9.1%
Mean	**−2.2%**	**Mean**	**−2.9%**

exacerbate the unacceptable racial disparities in our criminal justice system."[71]

The concentration of policing resources in poor, largely nonwhite urban communities practically ensures earlier and more numerous criminal justice contacts for blacks than for whites, without regard to actual rates of offending. Indeed, earlier contacts tend to generate later contacts simply because those with a record are "profiled," finding themselves subject to closer surveillance and greater suspicion. The harsh effects of such profiling are amplified when criminal history also becomes a central consideration in determining who gets probation, how intense supervision will be, who gets revoked, who gets paroled, and so forth. In principle, RNA should help to keep low-risk offenders in the community and out of prison, but we have to recognize that this more refined sorting is likely to make racial disparities in imprisonment worse. Harcourt points, for instance, to the racial effects of the deinstitutionalization of the mentally ill in the mid-20th century: the effort to reserve mental hospital commitments more rigorously for patients who posed a genuine danger led to a dramatic increase in the percentage of commitments of nonwhites.[72] JR may fall into a similar trap. Ironically and tragically for a movement that began with a vision of empowering disadvantaged communities, JR may prove to be just one more mechanism by which the structural racism in U.S. society is reinforced and perpetuated.

CHAPTER FIVE

Federal Sentencing in the Age of Bush and Obama

It was an historic and symbolically powerful moment. On July 16, 2015, Barack Obama became the first sitting president to visit a federal prison.[1] He was not there to celebrate the tight security or austere living conditions of the El Reno Federal Correctional Institution, nor to gloat over the misfortune of the offenders receiving their just deserts behind the prison's high, razor-wire-capped fences. Rather, Obama visited the medium-security institution outside of Oklahoma City in order to draw attention to the issue of mass incarceration and an emerging, bipartisan federal sentencing reform proposal to soften some of the excesses of the past generation.

In contrast to the Justice Reinvestment Initiative (JRI) crowd, President Obama seemed focused on not only the fiscal, but also the human, costs of the harsh sentencing laws of the late 20th century. Indeed, while at the prison, Obama met with six inmates, all incarcerated for drug offenses.[2] Reporters asked him afterward what struck him most about the experience. Obama's response made for a startling departure from the "othering" rhetoric employed reflexively by so many U.S. politicians when discussing crime and prisoners:

> Visiting with these six individuals. I've said this before—when they describe their youth and their childhood, these are young people who made mistakes that aren't that different than the mistakes I made and the mistakes that a lot of you guys made. The difference is they did not have the kinds of support structures, the second chances, the resources that would allow them to survive those mistakes.

And I think we have a tendency sometimes to almost take for granted or think it's normal that so many young people end up in our criminal justice system. It's not normal. It's not what happens in other countries.

What is normal is teenagers doing stupid things. What is normal is young people making mistakes. And we've got to be able to distinguish between dangerous individuals who need to be incapacitated and incarcerated versus young people who, in an environment in which they are adapting but if given different opportunities, a different vision of life, could be thriving the way we are.

That's what strikes me—there but for the grace of God. And that I think is something that we all have to think about.

Obama's empathetic take on mass incarceration seemed a breath of fresh air, but, in truth, the changes in federal criminal justice policies on his watch were hardly dramatic. Indeed, the federal prison population continued its long-term, unbroken upward trajectory throughout Obama's first term, even as the nation's *state*-level prison population actually began to fall.[3] Two years into his second term, the federal prison population was finally dropping, too, but remained slightly larger than the prison population he inherited from George W. Bush and *much* larger than the prison population Bush had inherited from Bill Clinton.

The federal criminal justice system operates in a quite different political and policy environment than any state system. Perhaps most importantly, the system operates with much looser fiscal constraints. For instance, Congress, unlike many state legislatures, is not legally required to adopt a balanced budget. In the absence of such constraints, the federal sentencing system became especially severe during the height of the tough-on-crime era, and retained that severity even as many states began their (halting) movement in the other direction in the new millennium. Then, when policy did finally start to soften, the changes were mostly limited to one particular area—drug sentencing, especially for crack cocaine offenses—in which the excessiveness of federal practices had become a political lightning rod. Obama himself exemplified the tendency to draw sharp distinctions between the nonviolent drug offenders and others in the system. "[T]here are people who need to be in prison," he declared at El Reno, "and I don't have tolerance for violent criminals."

As we have seen in earlier chapters, focusing sentencing reform on the demonstrably nonviolent greatly reduces its potential impact. But, even in the drug area, federal reforms proved quite modest, leaving prosecutors and judges with ample discretion to continue to send offenders away for very long prison terms. Thus, despite various unique features to the federal story, federal sentencing reform since 2000 has been limited in many of the same ways as state sentencing reforms.

Federal Criminal Justice: Structure and Politics

The federal system has not traditionally played a large role in the prosecution and punishment of crime in the United States. Before the 20th century, there was hardly any federal criminal justice system to speak of; federal jurisdiction was limited to a few small, specialized areas, such as crimes committed on federal lands and violations of federal revenue laws.[4] As the federal regulatory role in U.S. life grew during the Progressive Era, so, too, did the size and jurisdiction of the federal criminal justice system, culminating in a massive expansion during Prohibition. By the time Prohibition ended, a sizable federal component had become an entrenched part of U.S. criminal justice. It was not so clear, however, what exactly this federal component was supposed to do.

The federal system never acquired a general jurisdiction over the basic crimes that Americans most fear: murder, rape, assault, burglary, and the like. The ultimate responsibility for maintaining order on the street and safety in the home has always remained squarely with state and local authorities. One important federal job that did emerge was drug enforcement, which seemed to have a natural affinity with Prohibition enforcement. Indeed, not coincidentally, the long-time head of the Federal Bureau of Narcotics, Harry Anslinger, got his start as a Prohibition agent.[5] Another, overlapping area of federal specialization developed in the field of organized crime, propelled in part by Attorney General Robert Kennedy's crusade against the Mafia in the 1960s. Fighting criminal organizations, especially large, sophisticated ones, seemed to demand the special resources of the feds, including their ability to conduct investigations across state lines.

Despite the limited reach of federal jurisdiction, federal officials were unwilling to stand on the sidelines as public fear of crime reached a fever pitch in the late 20th century. It was hard for the feds to get at violent crime directly, but, given the association of violence with drug abuse and drug trafficking, the existing federal drug enforcement authority seemed a promising *indirect* path to fighting street crime. Additionally, drug trafficking could be targeted using existing federal tools and strategies developed to counter organized crime. Finally, new federal gun control laws provided another means of bringing the federal criminal justice system to bear against the offenses of greatest public concern.

Importantly, though, the federal system never grew large enough to challenge the crime-fighting preeminence of state systems. In 2000, for instance, the federal system employed only about one-twelfth as many correctional staff as state systems did collectively.[6] And, in 2001, the federal system employed only about one-eighth as many prosecutorial personnel.[7] Indeed, the federal system never purported to play a primary role in protecting public safety. When a crime victim calls 911, she does not expect to be connected with a federal official, but with the local police. And, when crime seems out of control, it is state and local officials who will be held accountable, not the feds. This lack of political accountability for the day-to-day business of responding to routine crime frees federal officials to cherry-pick cases. Typically, they see themselves targeting the worst of the worst—a premise that has greatly informed the development of federal sentencing law.

Federal law has also been marked by an absence of fiscal restraint. In their efforts to empower federal prosecutors to go after the worst of the worst, legislators have adopted a host of tough sentencing laws with no apparent regard for their impact on corrections budgets. As a general matter, of course, Congress has not particularly distinguished itself with its fiscal restraint in any policy area, but criminal justice expenses have been especially easy to disregard because they are such a miniscule portion of the federal budget. In 2001, for instance, the federal government's $4.3 billion in corrections expenditures were but a drop in a $1.8 *trillion* bucket.[8]

Federal Sentencing, 1984–2005

The story of federal sentencing in the two decades leading up to January 2005 can be summed up in three short phrases: tougher sentences, more prosecutorial power, and less judicial power. As we have seen, many states began to back away from these trends around 2000, but the federal government continued along its established trajectory without interruption for several more years.

Federal Sentencing Guidelines

Congress first established this trajectory in the Sentencing Reform Act of 1984 (SRA). The SRA abolished parole release for federal prisoners and authorized a new system of sentencing guidelines. Originally a *liberal* reform, the federal guidelines were initially championed in Congress by Senator Ted Kennedy (D-MA) in the 1970s.[9] In the early 1980s, however, Republicans controlled the Senate and the White House, and Kennedy's guidelines proposal underwent several rounds of modification at more conservative hands before its eventual passage. The end result was a sentencing guidelines system that differed markedly from the systems being adopted in many states at about the same time. The key features included the following:

- The guidelines would be drafted and then revised as necessary by a new United States Sentencing Commission, comprising commissioners nominated by the president and approved by the Senate.
- The commission was given numerous directives by Congress that would clearly have the effect of driving up federal sentences; for instance, Congress declared that the guidelines should ensure a "substantial term of imprisonment" for multiple repeat offenders and for certain drug offenses.
- Once the guidelines were in place, judges would be required to impose sentences within the narrow ranges recommended by the guidelines except to the extent that a particular case presented unusual circumstances that had not been considered by the commission in creating the guidelines.
- If a judge imposed a sentence below the guidelines range, the prosecutor could appeal, getting a higher court to reconsider whether the case really did present sufficiently unusual circumstances so as to warrant a "departure" from the guidelines.

The new commission promulgated its sentencing guidelines in 1987, with commissioner (and future Supreme Court Justice) Stephen Breyer playing a lead drafting role.[10] The complex federal guidelines employ a two-dimensional grid, with "offense level" along one axis and "criminal history category" along the other. Offense level is determined not only by the specific crime for which the defendant was formally convicted, but also by many additional factors, for example, whether a gun was used to commit the crime or, in drug cases, the amount of drugs involved. (This approach to guidelines, referred to as "real-offense sentencing," would eventually put the federal system into constitutional hot water, but not for another two decades.) These real-offense factors tended, almost without exception, to drive sentences up; in other words, there were many more aggravating than mitigating factors in the guidelines. By contrast, the guidelines strongly discouraged judges from taking into account anything about the offender's background and personal circumstances, other than criminal history.[11] Judges were thus more-or-less precluded from considering mitigating factors like a defendant's disadvantaged upbringing, military service and other civil contributions, and family responsibilities. This seemed to create an unbalanced system, of course, in which sentencing judges would tend to see only the negative side of the defendants before them: their current criminal conduct and their prior convictions.

In setting severity levels, the commission relied on existing sentencing practices, but only as a starting point.[12] Taking cues from the legislative directives in the SRA—but going beyond their literal requirements—the commission deliberately chose to inflate penalties for those convicted of drug, violent, or white-collar offenses, and for multiple recidivists. Collectively, these categories far outnumbered the remaining cases in the federal system.

The guidelines offered two main escape hatches from their general severity and rigidity, and both served in important ways to empower prosecutors. First, one provision offered a two-point discount (or in some cases, beginning in 1992, a three-point discount) in the offense level for "acceptance of responsibility." In essence, this really meant little more than pleading guilty.[13] This feature of the guidelines thus ensured that prosecutors would have considerable plea-bargaining leverage in the new system. Second, while the guidelines generally discourage departures, sentences below the guidelines range were expressly authorized for defendants who "provided substantial assistance in the investigation or prosecution of another person."[14] However, no departure on this ground was permissible without the prosecutor's express support. Prosecutors thus obtained a powerful tool to induce defendants to testify against one another—often a key component of law enforcement efforts to put criminal organizations out of business. More subtly, the substantial-assistance provision further amplified the prosecutor's plea-bargaining leverage. The guidelines provided little definition of "substantial assistance," giving prosecutors considerable leeway to dangle the promise of a departure before defendants who actually had little assistance of value to provide to law enforcement.

Statutory Minimums

Even as the guidelines were in gestation, Congress was starting to put together a separate and distinct federal sentencing system, one comprising a complex network of statutory mandatory minimums. Perhaps most notably, in 1986, at the height of the national cocaine panic, Congress adopted a tough new set of drug minimums.[15] The law singled out crack cocaine for the harshest treatment. Legislators understood little about this new drug threat, but Democrats and Republicans ended up in a sort of bidding war over who could be toughest against it.[16] They settled on a system that sharply distinguished the crack and powder forms of cocaine from one another: the quantity of powder required to trigger a minimum was 100 times greater than the quantity of crack required for the same minimum. This was the so-called 100:1 ratio that became quite controversial in the 1990s as it became apparent that blacks were being charged with crack offenses at rates far exceeding their proportion of the population; the high crack penalties thus particularly disadvantaged blacks, while the (relatively) moderate powder penalties were applied far more often to whites.

Congress adopted another notable mandatory minimum in 1984, the Armed Career Criminal Act. The law required a 15-year sentence for the possession of a firearm after three prior convictions of a serious drug offense or a violent felony. The same year, Congress also adopted a five-year minimum for carrying a firearm during a crime of violence, now contained in 18 U.S.C. § 924(c). The provision would be substantially broadened and toughened in subsequent years.

Congress regularly passed new minimum statutes over the ensuing two decades. Others included the following:

- 1986: extension of § 924(c) to carrying a firearm during a drug trafficking crime
- 1988: extension of drug minimums to conspiracy offenses; new minimum for simple possession of crack cocaine
- 1996: adoption of 10-year minimum for the production of child pornography (even longer for second or third convictions)
- 1998: extension of § 924(c) to mere possession of a firearm in furtherance of drug or violent crime; enhancement of 924(c)

minimums based on brandishing or discharging a firearm, or multiple convictions
- 2003: enhancement of minimums for production of child pornography; adoption of five-year minimum for receipt and distribution of child pornography, among other new minimums for various child sex crimes
- 2004: adoption of two-year minimum for aggravated identity theft
- 2006: further enhancement of minimums for various child sex crimes[17]

Collectively, the federal mandatory minimums constitute a second sentencing system layered on top of the guidelines. When a minimum statute calls for a higher sentence than the guidelines—no mean feat, considering the severity of guidelines—the minimum trumps the guidelines. Moreover, even when a judge decides that some unusual mitigating circumstance warrants a departure below the guidelines range, a statutory minimum still makes for a solid floor below which the judge may not normally go. Congress provides limited safety valves.[18] One statute mirrors the substantial-assistance guideline, permitting a below-minimum sentence with the prosecutor's support. Another statute permits below-minimum sentences in drug cases, but only for certain low-level offenders with minimal criminal history.

Crack and the 100:1 Ratio

As federal sentencing law grew increasingly tougher in the 1980s and 1990s, one aspect of the law drew a lion's share of the criticism. Congress first established the 100:1 ratio as part of the 1986 drug minimums, but the Sentencing Commission then chose to work the same approach into the guidelines. The commission's decision mattered because, in many cases, the drug guidelines provided higher penalties than the statutory minimums. However, the system attracted sharp criticism as it became clear that 100:1 produced massive racial disparities.

Although a complacent enabler of congressional excess for much of its history, the Sentencing Commission roused itself to move against 100:1 in 1995. Surveying the available medical and sociological evidence, the commission found little basis for distinguishing so dramatically between the crack and powder forms of cocaine.[19] Additionally, the commission noted the race problem: blacks accounted for more than 88 percent of federal crack cocaine distribution convictions in

1993, but only about 27 percent of powder convictions.[20] The commission declared, "Federal sentencing data lead to the inescapable conclusion that Blacks comprise the largest percentage of those affected by the penalties associated with crack cocaine."[21] The commission, by a 4–3 vote, decided to eliminate the crack–powder disparity in the guidelines.[22] (Of course, only Congress would be able to eliminate the *statutory* disparity.) The guidelines amendment, however, was rejected by Congress, exercising a veto power over guidelines changes that legislators had reserved for themselves when first establishing the system. The commission tried again in 1997 with a more modest position, calling on Congress to adopt a 5:1 ratio. However, Congress failed to act on this recommendation, and 100:1 remained the law into the new millennium.

From Clinton to Bush and Ashcroft

The growing severity of federal sentencing law in the 1990s reflected the continuing legacy of Willie Horton. Learning the lesson of the Michael Dukakis implosion in 1988, Bill Clinton resolved to take crime away from Republicans as a wedge issue. The strategy became clear early in his 1992 run for president, when Clinton took a break from the campaign trail in order to fly home to Arkansas to oversee the execution of Ricky Ray Rector.[23] It was a pathetic spectacle; a mentally impaired Rector had so little understanding of the proceedings that he asked to save the dessert from his last meal for the next day. However, Clinton's firm stand against a sentence commutation signaled that he was no Dukakis. "I can be nicked on a lot," he proudly declared, "but no one can say I'm soft on crime." As president, Clinton would push successfully for a federal three-strikes law, approve several expansions of the mandatory-minimum system, and sign the 1995 legislation that restored 100:1 in the guidelines.

By the time George W. Bush replaced Clinton in 2001, hardly any expert or practitioner outside the prosecutorial establishment viewed federal sentencing in a positive light. Bush, however, seemed unlikely to soften what was almost universally regarded as an excessively harsh and inflexible system. For all his talk of "compassionate conservatism," Bush, as governor of Texas, had presided over 152 executions—more than any other governor in a half-century.[24] As president, Bush confirmed that he would maintain this tough-on-crime stance through his appointment of a noted hard-liner, Senator John Ashcroft, as his attorney general.

The U.S. attorney general plays a far more important role in the federal criminal justice system than does the state attorney general in nearly any state criminal justice system. State prosecutorial functions tend to be highly decentralized, with each county electing its own district attorney. On the federal side, by contrast, the president appoints each of the 93 U.S. attorneys. While based in separate offices scattered throughout the country, the U.S. attorneys operate within a single prosecutorial bureaucracy, with the attorney general sitting atop the pyramid. The attorney general also oversees the federal prison system and prominent federal investigative agencies, including the FBI and the Drug Enforcement Administration.

Attorney General Ashcroft first made waves by adopting new Department of Justice (DOJ) policies intended to push federal prosecutors to seek the death penalty more aggressively, including in states that did not have or often use capital punishment in their own systems.[25] Federal courts could thereby step in and rectify what Ashcroft—a long-time, outspoken advocate of the death penalty—saw as a glaring deficiency in many state systems.

Although exceptionally high-profile, federal death-eligible cases had always been a rarity. Ashcroft's next move to stiffen federal prosecutorial practices applied much more broadly and consequentially. Through a pair of memoranda in 2003, Ashcroft sought to rein in excessive generosity in plea bargaining. This struck at a critical component of the federal sentencing system since, as we have seen, guilty pleas and cooperation with prosecutors were the most important escape hatches from the general severity of the guidelines. More specifically, the Ashcroft memoranda set forth these policies:

- Prosecutors were to charge and pursue "the most serious, readily provable offense or offenses" that were supported by the facts of each case.
- The use of mandatory minimums was "strongly encouraged"; prosecutors were directed to take any necessary steps to ensure that they were applied, except in certain limited circumstances when authorized to do otherwise by a supervisor.
- Prosecutors were required to disclose to the judge all aggravating facts about a case that would increase the sentence under the guidelines' system of "real-offense" sentencing; Ashcroft thus barred the practice of "fact-bargaining"—common in some federal districts—by which prosecutors would agree as part of a

plea bargain to withhold certain aggravating facts from the sentencing judge.

- Prosecutors were directed to oppose any requests for downward departures from the guidelines except in a few limited circumstances, and even then only with a supervisor's approval.[26]

White-Collar Sentencing

The Ashcroft DOJ did not limit its push for tougher sentences to internal memoranda. In 2002, in the midst of a recession that was widely blamed on high-level corporate malfeasance in companies like Enron, WorldCom, and Tyco, the DOJ lobbied the Sentencing Commission for an across-the-board increase in penalties for economic crimes, threatening to go to Congress for even more draconian increases if the commission did not comply.[27] Cynics saw the Bush administration's sudden interest in white-collar sentencing as a ploy to defuse political pressure for more extensive civil regulatory reform. However, it was characteristic of the administration to view tough deterrent threats as the tool of first resort in dealing with any troublesome problem—domestic or foreign. In any event, the commission—also acting true to form—mostly acceded to the pressure for longer sentences. Notably, these increases reached far beyond Enron-level crimes to the much larger number of routine, low-dollar frauds that can find their way into federal courts. Notably, too, the increases overrode a thoughtful, comprehensive reworking of the sentencing guidelines for economic crimes that had been adopted in 2001 after more than five years of study and deliberation.

The hastily adopted, knee-jerk toughening of white-collar sentences was a sad and troubling moment for federal sentencing policy. The whole point of having a Sentencing Commission had been to depoliticize sentencing policy, establishing a system by which sentencing rules would reflect science and expertise, not partisan grandstanding and the public passions of the moment. However, the habitual adoption of new statutory minimums and the override of the commission's 1995 crack amendment revealed that Congress had little respect for the depoliticization ideal. Now, the DOJ was also piling on, further demonstrating the commission's marginalization as a meaningful policy-making body.

DOJ's War on Departures and the Feeney Amendment

An even sadder and more troubling episode was already taking shape. Its roots lay in the Supreme Court's 1996 decision in *Koon v.*

United States, which involved the sentences of Los Angeles police offi-cers convicted of civil rights violations for the infamous beating of Rodney King, an African American motorist. Although the guidelines called for a prison term of 70–87 months, the judge departed down-ward and imposed sentences of 30 months on each of the police offi-cers. The principal reason given was the wrongful conduct of the victim, King, who had led police on a high-speed chase and then, once stopped, failed to obey officers' orders to lie down. The government appealed the departure and won. The officers then appealed further to the Supreme Court, arguing that the first-level appeals court should have been more deferential to the lenient decision of the original sen-tencing judge. The Supreme Court agreed, holding that a departure decision should only be reversed when the sentencing judge abuses her discretion—an established standard of review that, as all lawyers recognize, produces few appellate reversals. In effect, *Koon* seemed to reduce the power of prosecutors to force sentencing judges to adhere to the guidelines.

By 2000, federal prosecutors were griping to Congress about the high rates of departures in some districts.[28] In truth, departure rates had begun to rise even before *Koon*, but the Supreme Court's decision legitimized the trend, which continued unabated over the ensuing years. In 1999, for instance, more than one-third of sentences were outside the guidelines range. Of course, many of these departures were sponsored by the government for substantial assistance reasons. It was the nonsubstantial assistance departures that were of particular con-cern—like the one in *Koon*—because these departures undermined the DOJ's preeminent role in controlling the guidelines escape hatches.

The Ashcroft DOJ wasted little time in taking aim at departure rates, repeatedly raising the issue in statements to the Sentencing Commission and congressional committees.[29] The DOJ got its oppor-tunity for legal change in the form of the Prosecutorial Remedies and Tools against the Exploitation of Children Today (PROTECT) Act of 2003.[30] The bill included the now-familiar AMBER alert system for responding to child abduction, among other provisions intended to protect children from kidnapping and sexual abuse. A popular bill with little apparent opposition, the PROTECT Act easily passed the Senate and was clearly headed for rapid approval in the lower cham-ber, too. The bill thus provided a perfect vehicle for quietly smuggling some seemingly technical, but practically quite significant, changes into federal sentencing law. At the DOJ's behest, Tom Feeney, a fresh-man Republican from Florida with no particular background in the field of federal sentencing, introduced an anti-departure amendment, which was adopted by the House after just 15 minutes of debate. This was accomplished without any input from the Sentencing Commission—supposedly Congress's expert agency on sentencing policy—or, for that matter, the judiciary, the criminal defense bar, corrections officials, or academic experts.

In its original form, as passed by the House, the so-called Feeney Amendment would have dramatically curtailed the ability of judges to depart below the guidelines. Key changes included the following:

- A flat-out ban on certain established grounds for departure, such as the defendant's extraordinary family responsibilities;
- A ban on departures based on any grounds not specifically approved by the Sentencing Commission;
- A requirement of prosecutorial approval for the defendant to receive the full three-point reduction for acceptance of responsibility;
- A requirement that the DOJ report every nonsubstantial assistance departure to Congress within 15 days (an apparent effort to intimidate departure-granting judges); and
- A heightened standard of appellate review for departure decisions (effectively overturning the Supreme Court's decision in *Koon*).

Adoption of the Feeney Amendment meant that the House and Senate had passed different versions of the PROTECT Act, thereby setting the stage for a conference committee to iron out the differences. Although caught off guard by the swift introduction and passage of the Feeney Amendment, supporters of judicial discretion—judges, defense lawyers, academics, the National Association for the Advancement of Colored People (NAACP), corporate interests then feeling themselves in the crosshairs of white-collar prosecution, and even the Sentencing Commission itself—quickly rallied to urge the conference committee to jettison the sweeping changes to federal sentencing law.[31]

In the end, the Feeney Amendment was pared back, but, in final form, remained the most significant set of legislative changes of the guidelines system since its creation in 1984. The new limitations on grounds for departure were confined to child-victim and sexual offenses. However, all departures were made subject to the new, more rigorous standard of appellate review, and the DOJ was given power over the third point for acceptance. Perhaps most notably, the amendment authorized the DOJ to set up new early disposition, or "fast-track," programs, in which defendants could get a departure in return for a very quick guilty plea and waiver of legal rights. Congress thus created another escape hatch from the guidelines, and once again gave prosecutors the key.

The Feeney Amendment wrought several important changes in federal sentencing policy, but, in retrospect, even more important may have been a subtle shift in federal sentencing *politics*. Before 2003, legislators might have thought the politics simple and straight-forward: any changes that increased the system's severity carried only upside benefits. However, the vigorous, broad-based pushback against the Feeney Amendment seemed to reveal that a limit had been reached. The judiciary seemed firmly opposed to any further marginalization of its role at sentencing. Among the judges speaking out against the Feeney Amendment were at least two very prominent, law and order Republicans: Chief Justice William Rehnquist of the U.S. Supreme Court and Judge William Wilkins of the Fourth Circuit Court of Appeals, a protégé of the arch-conservative Senator Strom Thurmond and a former chair of the United States Sentencing Commission. Additionally, the business community, a key Republican constituency, also seemed increasingly skeptical of the guidelines system. An unintended consequence of the DOJ's push to boost the severity of the white-collar guidelines may have been to give business leaders a much greater stake in preserving the judicial departure power. Finally, by 2003, 100:1 had become a major civil rights issue. The crack–powder disparity tainted the entire guidelines system with the stench of racism—a point highlighted by the NAACP's opposition to the Feeney Amendment. In short, the controversy engendered by the Feeney Amendment demonstrated that any further efforts to tighten the guidelines system would be opposed by many groups with far more political clout than just the criminal defense bar.

The Guidelines at 15

Despite the scaling back of the Feeney Amendment, federal sentencing remained uniquely rigid, tough, and prosecutor-dominated as President Bush's first term wound down in 2004. The same month that Bush eked out his narrow reelection victory, the Sentencing Commission published a voluminous report assessing the guidelines' impact over their first 15 years in force (1987–2002). Among the eye-catching findings were these:

- The percentage of federal defendants receiving probation dropped by a third over the guidelines era.[32]
- The vast majority (86 percent) of convicted federal defendants were now being sent to prison.[33]
- Average sentence lengths were also up, with the typical federal defendant now spending nearly 50 months in prison—nearly twice as long as in the preguidelines era.[34]
- Drug trafficking offenses continued to make up the largest share of the federal criminal docket, as they had since the 1970s; in 2002, drug trafficking constituted more than 40 percent of federal criminal cases.[35]
- Drug trafficking sentences had grown especially severe in the guidelines era; in 2002, 95 percent of federal drug trafficking offenders were given a prison term, with time served averaging about 65 months.[36] By contrast, when the guidelines system was adopted in 1984, only about 80 percent were getting prison, with an average time served of about 30 months.
- The proportion of minority defendants (particularly blacks and Hispanics) in the federal system grew over the guidelines era.[37]
- Since the mid-1980s, the racial disparities in federal sentencing had grown more pronounced.[38]
- The typical black drug trafficking defendant received a sentence that was about seven months longer than his white counterpart; similar disparities were also found for Hispanics.[39]

These numbers translated into a sharp increase in the federal prison population in the guidelines era. Figure 5.1 compares the federal imprisonment numbers with those of Texas and California, the two largest state systems.[40] The two states had larger prison populations through most of the 1990s, but both moved into a long-term stabilization mode in about 2000. By contrast, the federal system continued to grow swiftly. Thus, in 2002, the federal system eclipsed both Texas and California and has remained easily the nation's largest prison system ever since.

Figure 5.2 further illuminates the distinctive nature of the federal system, as it existed when the commission was preparing its "15-Year Report."[41] Drug offenders constituted a majority of the federal population, with large shares also coming from public order

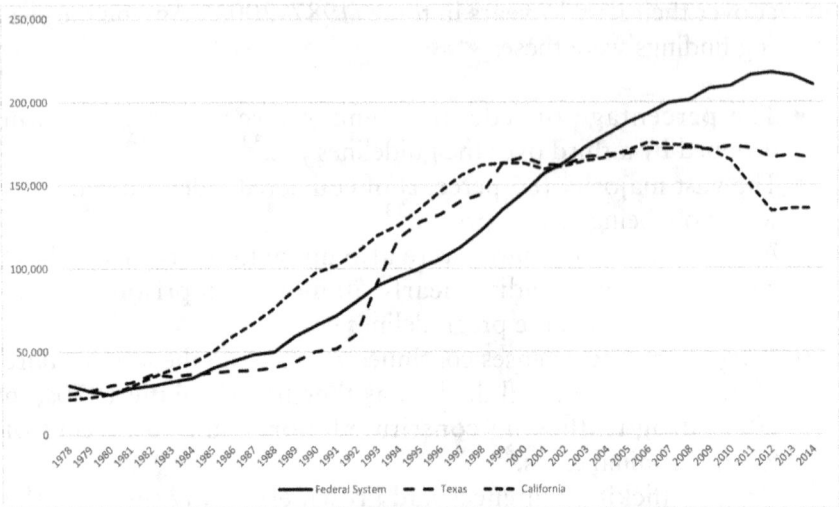

Figure 5.1 Year-end Prison Populations, Federal System, Texas, California, 1978–2014

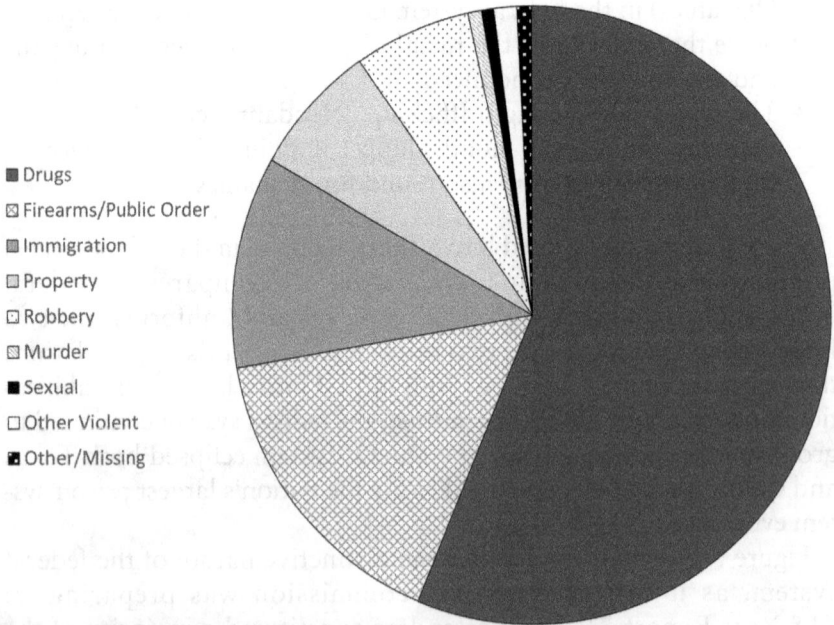

- Drugs
- Firearms/Public Order
- Immigration
- Property
- Robbery
- Murder
- Sexual
- Other Violent
- Other/Missing

Figure 5.2 Federal Prisoners by Offense, Year-end 2003

■ Drugs
□ Firearms/Public Order
■ Property
■ Robbery
□ Murder
■ Sexual
▨ Other Violent
□ Other/Missing

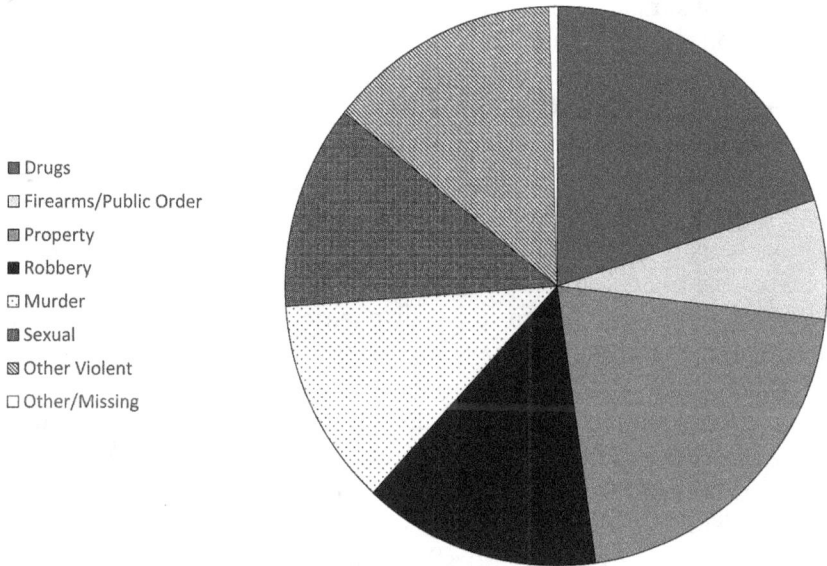

Figure 5.3   State Prisoners by Offense, Year-end 2003

offenses (chiefly violations of firearms laws) and immigration offenses. Together, the federal Big Three—drug, gun, and immigration offenses —accounted for more than 83 percent of the prison population. By contrast, Figure 5.3 shows a very different, and much more balanced, population in state prisons.[42] The drug and public order categories were much smaller, while the immigration category—an exclusively federal area of crime—did not exist. On the other hand, the property, robbery, murder, and other sexual and violent offenses categories were much larger. This helps to explain continued federal growth long past the time when most state systems were stabilizing. State systems are primarily oriented to responding to traditional victimizing crimes; when those crimes fall, as they did in the 1990s, one would expect to see reduced population pressures in the state systems. However, the federal system was not dependent on a steady stream of 911 calls, but instead relied on abundant offenses (drugs, weapons, immigration) whose discovery was simply a function of law enforcement effort.

More than such imprisonment numbers, though, the commission's 15-Year Report focused particularly on the question of whether the guidelines had reduced sentencing disparities in the federal system, that is, whether offenders with similar criminal histories who were

convicted of similar crimes were more likely to receive similar sentences. Back in the 1970s and 1980s, when the federal guidelines system
had been first developed, disparity had been the most-discussed concern of policy makers. More recently, the DOJ had been arguing that
increased departure rates were leading to a resurgence of disparity in
the federal system. The commission's disparity analysis was thus the
most eagerly awaited portion of the new report.

Reviewing multiple studies conducted by its own staff and outside
researchers, the commission found convincing proof that the guidelines had reduced judge-to-judge disparities.[43] Using sophisticated
new analytical techniques, the commission found that legally relevant
variables—that is, the sentencing factors given particular weight by
the guidelines and statutes—were, in fact, the major drivers of sentences in the federal system.[44] The assignment of a case to one judge versus another accounted for less than 3 percent of the variation in
sentence lengths. By contrast, the use of substantial assistance departures (controlled by prosecutors) accounted for a much larger share
of the variation (4.4 percent). More generally, while hard to quantify
fully, it seemed that *prosecutorial* discretion was now playing a more
important role than *judicial* discretion in causing similarly situated
offenders to receive different sentences. "Plea bargaining," the commission concluded, "is reintroducing disparity into the system."[45]
"Get your own house in order," the commission seemed to be telling
the DOJ, "before coming after the judges and us."

The commission also got in its digs against the 100:1 ratio. Crack
defendants were getting an average sentence of 119 months, while powder defendants received an average of only 78 months.[46] This did not
constitute a disparity as the commission defined the term, since crack
versus powder was a legally relevant variable. Still, the racial effects were
dramatic and troubling. "This one sentencing rule," the commission
concluded, "contributes more to the differences in average sentences
between African-American and White offenders than any possible effect
of discrimination [by judges]. Revising the crack cocaine [guideline]
would better reduce the gap than any other single policy change, and it
would dramatically improve the fairness of the federal sentencing
system."[47]

The *Booker* "Revolution"

The U.S. Supreme Court engages with sentencing policy in two distinct ways. First, the Court decides what limitations the Constitution

imposes on sentencing. These limitations—which apply to all U.S. sentencing systems, state and federal—will be discussed in the next chapter. Second, the Court decides how federal sentencing laws, such as mandatory minimum statutes and the guidelines, should be interpreted and applied. These latter decisions, of course, pertain only to the federal sentencing system. We have already encountered an example: the Court's 1996 ruling in *Koon v. United States* that appellate courts should defer to the departure decisions of sentencing judges. The Court's most important case on federal sentencing law, *United States v. Booker*, occurred nearly a decade later—the culmination of a long-running battle over the guidelines' "real-offense" rules. Defense lawyers had long objected to the seeming unfairness of increasing punishment based on facts found by a judge at the sentencing hearing, rather than by a jury at trial.

As we will see in the next chapter, a key breakthrough occurred in 2000, when the Supreme Court held, as a matter of constitutional law, that any fact that increases the maximum punishment to which a defendant is exposed must be proven to a jury beyond a reasonable doubt. Then, in 2004, in *Blakely v. Washington*, the Court ruled that the same principle applies to sentencing guidelines. If a fact increased a defendant's guidelines range, then regular trial procedures would have to be followed. Although *Blakely* dealt with state sentencing guidelines, most experts immediately recognized that the federal guidelines system would also run afoul of the new decision's logic. The question was, how would the Court remedy the constitutional problem. Would the Court throw out the SRA in its entirety, or just particular portions of the statute? If the latter, which portions exactly would be retained?

Lawyers and lower-court judges were not kept long in suspense. In January 2005, in *United States v. Booker,* a closely divided Supreme Court chose a moderate remedy. Writing for a bare 5–4 majority, Justice Stephen Breyer proved remarkably successful in salvaging much of the guidelines system that he himself had played a key role in designing two decades earlier. Breyer decided that sentencing judges could and should continue to calculate real-offense guidelines sentences just as they had been doing for years, so long as the guidelines were merely "advisory," not presumptive. *Booker* thus clearly increased the discretion of sentencing judges, but the extent of this newfound discretion remained something of a mystery. *Booker* required judges to "consider" the guidelines and retained the ability of prosecutors to appeal sentences that were below the guidelines range. On the other hand, *Booker* threw out the Feeney Amendment's new, more rigorous standard of appellate review.

Under *Booker,* appellate courts would have to determine whether sentences were "unreasonable"—whatever that meant.

Despite its ambiguities, *Booker* was welcomed enthusiastically by defense lawyers and other guidelines critics. "In the immediate aftermath," recall two scholars, "some commentators were 'ecstatic' and 'elated' with a 'wise and careful decision,' ending two decades of 'unjust, irrational sentences" and replacing them with a 'marvelous' and 'ideal sentencing system' where 'federal judges can be federal judges again.' "[48] Not surprisingly, prosecutors took a much dimmer view of the Supreme Court's handiwork. Outgoing attorney general Ashcroft—soon to be replaced by Alberto Gonzales as President Bush moved into his second term—predicted that prosecutors would lose leverage over suspects and judges would hand out more lenient sentences.[49] He called *Booker* "a retreat from justice that may put the public's safety in jeopardy."

The DOJ asked Congress, in effect, to reinstitute the pre-*Booker* guidelines system, taking advantage of a curious asymmetry in the underlying constitutional law.[50] Although it was unconstitutional to have guidelines that increased a defendant's *maximum* possible sentence based on a judge's findings of fact, there was (at the time) no constitutional barrier to increasing a defendant's *minimum* sentence. The DOJ thus asked Congress to convert the guidelines into a system of mandatory minimums. Judges would then face the same prohibitions they faced pre-*Booker* on imposing below-guidelines sentences. There would, however, be no restrictions on *above*-guidelines sentences.

In contrast to the swift adoption of the Feeney Amendment two years earlier, the DOJ's new proposal for "topless" guidelines in 2005 went nowhere. In retrospect, it is striking that Congress did not respond to the public safety dog whistle. Why did 2005 play out so differently than 2003? In part, the answer is that the broad-based, anti-Feeney mobilization was still a fresh memory, and the anti-guidelines forces were ready this time; prosecutorial predictions of disaster were met immediately with calls by respected authorities to give the new system a chance to work. A particularly prominent and important voice urging caution was that of Judge Paul Cassell of Utah, a conservative appointee of President George W. Bush who was one of the nation's leading advocates for the rights of crime victims.

More generally, despite the DOJ's suggestion of an imminent wave of lenient sentences by liberal judges, the fact was that a generation of Republican domination of the White House—including 24 of the previous 36 years—gave Republicans a leading position on the federal bench, a position that would clearly be strengthened, thanks to President Bush's recent reelection. (By the end of Bush's second term, Republicans would hold nearly 60 percent of all federal judgeships.[51]) Notably, Republican judges seemed no happier than Democrats about limits on their discretion. Their opposition to a revival of the pre-*Booker* system stood out, since it strained credibility to argue that they intended to use their newly expanded discretion to hasten the return of dangerous offenders to the streets.

Then, too, 2005 was a difficult year for the Bush administration, full of distractions and crises, and not the time for a pitched battle over sentencing policy. The president's push for Social Security reform foundered, indecisive wars in Iraq and Afghanistan dragged on, and the bungled federal response to Hurricane Katrina widened doubts about the administration's competence. With black residents of New Orleans particularly hard hit, the Katrina fiasco also had a racial dimension, exacerbating perceptions that the administration was indifferent to the interests of people of color. In this context, a fight to restore the binding sentencing guidelines—including, of course, the notorious 100:1 crack–powder ratio—would have seemed especially ill-timed.

Additionally, for all of the DOJ's post-*Booker* bluster, there seemed a modest softening of the Bush administration's criminal justice policies over time. Perhaps the first indication of a change in tone came in the 2004 State of Union address, in which Bush highlighted the increasingly prominent issue of prisoner reentry. A predictable legacy of the great imprisonment boom, an ever-swelling wave of ex-cons was returning to free society. "We know from long experience," Bush warned, "that if they can't find work, or a home, or help, they are much more likely to commit crime and return to prison."[52] He called for a $300 million program to provide social services for reentrants—a tiny drop in an enormous bucket of unmet needs, but still a notable rhetorical shift from the dominant emphasis of politicians for a generation on deterrence and incapacitation as the nation's chief crime-control strategies. Bush's initiative would culminate in the passage of the Second Chance Act of 2007, which authorized new grants for state and local governments to support reentry projects.[53] Maybe the notion of "second chances" came naturally to a president who, himself, was a convicted offender for driving under the influence in 1976.[54] Moreover, the ideal of forgiveness and mercy may have resonated with many of the evangelical Christians who comprised a core Bush administration constituency.[55] In any event, there would have been at least a little cognitive dissonance for a president who spoke glowingly of second chances also to go to bat for the DOJ's proposal to restore the mandatory character of the draconian federal sentencing guidelines.

Over time, though, the most compelling argument against a congressional override of *Booker* was that it proved unnecessary. Simply put, *Booker* had only a very modest impact on federal sentencing practices. To be sure, comparing the three years following *Booker* with the year preceding *Blakely*, the proportion of within-guidelines sentences dropped from 70 percent to 60 percent.[56] Still, the great majority of sentences remained within the guidelines, and the average sentence length actually *increased* slightly after *Booker*, from 53 to 54 months. Moreover, much of the increase in below-guidelines sentences came not from judges taking advantage of their new discretion, but from prosecutors implementing the new "early disposition" programs that were authorized by the Feeney Amendment. In the two years following *Booker*, the proportion of cases with early disposition departures increased from less than 2 percent to more than 7 percent. More generally, as had been the case pre-*Booker*, judges proved very reluctant to give defendants a break without the agreement of prosecutors. Indeed, more than two-thirds of the below-guidelines sentences came at the behest of prosecutors. Judges independently chose to go below the guidelines in fewer than 13 percent of the post-*Booker* cases. Put differently, judges, by and large, continued to support the pre-*Booker* system that had so dramatically empowered prosecutors by giving them control over the guidelines escape hatches.

Why did judges not seize the *Booker* moment, reasserting their traditional preeminence in the sentencing process? The data likely reflect a number of underlying considerations. Perhaps most simply and powerfully, the pre-*Booker* system was familiar and comfortable; inertia favored its de facto perpetuation. In the words of retired district judge Nancy Gertner, "Twenty years of Guidelines sentencing has transformed the federal bench. . . . It is a tectonic shift in the way judges see the job of sentencing. Guidelines and mandatory minimum sentences have normalized sentences that would have been obscene years ago. We have come to view imprisonment as the appropriate punishment for all crimes with the only question being *how much*."[57]

Decisions from the various federal circuit courts of appeals helped to reinforce this inertia. In the federal system, 12 circuit courts handle criminal appeals from the district (trial-level) courts; these circuit courts stand between the district courts and the Supreme Court, serving as the lead interpreters of the Delphic pronouncements of the nine justices in Washington, DC. Although different circuits adopted slightly different approaches to implementing *Booker*, their overall response can best be described as minimalistic—the ambiguities of *Booker* were consistently resolved in favor of the status quo ante. Most circuits, for instance, adopted a "presumption of reasonableness" in favor of guidelines sentences.[58] The message to district judges was clear: follow the guidelines, and your sentence will not get overturned; deviate from the guidelines, and you risk the public rebuke of appellate reversal. Consistent with this message, most of the below-guidelines sentences that were appealed in the first year after *Booker* were overturned. Additionally, the circuit courts insisted that district judges *begin* their sentencing analysis by calculating the guidelines range.[59] Although this seemed merely a procedural requirement, critics quickly expressed concern about what psychologists call the "anchoring" effect: much research indicates that articulating a number at the start of a decision process—even a randomly selected number—can powerfully influence the final decision reached.[60] Thus, the procedural requirement may have also subtly reinforced the inertial tendencies of district judges. Finally, when it came to the guidelines' most controversial feature, most circuits held that district judges were still bound by the 100:1 crack–powder disparity; judges could not impose a below-guidelines sentence based simply on a disagreement with the 100:1 policy.[61]

The conservatism of district and appellate judges post-*Booker* highlights an important, but often misunderstood, reality of the federal judiciary. Because federal judges are appointed for life, not elected, it is often assumed that they are immune from the tough-on-crime political dynamics that otherwise so deeply affect the making of sentencing policy. This supposed immunity, however, is largely an illusion. For one thing, while federal judges do not face reelection themselves, they are appointed and confirmed by presidents and senators who do. These politicians naturally want to select judges who will reflect well on them, which means, among other things, judges who seem to share their attitudes about crime and punishment. Moreover, those judges who wish to move up the ladder—from district to circuit court, from circuit to Supreme Court—will have an additional reason to stick with the tough-on-crime approaches that politicians of both parties tend to favor. Even among those judges who have little expectation of advancement, no one can relish the thought of being called out as soft on crime in the media. Judges must also be wary of antagonizing Congress and the DOJ. For instance, as we saw with the Feeney Amendment, if the DOJ perceives an excess of judicial lenience, the department may prevail on Congress to adopt legislation that sharply curtails judicial discretion.

All of these considerations surely played into the post-*Booker* sentencing data, as did principled concerns regarding disparity. Federal judges had become accustomed to viewing the guidelines as a bulwark against unwarranted disparities (disregarding, of course, the fact that the guidelines themselves seemed to embrace various disparities of their own, such as 100:1). Routine deviations from the guidelines seemed to invite chaos—a return to the pre-SRA system famously derided by a federal judge in 1973 as "law without order."[62] Indeed, all of the circuits adopting the "presumption of reasonableness" of guidelines sentences cited as a justification the need to minimize disparity.[63]

In a pair of 2007 cases, the Supreme Court offered some modest pushback. In *Kimbrough v. United States*, the Court held that a district judge *could* impose a below-guidelines sentence in a crack case based on the judge's opinion that the crack guideline was too harsh as a general matter.[64] Then, in *Gall v. United States*, the Court scolded a circuit court for reviewing a below-guidelines sentence too rigorously.[65] The case presented a striking illustration of excessive prosecutorial zeal in fighting the War on Drugs. For a few months in 2000, University of Iowa sophomore Michael Gall participated in an Ecstasy-distribution business. By September of that year, he advised his co-conspirators that he wanted out, and he distributed no more drugs after that. He successfully graduated from college, moved to a different state, and became a master carpenter. However, the long arm of the law finally caught up with Gall four years after he stopped dealing drugs. Facing federal charges, Gall pled guilty. The prosecutor insisted that Gall be given the guidelines sentence of 30–37 months in prison, despite his complete, voluntary, sustained cessation of any illegal activity. The district judge instead ordered probation, and the government appealed. The circuit court overturned the below-guidelines sentence, but then the Supreme Court reversed, holding that the circuit court failed to show the "requisite deference" to district judge's opinion. Combined with *Kimbrough*, *Gall* sent a strong signal to the circuit courts that they would have to soften their review of below-guidelines sentences.

Appellate courts got the message. As some circuit court judges put it at the time, the "Court of Appeals is out of the sentencing business."[66] Indeed, perhaps the strongest indication of the new appellate environment was that prosecutors, for the most part, decided it was no longer worthwhile to appeal sentencing issues. The number of prosecutorial sentencing appeals dropped by about three-quarters between 2006 and 2009.[67]

Yet, even without the circuit courts enforcing the guidelines much anymore, changes at the district level were hardly dramatic. Comparing the four years after *Gall* with the three years before, the proportion of guidelines sentences dropped another six percentage points, but still remained a clear majority at about 54 percent.[68] Moreover, most of the below-guidelines sentences continued to be prosecutor-sponsored; judges independently went below the guidelines in barely 17 percent of cases. Average sentence length dropped to 49 months, but this reduction was mostly driven by changes in the composition of the federal criminal docket and by reductions in the guidelines ranges, not by increased judicial generosity. In cases in which the judge reduced a sentence without prosecutor support, the average amount of the reduction increased only slightly from 20 months pre-*Gall* to 21 months afterward. This figure was dwarfed by the average 45-month reduction in cases in which the prosecutor made a substantial assistance motion.

In short, despite *Gall* and the retreat of appellate review, district judges continued to support the federal system of harsh, prosecutor-dominated sentencing—a striking testament to the power within the federal judiciary of institutional inertia, anchoring effects, and tough-on-crime politics. As Judge Gertner put it,

> By announcing that the Sentencing Guidelines were advisory, the Supreme Court in *Booker* surely opened the door to more judicial discretion in sentencing than had existed when the Guidelines were vigorously enforced. But "more" does not mean "much." Judges are exercising discretion around the margins of the Federal Sentencing Guidelines, what I like to call variations on the theme of guidelines. Some are not even trying: Go to numbers of courts around the country and you will find *Booker* is a mantra to be repeated, not a meaningful change in sentencing.[69]

Reform of Federal Drug Sentencing and the Obama Years

The dogged prosecution of the reformed drug dealer Michael Gall neatly symbolized the continued vigor of the federal War on Drugs during the George W. Bush era. Increasingly, though, the hyper-punitive federal sentences for drug crime seemed out of step with state-level trends. As we saw in Chapter 2, there were many signs in the early and mid-2000s of a turn toward more nuanced, treatment-oriented responses to drug offenses. California adopted Proposition 36 the very year Bush was first elected president, Michigan and New York scaled back or eliminated particularly notorious drug minimums over the next few years, many states adopted medical marijuana laws, and the number of drug treatment courts continued to skyrocket. Ironically, the federal DOJ administered the drug court grants that fueled the development of new rehabilitative programs around the country, even as the department simultaneously pressed for long prison terms as a matter of course in *federal* drug prosecutions. Increasingly commonplace in state systems, drug courts were still a stranger to the federal system.

By way of justification, prosecutors trotted out the old line that the feds only went after the worst of the worst. Drug court diversions might be suitable for the petty criminals who found themselves charged in state court, but not for the violent gangsters and drug king-pins singled out for federal prosecution. The reality, however, was far more complex than this idealized federal–state division of labor might suggest. For instance, in 2007, the year *Gall* was decided, more than half of the drug offenders sentenced in federal court were in the lowest criminal history category in the guidelines system, belying any sugges-tion that they were hardened career criminals.[70] Moreover, barely 17 percent of the offenders were found in possession of a weapon, while fewer than 6 percent were given an "aggravating role enhance-ment" for playing a managerial role in a criminal organization with at least five participants.[71] The fact was that the federal War on Drugs cast a very wide and seemingly indiscriminate net, as Michael Gall discovered to his chagrin. Arguably, in some cases, going hard after the little fish might have been justified as a way to force their co-operation in efforts to identify and take down the real sharks. Other cases, however, just seemed to demonstrate the irresistible lure of an easy "win" for federal law enforcers.

By 2007, federal drug sentencing and incarceration seemed increas-ingly unsupportable. Correcting these excesses would prove to be the top priority of federal reformers for the next decade. They would achieve some significant breakthroughs, but in a frustratingly slow and disjointed fashion.

2007: A First Step toward Crack Reform

An obvious first target was the 100:1 crack–powder ratio—a glaring injustice that had hardly any remaining defenders and that, due to its racially disparate effects, seemed in some important way to threaten the very legitimacy of the federal system. The Sentencing Commission tried to equalize crack and powder sentences in 1995, but had been rebuffed by Congress. The commission grew more timid for many years afterward, and, in the wake of the Feeney Amendment and *Booker*, seemed to become almost irrelevant as a player in federal sentencing policy. By 2007, however, the commission was finally ready to reassert itself and try once more to fix the crack problem. In April, the commission adopted an amendment to the guidelines that reduced crack sentences by two offense levels across the board.[72] Thus, for instance, the guidelines minimum for a first-time offender convicted of dealing 5 grams of crack would drop from 63 to 51 months, while the guidelines minimum for a 50-gram dealer would drop from 121 to 97 months.[73] This was not nearly so dramatic a change as the commission had proposed in 1995, but it was a notable first step toward reform in an area that had proven a political third rail in the past.

In stark contrast to 1995, the commission's crack amendment of April 2007 provoked little controversy, partly because of its modest scale and partly because the public conversation about crack and crack sentencing had changed considerably over the previous dozen years. The commission's next move, though, proved somewhat more provocative. Normally, changes in sentencing law are "prospective" only, that is, they do not do anything to help or hurt the offenders who have already been sentenced under the earlier version of the law. However, in December 2007, the commission invoked a little-known, seldom-used provision of the SRA that gave it the power to make guidelines amendments retroactive—a move that might result in sentence reductions for nearly 20,000 federal inmates.[74] In this sense, the potential reach of this decision was extraordinary, although, in truth, only a small percentage of the beneficiaries would be able to gain *immediate* release given the limited size of the potential sentence reductions. Moreover, no inmate would be *entitled* to a reduction;

district judges would have discretion to refuse a reduction or to order something less than the full reduction.

Despite these limitations, the Bush DOJ and a few House Republicans made a show of opposition, warning of dire public safety consequences and the heavy burden that would be imposed on prosecutors and court personnel if they had to deal with thousands of resentencing proceedings.[75] However, following their sweeping 2006 election victories, Democrats now controlled Congress, and, in the post-Clinton era, Democrats had come around to seeing excessive crack sentences as an important civil rights issue. The Republican anti-retroactivity bill went nowhere. (Notably, Hillary Clinton, on the presidential campaign trail, hewed to her husband's tough-on-crime approach and voiced criticism of the crack retroactivity amendment.[76])

The Sentencing Commission carefully tracked the results of retroactivity, which proved better than the DOJ doomsayers had predicted. In the end, district judges granted 16,511 applications by crack offenders for a reduced sentence, amounting to about 64 percent of the applications received.[77] Blacks accounted for more than 86 percent of the beneficiaries, indicating that crack reform was having the intended effect of (partially) rectifying a terrible racial injustice.[78] Beneficiaries received, on average, a 17 percent reduction in their prison terms.[79] Put differently, the typical offender was able to decrease his sentence from 12 years to 10 years. Moreover, the retroactivity beneficiaries did not reoffend at any higher rate than did similar offenders who had to serve out their full term before the crack reforms took effect.[80] These positive results from the 2007 guidelines amendments helped to validate subsequent reform efforts.

And further reform was clearly needed. Among other things, the guidelines changes did not affect the statutory minimums, which established a floor below which judges could not normally go. This was an important limitation. In 2007, for instance, more than 80 percent of sentenced federal crack offenders were subject to a statutory minimum, in most cases a minimum of 10 years or more.[81] As long as the statutory minimums remained in place, the predominantly black crack defendants would continue to get substantially longer sentences than the predominantly white powder defendants.

A New President and the Fair Sentencing Act

Barack Obama's election in 2008, combined with continued Democratic control of Congress, finally created the opening for statutory reform. To be sure, crime and punishment did not play a prominent role in a presidential campaign focused more on the catastrophic economic recession and ongoing wars in the Middle East.[82] Yet, Obama's statements on the topic did suggest a genuine desire to reorient the federal criminal justice system, especially when it came to drug crime and racial disparities. For instance, in a 2007 address at Howard University, candidate Obama argued that we should not "accept a country where too many African-American men end up in prison because we'd rather spend more to jail a 25-year-old than to educate a five-year-old."[83] Obama charged that "we have a system that locks away too many young, first-time, non-violent offenders for the better part of their lives—a decision that's made not by a judge in a courtroom, but by politicians in Washington. ... [W]e have certain sentences that are based less on the kind of crime you commit than on what you look like and where you come from."[84] Lest the implicit reference to 100:1 be missed, Obama also declared, "[L]et's not make the punishment for crack cocaine that much more severe than the punishment for powder cocaine when the real difference between the two is the skin color of the people using them. ... That will end when I am President."[85]

True to Obama's word, in April 2009, just three months into the new president's first term, Assistant Attorney General Lanny Breuer was dispatched to Capitol Hill to urge Congress to *equalize* the crack and powder penalties.[86] Consistent with candidate Obama's remarks, and in contrast to the rhetoric surrounding so much of the post-2000 reform at the state level, Breuer emphasized not the fiscal benefits of reducing crack sentences, but "fundamental fairness" and the need to enhance public trust in the criminal justice system.[87] Still, even with the president's support and Democratic control of Congress, the crack reforms stalled for about a year, overshadowed by other priorities, such as the president's economic stimulus package and health care reforms.

Moreover, the bill that finally emerged in 2010 plainly reflected some important behind-the-scenes compromises. Most notably, the "Fair Sentencing Act of 2010" failed to equalize crack and powder penalties, but merely lowered the disparity from 100:1 to 18:1.[88] Additionally, even this more modest change was made only on a prospective basis; the bill did not provide for retroactive application to help those offenders still serving lengthy prison terms that were now implicitly recognized as unfair. Finally, the bill directed the Sentencing Commission to amend the guidelines so as to *increase* crack penalties in cases involving violence or one of several other aggravating circumstances. To be sure, under *Booker, Kimbrough,* and *Gall,* district judges could effectively ignore these new guidelines provisions if they wanted, but, as we have seen, district judges have mostly continued to follow the guidelines in the absence of prosecutorial acquiescence to a lower sentence.

These compromise, tough-on-crime gestures in place, the crack bill sailed swiftly through Congress. Indeed, only a single member of Congress voiced clear opposition. However, the lone opponent was a notable one: Representative Lamar Smith of Texas, an influential Republican who would become chair of the House Judiciary Committee after the GOP's big win in midterm elections. His remarks on the House floor against the Fair Sentencing Act demonstrated that the tough-on-crime attitudes of the 1980s and 1990s had not died out, but remained a mainstream view within the Republican Party. Smith repeatedly associated crack dealing with violent crime, claimed that violence rates had fallen since the 1980s, "thanks in large part to the enactment of tough penalties for drug trafficking and other offenses," and accused the crack reformers of "coddling some of the most dangerous drug traffickers in America."[89] Smith plainly welcomed the opportunity Obama was handing Republicans to restore crime's pre-Clinton role as a wedge issue. The Democratic Party, he crowed, "teeters on the edge of becoming the face of deficits, drugs, and job destruction."[90] He even revived the Willie Horton premise, suggesting that those who voted for reform would be morally accountable for any crimes committed by the beneficiaries: "I hope, sincerely, that those who support this legislation are prepared to take responsibility if cocaine trafficking increases, if our neighborhoods and communities once again become riddled with violence, and the lives of Americans are unnecessarily destroyed."[91] Smith's remarks foreshadowed the partisan gridlock that would soon stymie further sentencing reform in Congress.

Beyond Crack: Further Efforts to Reduce Drug Imprisonment in the Obama Years

As President Obama signed the half-a-loaf Fair Sentencing Act into law in August 2010, did he realize this would be the last sentencing reform bill he would sign? Although candidate Obama had focused particular attention on crack sentences, his critique of drug sentencing had been broader. At Howard University in 2007, he had said, "I think it's time we also took a hard look at the wisdom of locking up some first-time, non-violent drug users for decades. ... We will review these sentences to see where we can be smarter on crime and reduce the blind and counterproductive warehousing of non-violent offenders."[92] With continued Democratic control of Congress and the heavy lifting of health care reform behind him, perhaps President Obama would have turned his attention after 2010 to more fundamental legislative changes in federal drug sentencing. However, continued Democratic control was not to be, and it soon became clear that Obama would hardly be able to advance *any* of his agenda in the new Congress.

No matter, drug sentencing reform proceeded along other lines, albeit not until after Obama won reelection in 2012, which effectively insulated him from any potential political fallout. Obama's attorney general, Eric Holder, took the lead.

Holder, the nation's first African American attorney general, contrasted sharply with John Ashcroft, his predecessor from President George W. Bush's first term. Where Ashcroft had come to the attorney general's office as a career politician with a long history of tough-on-crime posturing, Holder had never held elective office. His pre–attorney general career included work as a prosecutor, trial-court judge, high-level official in the Clinton DOJ, and corporate lawyer. A product of New York City who then served as a judge and prosecutor in Washington, D.C., Holder had a keen sensitivity to the difficult realities facing urban minority communities.[93] Although hardly a bomb-thrower, he would become the Obama administration's most prominent spokesperson on issues of race. Indeed, early in his tenure, he earned a rebuke from Obama himself for an address to DOJ employees in which he said that "though this nation has proudly thought of itself as an ethnic melting pot, in things racial, we have always been and we, I believe, continue to be in too many ways essentially a nation of cowards."[94]

Although quiet on sentencing issues during Obama's first term, Holder was finally ready to advance his reform agenda in 2013. He spelled out this agenda in a notable August address to the American Bar Association, a speech that echoed and expanded on Obama's 2007 address at Howard University. "Our system," Holder declared bluntly, "is in too many respects broken."[95] "It's clear," he continued, "that too many Americans go to prison for far too long, and for no truly good law enforcement reason."[96] He also noted racial disparities and the resulting disrespect for the criminal justice system in some communities. In light of these concerns, he announced three reform priorities for the DOJ: reduced use of mandatory minimums in drug cases, greater use by the Bureau of Prisons of compassionate release for medical reasons, and the development of drug treatment courts and other diversion programs for the federal system. He dubbed these reforms the "Smart on Crime" initiative, using a phrase from Obama's Howard speech.

At the same time, Holder issued a memorandum to federal prosecutors in order to implement the new approach to minimums—a memorandum that countermanded key components of the Ashcroft memoranda of a decade earlier. "We must ensure," he urged, "that our most severe mandatory minimum penalties are reserved for serious, high-level, or violent drug traffickers."[97] More specifically, Holder set forth various new criteria that prosecutors would have to consider case by case before pursuing mandatory minimums based on drug quantity or prior convictions, a distinct contrast from Ashcroft's "strongly encouraged" policy on minimums. Importantly, though, the policy did not apply to minimums in general, but only two types of minimums specific to drug cases. For instance, use of the draconian § 924(c) minimum for firearm possession remained unaffected. The memo thus adhered to a consistent Obama–Holder theme: reform would focus first and foremost on nonviolent, low-level drug offenders.

Seen in one light, the Holder memo seemed a striking reform initiative. Established DOJ policy and practice did not necessarily insist on the use of minimums in all cases in which they were available, but did reflect the view that defendants should have to earn relief. A prosecutor's restraint in the pursuit of minimums was offered as a quid pro quo for the defendant's guilty plea and cooperation. Now, however, Attorney General Holder was saying restraint was simply the right thing to do in some cases. To be sure, many frontline prosecutors had been doing this all along, but now official DOJ policy was expressly legitimizing that position.

Yet, seen in another light, the Holder memo may have carried greater symbolic than practical importance. Its limitation to certain kinds of offenders facing certain kinds of minimums precluded any dramatic impact on federal imprisonment rates. By one estimate, the Holder memo would have resulted in reduced sentences for only 530 defendants in 2012.[98] To put that number into perspective, federal courts sentenced more than 25,000 drug offenders that year, more than 15,000 of whom were subject to statutory minimums.[99]

In short, even after the Holder memo, there remained much reform work to be done if truly significant reductions in federal drug imprisonment were to be achieved. It was the Sentencing Commission that made the next move, doubtlessly emboldened both by its success with crack reform in 2007 and by the fresh breeze blowing in from the DOJ. In January 2014, the commission proposed broader changes in the drug guidelines, featuring a general two-level reduction for all drug types and quantities. This reform promised to have a greater impact than the Holder memo. The average drug offender would face about a year less in prison, leading to a 6,550-inmate reduction in the federal prison population in five years.[100] Holder quickly signaled his approval, and the commission formally adopted the reform in April.

This decision left open the key question of retroactivity—what of the tens of thousands of drug offenders still serving time in federal prisons on sentences imposed in the old system? The success of crack reform retroactivity paved the way for the same approach to the 2014 reform. The commission's July approval of retroactivity initiated a lengthy process of sentence reexamination in the federal courts. By March 2016, district judges had granted reductions to nearly 27,000 prisoners.[101] The average reduction was two years, which still left the average sentence for successful applicants at nearly 10 years.[102] Many of these applicants would still have years to serve even after winning their sentence-reduction motions.

As the "drugs minus two" story played out in the Sentencing Commission over the first half of 2014, the Obama administration launched a separate initiative to further reduce drug imprisonment. This initiative aimed to use the president's clemency power.

From the start, U.S. presidents have had the constitutional authority to show mercy to criminals, either in the form of a pardon, which would erase a conviction entirely, or a commutation, which would keep the conviction in place but reduce the sentence. Some presidents used the clemency power liberally, but, with the advent of the tough-on-crime era, prevailing political currents pushed in the opposite direction.[103] Presidents would only grant clemency very sparingly, and almost exclusively at the very end of their time in office.

President George W. Bush, no doubt inadvertently, spurred a revival of interest in commutation through his 2007 grant of clemency to a high-level national security adviser, I. Lewis "Scooter" Libby. Libby had been convicted in connection with a leak of classified information and sentenced to 30 months in prison and a hefty fine.[104] Bush then used his clemency power to eliminate the prison portion of the sentence.

Libby's case was highly unusual in many respects, but it served to remind critics of mass incarceration of the clemency power and prompted questions about whether that power could be used on a wider scale to correct more routine injustices. After Obama succeeded Bush, calls were soon made for the systematic use of commutations to draw down drug imprisonment. One group of particular concern was the crack offenders who were sentenced before adoption of the Fair Sentencing Act; since the act was not made retroactive, many of these offenders were serving more time than they would have if they had been convicted of the same conduct a little later.[105] Clemency seemed an appealingly flexible and efficient mechanism for addressing this unfairness.

In April 2014, the administration finally announced the criteria for a new commutation initiative. In effect, the goal was to give a break to all long-serving, low-level, nonviolent offenders who got longer sentences than they would get today. As we have seen, there were several ways in which the federal sentencing system had grown at least a little more lenient in the previous decade, beginning with *Booker*, proceeding through the Holder memo, and including the Fair Sentencing Act and various changes to the guidelines. Obama signaled his willingness to entertain clemency petitions from prisoners who might have benefited from *any* of these changes, provided they had no record of violence and had already served at least 10 years.

As with the Holder memo, the clemency initiative only seemed bold by comparison to what preceded it; the limiting criteria would result in a rather modest practical impact. In order to support the initiative, five organizations with an interest in reducing mass incarceration collaborated to establish a screening process for petitioners. The organizations—the American Bar Association, American Civil Liberties Union, National Association of Criminal Defense Lawyers, Families against Mandatory Minimums, and the federal public defenders—called their effort Clemency Project 2014 (CP2014), and enlisted the aid of nearly 4,000 volunteer lawyers.[106] More than 36,000 federal prisoners expressed an interest in assistance by "CP2014," but it turned out that few met the administration's criteria—even when assessed by the presumably sympathetic CP2014 reviewers. As of early November 2016, CP2014 had completed the screening of more than 34,000 applicants, but had filed only about 2,150 commutation petitions. Even if all of these were to be granted, the impact on the 200,000-inmate federal prison population would hardly be noticed.

Nor was there any guarantee that all of the CP2014-approved petitions would be granted by the president, or even fully reviewed by the time his term ended. As of early 2016, the administration's clemency process seemed in disarray. Petitions are initially submitted to the United States Pardon Attorney, an official in the DOJ. While Attorney General Holder had seemed enthusiastic about the clemency initiative, he left office in April 2015, and his successor, Loretta Lynch, a federal prosecutor from New York City, seemed much less supportive. By January 2016, Pardon Attorney Deborah Leff had had enough. She submitted a blistering resignation letter to Deputy Attorney General Sally Yates (Lynch's second in command), which became public two months later.[107] Leff declared:

> [G]iven that the Department has not fulfilled its commitment to provide the resources necessary for my office to make timely and thoughtful recommendations on clemency to the President, given your statement that the needed staff will not be forthcoming, and given that I have been instructed to set aside thousands of petitions for pardon and traditional commutation, I cannot fulfill my responsibilities as Pardon Attorney.

Under the leadership of Robert Zauzmer, Leff's successor, the pace of commutations finally picked up later in 2016. Indeed, with 72 grants on November 4, President Obama reached a total of 944 with a little over two months still left in his term. Advocates hoped for a further acceleration in grants after the election date of November 8, but chances seem remote that the clemency initiative would ever emerge as anything more than a modest adjunct to the other drug sentencing reforms of the Obama era.

Continued Reform Efforts in Congress

Obama's final year in office also witnessed a final push to achieve mandatory minimum reform in Congress, stalled since the passage of the Fair Sentencing Act six years earlier. Momentum for legislative reform had waxed and waned repeatedly throughout Obama's second term. Initially leading the way were Senators Dick Durbin of Illinois and Mike Lee of Utah. The odd-couple pairing of a liberal stalwart (Durbin) and a Tea Party Republican (Lee) drew immediate attention and raised hopes that reform might actually be accomplished, even in an era of divided government and toxic partisanship. Their "Smarter Sentencing Act," introduced in late July 2013, included three components: (1) an expansion of the "safety valve" for drug mandatory minimums, giving judges discretion to go below the minimum for a somewhat wider set of nonviolent offenders; (2) a halving of the drug minimums; and (3) an expansion of the Fair Sentencing Act to include full retroactivity.[108]

In their arguments for the bill, Durbin and Lee particularly emphasized fiscal considerations—the "strain on our prison infrastructure and federal budgets"—rather than the racial justice and system legitimacy themes that Attorney General Holder was pressing at the same time through his similarly named Smart on Crime initiative.[109] In essence, Durbin and Lee employed the same rhetoric being used in many states at the same time in support of bipartisan JRI reforms. Their bill attracted endorsements from an impressively wide range of organizations, including the National Association of Evangelicals, American Civil Liberties Union, NAACP, American Bar Association, the conservative Heritage Action, and the noted antitax agitator Grover Norquist. The coalition recalled the hastily assembled alliance that had come together to soften the Feeney Amendment a decade earlier. Conservative support for criminal justice reform clearly owed a lot to concern over the fiscal burden of mass incarceration, but also reflected libertarian values—particularly in light of the growing potential for criminal enforcement of business regulatory laws—and the apparent tension between inflexibly harsh prison sentences and Christian values like mercy, forgiveness, and reconciliation.

With Democrats still in control of the Senate and Attorney General Holder signaling administration support, the Senate Judiciary Committee approved the Smarter Sentencing Act in January 2014, but not without a telling set of amendments. The panel's senior Republican, Charles Grassley of Iowa, successfully moved to have several *new* mandatory minimums added to the bill. Thus amended, the Smarter Sentencing Act took on the same two-steps-forward-one-step-back character as the Fair Sentencing Act. It seemed that minimums could not be relaxed for one group of offenders without offsetting sentence enhancements for others. (In Chapter 2, of course, we saw precisely this pattern in many state-level efforts to reform drug minimums.)

Even with his amendments in place, Senator Grassley continued his dogged resistance to the bill as the fight moved out of committee. Joined by fellow Republicans Jeff Sessions of Alabama and John Cornyn of Texas, Grassley circulated a lengthy critique of the Smarter Sentencing Act in May.[110] Their arguments echoed those made by Representative Lamar Smith in opposition to the Fair

Sentencing Act, equating drug crime with violent crime. "The notion that drug traffickers are non-violent is simply incorrect," they asserted. "Violence and threats are the norm." Thus, they declared, reducing sentences for drug traffickers would "put more dangerous criminals back on the streets sooner." They also pointed to the increasingly visible heroin problem of the United States as another reason why legislators should be especially reluctant to reduce drug penalties.

Grassley and other reform opponents in Congress were joined by an unusual uprising of frontline prosecutors. Many were understandably stung by the implicit public criticism coming from their nominal boss, Attorney General Holder. When Holder declared the system "broken" and decried its racial disparities, this could hardly sit well with the many prosecutors who spent their careers in the system, routinely charging people of color with the best of intentions to help, not harm, disadvantaged minority communities. When the National Association of Assistant United States Attorneys (the career prosecutors) surveyed its members in the wake of Holder's August 2013 speech to the American Bar Association, more than 80 percent rejected his claim that the system was broken, and nearly the same number denied there was disproportionate punishment of people of color.[111] With 60 percent also voicing opposition to the Smarter Sentencing Act, the National Association of Assistant United States Attorneys (NAAUSA) decided to take an official position against the bill, a highly unusual effort by the organization to engage with a policy question. "We believe the merits of mandatory minimums are abundantly clear," they wrote. "They reach only the most serious of crimes. They target the most serious criminals. They provide us leverage to secure cooperation from defendants. They help to establish uniformity and consistency in sentencing. And foremost, they protect law-abiding citizens and help to hold crime in check."[112]

With such soft-on-crime charges in the air, Congress had no stomach to move ahead with reform in an election year. The Smarter Sentencing Act died quietly without ever receiving a vote by the full Senate.

Supporters promptly reintroduced the measure in 2015, but in a very different political environment. Most notably, Republicans took control of the Senate, which meant that the key Judiciary Committee was now chaired by none other than Charles Grassley, the diehard reform opponent. Still, the same strange bedfellows, left–right coalition that had attracted so much attention in 2013 and early 2014 reappeared, buttressed by the formidable Koch brothers, the power-house Republican donors.[113] Surprisingly (or maybe not), Grassley proved willing to negotiate with the reform proponents, so long as they started from scratch and not with the Smarter Sentencing Act as a template.[114]

The resulting bill, unveiled in October 2015 as the Sentencing Reform and Corrections Act (SRCA), was far more complex than its predecessor, including many provisions that had nothing to do with mandatory minimums.[115] Indeed, it was clear that the price of Grassley's support had been high. The SRCA did not include any reduction in the basic 5- and 10-year drug minimums. However, the bill did include an expansion of the safety valve and retroactivity for the Fair Sentencing Act. Other notable provisions included the following:

- Softening of the mandatory minimums for repeat drug offenses
- Softening of the § 924(c) minimums for possessing a firearm in connection with a drug or violent crime
- Elimination of life without parole sentences for juveniles
- Expansion of compassionate release for elderly or ill inmates
- Creation of earned time program for federal inmates

Importantly, key changes were made retroactive, creating a potential for an estimated 6,500 inmates to petition for resentencing.[116] However, in what had become a familiar move, the scaling back of some minimums was coupled with the creation of new minimums.

The SRCA swiftly passed through the Judiciary Committee, but not without an ominous brush with presidential campaign politics. Senator Ted Cruz of Texas, a candidate for the Republican nomination, attempted to delete retroactivity for the new sentencing provision, even though he had been a sponsor of the Smarter Sentencing Act, which would have made crack sentencing reforms retroactive. Cruz was plainly positioning himself as an unreconstructed tough-on-crime conservative, and in so doing signaled that campaign opponents who jumped on the "smart-on-crime" bandwagon risked Willie Horton–style attacks. Cruz warned his colleagues that they would be held accountable by their constituents when prisoners were released early and committed new crimes.[117] After Cruz's proposed amendment failed, he voted against the bill. Although Cruz had few close allies in the Senate, his growing strength in the presidential campaign through early 2016 made it unlikely that the SRCA would advance until the nomination picture was clearer.[118]

Judiciary Committee approval put the reform ball in the court of Senate majority leader Mitch McConnell, who would have to decide whether to schedule the matter for floor debate. With his own caucus closely divided on the SRCA, McConnell stalled, asking that the bill be revised to win over more Republicans. Grassley, Durbin, and other proponents obliged with a variety of changes in April 2016, including new mandatory minimums for offenses involving the potentially deadly heroin additive Fentanyl. Still, McConnell failed to act, as did his counterpart House Speaker Paul Ryan, who had a closely parallel sentencing reform bill on his plate. If Cruz's waning presidential prospects in the spring of 2016 created any renewed sense of hope, the picture became gloomier in late May, when presumptive nominee Donald Trump signaled that he would take a tough-on-crime stance in the general election, accusing presumptive Democratic nominee Hillary Clinton of wanting to let violent criminals out of prison.[119] At about the same time, Republican senator Tom Cotton of Arkansas, a particularly strident opponent of the SRCA, declared that sentencing reform was dead in the 114th Congress.[120]

Conclusion: President Obama's Legacy on Federal Sentencing

As of this writing, it is not yet entirely clear what the fate of the SRCA will be, but, even if it does achieve passage, President Obama's sentencing reform legacy will remain a disappointment to those who were stirred by his 2007 address at Howard University. Candidate Obama spoke of a "new dawn of justice in America" and promised to "brave the politics and make it right" when it came to crack cocaine sentencing. However, crack and powder sentences were never equalized, and even the more modest reform of 2010 was not made retroactive. Moreover, by Obama's last year in office, hopes that he would sign more meaningful legislative changes were pinned on a bill that had been repeatedly watered down and offered no reform at all to the key 5- and 10-year drug minimums, including those for crack. For his part, Attorney General Holder said that the failure to achieve further crack reform was the greatest disappointment of his six years under Obama.[121]

To be sure, a president has other ways to affect sentencing besides pushing for and signing reform legislation. By mid-2016, the Obama administration could point to some significant nonlegislative accomplishments that were helping to draw down the swollen federal prison population. Holder's 2013 memo to federal prosecutors called for greater restraint in the use of mandatory minimums. Then, in 2014, the administration supported the "drugs minus two" amendment to the sentencing guidelines, which resulted in reduced sentences for nearly 27,000 inmates. In 2014, the administration also launched an unprecedented clemency initiative in order to give a break to low-level, nonviolent offenders being held on decade-plus sentences. Collectively, such nonlegislative achievements were hardly trivial. But nor did they quite seem a "new dawn of justice."

The numbers are telling. In May 2016, the federal prison population stood just a little under 196,000. This represented a net drop of only 3 percent from 2008, the year Obama was elected. As we saw in Table 4.2, many states were doing far better in reducing their prison populations. Indeed, the federal system still had *tens of thousands* more prisoners than the Texas and California systems, both of which had been larger than the federal system when George W. Bush became president.

Figure 5.4 breaks the federal numbers out by the six most important offense types.[122] Obama and Holder clearly identified drug imprisonment as their greatest category of concern. Consistent with that emphasis, it is clear that the net reduction from 2008 to 2016 was driven overwhelmingly by a 10,000-inmate drop in drug imprisonment. Even with this change, however, drug imprisonment remained by far the largest contributor to the federal prison population in 2016. And federal prosecutors were continuing to send large

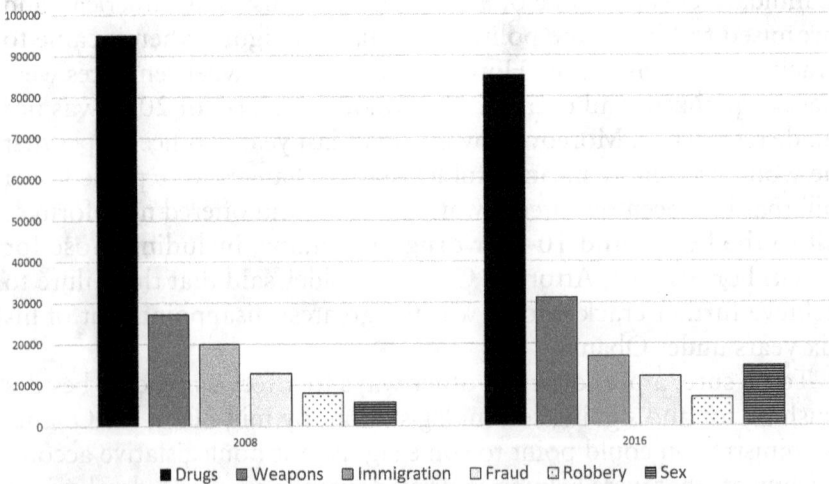

Figure 5.4 Federal Prisoners by Offense, 2008 and 2016

numbers of drug offenders to prison for long periods of time. In FY2015, more than 20,000 offenders were sentenced in federal court for drug trafficking, receiving an average (mean) sentence of 67 months—more than five and half years.[123]

In trying to explain why Obama did not have a more dramatic impact on federal imprisonment numbers and sentencing policy, at least four reasons are apparent. First, and most obviously, sentencing reform was simply not at the top of his agenda during his first two years in office, when his ability to influence Congress was at its zenith. Instead, he chose to spend his political capital on a highly controversial set of health care reforms. In the wake of that legislation, Obama's party lost control of the House and the ability to override Republican filibusters in the Senate. By the time his administration was ready to make a real push for sentencing reform in 2013, the president no longer had much say in the legislative process beyond his ability to veto legislation he did not like.

Second, despite the outspoken support of sentencing reform by a few high-profile conservative activists, rank-and-file Republicans remained skeptical of any softening of punishment. The sentencing reform story seemed to foreshadow the divide within the GOP that was so dramatically exposed by Donald Trump's insurgent presidential campaign in 2016—that sharp divide between District of Columbia–based, policy-oriented elites and the ordinary party members who cared less about research and data than tough talk. With a divided caucus, Republican legislative leaders could still probably have enacted sentencing reform if they had been willing to pass a bill with more Democratic than Republican support; however, party leaders were unwilling to proceed on that basis during a time of extraordinarily intense partisanship. The backbench revolt that ended John Boehner's tenure as Speaker of the House demonstrated the political risk to Republican leaders of collaborating with Democrats. Meanwhile, for their part, congressional Democrats hardly seemed anxious to press Republicans on sentencing reform. As long as crack sentencing was seen as a major civil rights issue, Democrats felt pressure to do something about it. Once the Fair Sentencing Act was passed, however, their interest seemed to flag. As Lamar Smith so pointedly reminded them in 2010, further reform risked a revival of the soft-on-crime charges that Republicans had deployed so effectively against Democrats in the past.

Third, Obama's own DOJ bureaucracy was resistant to change, as illustrated most clearly by the NAAUSA's active opposition to sentencing-reform legislation supported by the president. Federal prose-cutors proved no less subject to the power of inertia than had the many federal judges who proceeded with their business after *Booker* as if noth-ing had really changed. Ever since the implementation of mandatory minimums and mandatory guidelines in the 1980s, prosecutors had enjoyed an extraordinary degree of power in the federal system. A tough, rigid sentencing system gave prosecutors tremendous leverage to extract guilty pleas and other forms of cooperation from defendants. They would not let go of that leverage easily.

Fourth, and finally, Obama himself seemed unwilling to follow fully his own best instincts. Repeatedly, his administration embraced reforms that were narrowly limited to low-level, nonviolent offenders, especially drug offenders. This restrictive approach to policy making contrasted with Obama's remarkable statement in 2015 when he became the first president to visit a federal prison—a statement in which he seemed to be pushing the United States toward a genuine moral reckoning with mass incarceration. The people in prison, he observed, differed from the rest of us not because they made mistakes, but because they lacked the "support structures, the second chances, the resources that would allow them to survive those mistakes." "[T]here but for the grace of God," he said—that "is something we all have to think about." There is no reason, though, that such an empathetic response should be limited to one class of offenders.

Eight years earlier, when Obama gave his Howard University address, he focused many of his comments on a case that was then very much in the news—that of the so-called Jena Six. The case involved six black high school students from Louisiana who severely beat a white classmate.[124] When five were charged with attempted murder, the prosecutor's decision drew outraged responses from civil rights activists and African American leaders from across the United States, including Obama. Of course, the criticism was *not* that these were nonviolent offenders facing long prison terms, but that they were nonetheless being treated too harshly in light of all of the circum-stances, including their youth and the fact that white students at the same high school had apparently taken some racially provocative actions of their own. In 2007, then, Obama at least implicitly recog-nized that empathy could extend to violent offenders, too.

To be sure, given the unusual orientation of the federal system to drug crime, a presidential focus on reducing drug sentences might accomplish much more than a similar reform agenda on the state level. Still, it is important to remember there is no crisp, clear dividing line between "drug" offenders and "violent" offenders. What of the drug dealer who kept a pistol under his mattress at home—should he be categorized as "violent"? How about the dealer who once got arrested for domestic violence or a barroom fistfight? What about the dealer who has never engaged in violence herself, but who is part of a gang that has been known to use force? If violence exclusions are interpreted broadly enough, there might not be many drug offenders left to benefit from reforms, and those who are will likely not be serving long prison terms anyway. Recall Senator Grassley's view that drug dealing and violence are so inherently intertwined that there is no point even talking about reform for "nonviolent" traffickers. Given such beliefs, Obama's reinforcement of harsh attitudes toward "violent" offenders may have undermined his efforts to moderate the punishment of drug offenders.

And so the federal criminal justice system continues to lumber along as it has for years, plagued by its inherent contradictions. The system grew large and powerful in the late 20th century, as federal politicians sought to bring the system to bear in the war on street crime. But the desire to have federal law enforcement officers fight the war was never strong enough for them to be given the resources and legal authority they needed to truly supplant state and local officials as the key frontline troops. Such a change would be far too radical a departure from U.S. traditions of federalism. Nor were the feds permitted to combat violent crime through vigorous gun control, which might have provided the federal government with a uniquely valuable role to play given the national scope of the gun manufacturing and distribution business. No, the feds would be largely relegated to fighting on the drug front—at best an oblique way of getting at the underlying problem of predatory violence.

By the time George W. Bush took office, these arrangements seemed increasingly unsatisfactory. Violence was down sharply and no longer seemed so compelling a justification for maintaining a mostly redundant federal criminal justice system. Moreover, public attitudes toward drugs were changing. Grassley notwithstanding, the simple equation of drugs and violence was no longer so widely accepted as it had been a decade earlier. But, without the War on Drugs, what would the federal criminal justice system do? After 9/11, national security beckoned, but it seemed there were far fewer terrorists to go after than drug dealers. After the Enron meltdown and other corporate scandals, white-collar crime also seemed to merit increased attention. However, for ideological reasons, the probusiness Bush administration was unlikely to push hard on that front. And, in any event, white-collar prosecutions were far more complex and uncertain in their outcome than drug prosecutions. Voter fraud, child pornography, immigration, and human trafficking also inspired some prosecutorial enthusiasm, but nothing ever really emerged as a satisfactory substitute for the War on Drugs. The federal system had vast, accumulated investigative and prosecutorial expertise in this area; coming overwhelmingly from the poor, marginalized sectors of society, the defendants were politically easy targets; and the structure of federal sentencing law practically guaranteed guilty pleas in nearly all cases.

Thus, drug war de-escalation has come to the federal system much more slowly and shallowly than it has come to state systems. Without the budgetary or public safety accountability of state systems, there is no clear reason why the federal system cannot continue to hold tens of thousands of drug offenders in prison in perpetuity. The entire system cries out for a fundamental rethinking of its mission, but there is nothing at this point to suggest that the incoming president will be any more likely to engage in that process than the outgoing.

CHAPTER SIX

Sentencing in the Supreme Court

The U.S. Supreme Court was little more than a passive observer to the unprecedented explosion of the national prison population through the end of the 1990s. This stance was not for lack of legal authority to regulate excessive punishment. Most notably, the Eighth Amendment prohibits the imposition of "cruel and unusual punishments." Yet, after one brief foray in 1983, a closely divided Court backed away from using the Eighth Amendment as a tool to rein in long terms of imprisonment. Since 2000, the Court has revived the Eighth Amendment, but more to regulate capital punishment than to address mass incarceration. In 2010, the Court finally adopted for the first time a clear, constitutional restriction on LWOP (sentences of life in prison without the possibility of parole). However, the Court has thus far declined to build much on that narrow precedent, and the *length* of prison terms remains almost entirely beyond the scope of constitutional protections. (The *conditions* of prison terms are another matter, as we will see in the next chapter.)

In order to understand the Court's engagement with sentencing issues since 2000, it is necessary first to consider the Court's last great effort to give the Eighth Amendment real meaning—the Court's short-lived abolition of the death penalty in the 1970s.[1] This initiative provoked a great backlash against the Court that continues to cast a shadow over the justices' work on sentencing issues. In this chapter, we thus begin with a consideration of capital punishment. Although this book is more concerned with imprisonment than death sentences, the constitutional jurisprudence in these two areas is deeply intertwined. Not only did the Court's backing down on the death penalty in the 1970s foreshadow its subsequent diffidence on imprisonment, but also its more active, post-2000 approach to regulating the death penalty laid the groundwork for its subsequent LWOP cases.

After covering the death penalty, we will move to the Court's efforts to engage with imprisonment. These cases fall into two categories. The Court's Eighth Amendment decisions have very recently imposed new substantive and procedural restrictions on the use of LWOP with juvenile offenders. Meanwhile, another line of Sixth Amendment decisions has established new procedural protections for defendants facing mandatory minimums or enhanced maximum sentences. The Sixth Amendment cases have actually affected many more defendants than the Eighth Amendment cases, but in more subtle and uncertain ways. In the end, neither set of decisions has done much to alter the institutional dynamics that caused and continue to sustain mass incarceration.

For ease of reference, Table 6.1 summarizes the key aspects of the various Supreme Court decisions discussed in the chapter.

The Supreme Court and the Death Penalty

The Eighth Amendment before Furman

Before the 1970s, the Supreme Court invalidated very few punishments as "cruel and unusual" under the Eighth Amendment.[2] However, a 1958 opinion in the case of *Trop v. Dulles* by Chief Justice Earl Warren planted the seeds for a new, more expansive understanding of the Cruel and Unusual Punishments Clause. In support of a ruling that the government could not constitutionally strip a military deserter of his citizenship, Warren wrote, "The basic concept underlying the Eighth Amendment is nothing less than the dignity of man. While the State has the power to punish, the Amendment stands to assure that this power be exercised within the limits of civilized standards. ... [T]he words of the Amendment are not precise, and ... their scope is not static. The Amendment must draw its meaning from the evolving standards of decency that mark the progress of a maturing society."[3]

Warren's "evolving standards" ideal created a basis for the Court to strike down penalties that had long been accepted. This jurisprudential move, however, was bitterly opposed by the Court's "originalists," who felt that the Eighth Amendment only prohibited those punishments that the amendment's framers would have characterized as cruel and unusual in 1791. "Evolving standards" also gave rise to a new intellectual conundrum for the Court: how exactly were the justices to know when standards had evolved to a point requiring the invalidation of an established punishment? The most reliable indicator

Table 6.1 Timeline of Key Supreme Court Cases*

Year	Case	Holding
1949	*Williams v. New York*	Declined to extend the defendant's recognized trial rights (including the right to confront and cross-examine opposing witnesses) into the sentencing hearing
1958	*Trop v. Dulles*	Established the ideal that the Eighth Amendment "draws its meaning from the evolving standards of decency that mark the progress of a maturing society"
1962	*Robinson v. California*	Embraced ideal of proportionality as a requirement of the Eighth Amendment: the constitutionality of a punishment depends in part on its severity relative to the seriousness of the offense being punished
1972	*Furman v. Georgia*	Effectively invalidated most or all death penalty laws in the United States
1976	*Gregg v. Georgia*	Approved "guided discretion" death penalty statutes
1977	*Coker v. Georgia*	Banned death penalty for the rape of an adult woman
1982	*Enmund v. Florida*	Banned the death penalty for defendants who had no intent to kill and were just peripheral accomplices to a killing
1983	*Solem v. Helm*	Overturned an LWOP sentence for a defendant who had passed a bad $100 check, applying the proportionality analysis from *Robinson*
1986	*Ford v. Wainwright*	Prohibited execution of the insane
1986	*McMillan v. Pennsylvania*	Permitted mandatory minimum to be imposed based on facts not found beyond a reasonable doubt, effectively reaffirming *Williams*
1988	*Thompson v. Oklahoma*	Declined to adopt a bright-line constitutional rule against capital punishment for crimes committed by persons younger than 16
1991	*Harmelin v. Michigan*	Upheld Michigan's 650-Lifer law, effectively narrowing *Solem* and softening Eighth Amendment proportionality requirement for prison sentences

(Continued)

Table 6.1   (Continued)

Year	Case	Holding
1998	*Almendarez-Torres v. United States*	Held that sentence enhancement based on a prior conviction is not subject to the constitutional protections governing criminal trials, effectively reaffirming *McMillan* and *Williams*
2000	*Apprendi v. New Jersey*	Held that defendants have a right to jury trial on most facts that increase punishment, distinguishing and narrowing *Williams*, *McMillan*, and *Almendarez-Torres*
2000	*Williams v. Taylor*	Overturned death sentence on Sixth Amendment grounds, highlighting poor legal representation provided to many capital defendants
2002	*Atkins v. Virginia*	Banned death penalty for the intellectually disabled
2003	*Ewing v. California*	Upheld life sentence for stealing three golf clubs, affirming narrow interpretation of Eighth Amendment proportionality requirement from *Harmelin*
2004	*Roper v. Simmons*	Banned death penalty for crimes committed when the defendant was under the age of 18
2004	*Blakely v. Washington*	Held that *Apprendi* right to jury trial on facts that trigger sentence enhancements applies to presumptive sentencing guidelines
2005	*United States v. Booker*	Converted federal sentencing guidelines from presumptive to discretionary in light of *Apprendi* and *Blakely*
2008	*Kennedy v. Louisiana*	Banned death penalty for rape of a child
2010	*Graham v. Florida*	Held that juvenile offenders cannot be sentenced to LWOP for nonhomicide offenses
2012	*Miller v. Alabama*	Banned mandatory LWOP for all juveniles, even those convicted of homicide offenses
2013	*Alleyne v. United States*	Applied *Apprendi* rule to facts triggering mandatory minimums, effectively overruling *McMillan*

*I am grateful to Elisabeth Thompson for suggesting this timeline and preparing a first draft of it.

seemed to be the decisions of the 50 democratically elected state legislatures of the United States. Yet, if the Court waited to ban a punishment until after it had already been banned by all of the states, then the constitutional protection was effectively meaningless. On the other hand, if fewer than 50 states were required to trigger a constitutional ban, how many would be enough? And, if the states were divided, could other evidence of evolving standards be considered? If so, what would count and how would it be weighed?

Four years later, the Court added another dimension to its "evolving" Eighth Amendment jurisprudence in *Robinson v. California* (1962). In *Robinson*, the Court overturned a state law that criminalized the status of being addicted to narcotics (as opposed to the act of using or possessing drugs). This decision went beyond *Trop* because, in contrast to a loss of citizenship, there was nothing unusual or inherently controversial about the form of punishment triggered by the California statute: a short term of incarceration. The Court conceded that "imprisonment for ninety days is not, in the abstract, a punishment which is either cruel or unusual. But the question cannot be considered in the abstract. Even one day in prison would be a cruel and unusual punishment for the 'crime' of having a common cold."[4] Implicitly, the Court incorporated a proportionality ideal into the Eighth Amendment—the constitutionality of a punishment would depend not only on the intrinsic character of the punishment itself, but also on its severity relative to the seriousness of the underlying offense.

Furman *and Its Aftermath, 1972–2000*

The "evolving standards" seeds planted by Chief Justice Warren in 1958 did not fully blossom until 1972, when the Court overturned three death sentences on Eighth Amendment grounds in *Furman v. Georgia*. Although *Furman* lacked a majority opinion—that is, a majority of the justices could not agree on a single rationale for the holding—the decision was widely understood at the time to invalidate most or all of the existing death penalty laws in the United States. Even after *Trop* and *Robinson*, this seemed a stunningly strong repudiation of the originalist interpretation of the Eighth Amendment, for the Constitution itself plainly contemplated the use of capital punishment.[5]

Furman provoked a powerful political backlash. Indeed, perversely, the Court's decision may have ensured the death penalty's survival over the long run. Prior to *Furman*, the U.S. death penalty had been fading away without any apparent need for Supreme Court intervention. Public opinion polls showed declining support for capital punishment in the 1960s, with a low of 42 percent reached in 1966.[6] A handful of states abolished the death penalty in that time period, while others strictly limited the number of eligible crimes.[7] In the 1950s, the United States averaged 72 executions per year, but, by 1967, the number of executions dipped to just 2. In fact, those two would prove to be the last two for a decade.

Yet, in the first Gallup poll after *Furman,* support for capital punishment surged to 57 percent—the highest level in two decades.[8] For their part, politicians wasted little time attacking the Court's decision. President Richard Nixon declared, "The time has come for soft-headed judges and probation officers to show as much concern for the rights of innocent victims as they do for the rights of convicted criminals."[9] Alabama's governor was even more derisive, charging that a "majority of this nation's high court has lost contact with the real world."[10] Georgia's lieutenant governor called *Furman* a "license for anarchy, rape and murder."[11]

Less than six months after *Furman* was decided, Florida enacted a new death penalty law.[12] Other states followed in quick succession. Nor was the backlash confined to the conservative South; even the legislature in liberal Massachusetts passed a new death penalty bill, although it was later vetoed by the state's governor.[13] By 1974, polls were showing that about two-thirds of Americans supported capital punishment, and 29 states had enacted new death penalty laws, even though the constitutionality of the death penalty was still very much in doubt. The U.S. people seemed to respond to *Furman* like obstreperous children; told they could not have the death penalty, they only then decided that it was something they really wanted.

Furman makes for an interesting comparison with *Roe v. Wade* (1973), the Supreme Court case establishing a constitutional right to terminate pregnancy. Decided just a few months after *Furman, Roe* also famously provoked a furious public backlash. Yet, *Roe* proved far more durable than *Furman.* While the constitutional abortion right persists to this day, *Furman*'s death penalty moratorium did not even last to the end of the 1970s. Among other things, *Furman*'s quicker demise reflected the Court's greater ambivalence toward the decision from the start: where *Roe* had a healthy 7–2 majority, *Furman* was decided by a much more tenuous 5–4 majority.

Perhaps even more importantly, and also in contrast to *Roe,* the justices in the *Furman* majority could not agree on a single rationale for their holding. Each wrote his own opinion, emphasizing his own particular concerns with the death penalty.[14] Justice William Brennan invoked the idea of human dignity that Chief Justice Warren had said was at the core of the Eighth Amendment. Justice William Douglas focused on racial discrimination in the administration of the death penalty. Justice Thurgood Marshall attacked the concept of retribution. Finally, Justices Potter Stewart and Byron White both emphasized the arbitrariness and unpredictability of the death penalty, using the very infrequency of its application against it.

Perhaps *Furman* would have garnered more respect if had contained a short, simple, unified statement against the death penalty, in the spirit of the Court's 1954 ruling against school segregation in *Brown v. Board of Education*—a decision that was also fiercely opposed when it first came out, but that became almost universally revered within a generation. As it was, the jumbled set of *Furman* opinions ran to 66,233 words—the longest decision up to that time in the history of the Supreme Court.[15] There was little likelihood that many people would even read the Court's handiwork, let alone be persuaded by it.

Finally, in 1976, just four years after *Furman*, the Court backed down on capital punishment and gave its constitutional blessing to the new generation of "guided discretion" death penalty statutes. Like the pre-*Furman* laws, the new statutes gave juries the discretion to choose death, but now provided juries with standards to apply. Additionally, the laws incorporated new procedural safeguards, like closer appellate review of the appropriateness of death sentences. In truth, though, the new laws did little to tie the jury's hands. Although juries were required to find at least one aggravating factor as a prerequisite to choosing death, the statutes typically permitted the use of various open-ended, highly subjective factors, such as whether the crime was especially heinous, atrocious, or cruel. If the concern in *Furman* had been arbitrariness in capital punishment, or the potential for racial bias to infect the death penalty, then the new laws should have provided little reassurance of improvement.

What changed between *Furman* and *Gregg v. Georgia*, the lead decision in 1976 that approved the guided discretion laws? For one thing, the liberal hero William Douglas had retired and been replaced by John Paul Stevens, a more centrist justice. For another, the justices were keenly aware of the public backlash against *Furman*. In 1972, Potter Stewart had voted with the majority against capital punishment, but in 1976 conceded that he had "misjudged the passion among voters."[16] In conference with his colleagues on *Gregg*,

Stewart observed, "There was more to say for [Justice] Bill Brennan's views at the time of *Furman* than there is now. Death statutes then were dead letters. But what thirty-five state legislatures have done since 1972 is focused on why there should be the death penalty for specific, serious offenses. This establishes what evolving standards of decency are in 1976."[17] His new colleague, Stevens, similarly felt that "standards of decency" had not yet evolved to a point that required abolition of the death penalty, although he thought they would get there eventually.[18]

Along with Justice Lewis Powell, Stewart and Stevens now constituted a middle-ground coalition that effectively controlled the outcome of the Court's pivotal death penalty cases in 1976 and, through a series of joint opinions, established a jurisprudential framework for such cases that remains largely intact to this day. Powell, one of the *Furman* dissenters, shared the personal reservations of Stewart and Stevens about the death penalty, but also instinctively favored judicial restraint and the ideal of letting state democratic processes work themselves out without interference from the Supreme Court. At the same time, he disliked upsetting precedent and was disinclined simply to overrule *Furman*.[19] All three members of the "troika" thus favored an approach affirming the principle that the Eighth Amendment limited how states could administer the death penalty—contrary to the originalist position—but also giving the states considerable leeway in how they did so. The basic constitutional requirements emerging from the 1976 cases were twofold: (1) states had to provide juries with at least some minimal guidance about when death was an appropriate sentence, but (2) states could not entirely strip all discretion from juries—in other words, states could not make death a mandatory sentence upon conviction of certain crimes, but had to give juries the opportunity to weigh the aggravating and mitigating circumstances in each case on an individualized basis.

Eighth Amendment death penalty law evolved little for the next quarter-century. Most notably, the Court began to chip away—very gingerly—at the categories of offenders and offenses eligible for the death penalty. In 1977, in *Coker v. Georgia*, the Court banned the death penalty for rape of an adult woman. A lead opinion, joined by Justices Stewart and Stevens, invoked the proportionality principle of *Robinson v. California*, the narcotics addiction case, and noted that Georgia was the only state authorizing the death penalty for adult rape at that time.[20] Five years later, in *Enmund v. Florida* (1982), the Court prohibited capital punishment for peripheral accomplices who had no intent to kill. (Enmund, for instance, had been the get-away car driver for a robbery that went bad and ended in a killing.) Once again, as in *Coker*, the practical impact of the ruling was extraordinarily limited. Only eight states authorized the death penalty for defendants like Enmund, and even those states rarely imposed the penalty.[21] In Florida, for instance, Enmund himself was the only defendant on death row who neither had an intent to kill nor partici-pated directly in a killing. A few years later, in *Ford v. Wainwright* (1986), the Court held that the Eighth Amendment prohibits execu-tion of the insane, but found that no state actually authorized such executions.[22]

Perhaps no case better illustrates the Court's diffidence as to capital punishment in the 1980s and 1990s than *Thompson v. Oklahoma* (1988). Oklahoma sentenced Thompson to die for a crime he commit-ted when he was just 15 years old. On appeal to the Supreme Court, Thompson argued that his sentence violated the Eighth Amendment proportionality requirement, reasoning that young people have dimin-ished understanding and self-control, and hence lessened culpability for their crimes. Essentially, the case was an invitation to the Court to put an age limit on the death penalty—but the Court declined.

It would have been easy for the Court to agree that 15-year-olds should be spared from execution, in the same sense that it was easy for the Court to rule as it did in *Coker, Enmund,* and *Ford*—these cases imposed only very marginal restrictions on capital punishment with little practical impact and little likelihood of provoking a public backlash. Similarly, a ruling that 15-year-olds could not be executed would, in practical terms, have spared only a very few lives. Among the states that had an explicit minimum age for the death penalty, not one set that age at less than 16.[23] Moreover, while 19 death penalty states did not have an explicit minimum age, that seemed more likely a matter of oversight than of conscious choice to expose 15-year-olds to death. Indeed, in practice, it was exceedingly rare for death sentences to be imposed for crimes committed at such a young age. Over one five-year period in the 1980s, only 5 out of 1,393 death sentences nationally were imposed in such circumstances.[24]

Yet, Thompson could not convince five justices to adopt a bright-line constitutional rule against capital punishment for crimes commit-ted by 15-year-olds. Although he won a reversal of his own sentence, the deciding fifth vote was cast by Justice Sandra Day O'Connor, who specifically limited her decision to the facts of his case and left open the possibility that a state legislature could permissibly adopt a law authorizing the execution of future defendants in Thompson's shoes.[25] (O'Connor had joined the Court after Potter Stewart's retirement and perpetuated his role as a key swing vote in death penalty cases for many years.)

Reviewing the Eighth Amendment cases from 1976 (*Gregg*) to 2000, it is clear that the Court was intent on accommodating the growing support of the U.S. public for capital punishment, which peaked at an astonishing 80 percent in 1994.[26] While the Court was never willing to entirely jettison the foundational premise of *Furman*—that is, that the Eighth Amendment applied to the death penalty—the Court was very hesitant about adopting clear limiting principles. The few it did embrace were almost meaningless in practice, for they simply prohibited states from doing things that states rarely had any interest in doing. But the Court's approach was not necessarily unprincipled. Rather, it reflected the dominant influence of a line of justices including Potter Stewart, Lewis Powell, and Sandra Day O'Connor, who embraced certain values of judicial restraint: respect for precedent, avoidance of sweeping rulings, preference for moral questions to be worked out through the democratic process, and preservation of state autonomy in the federal system of government. Moreover, the accommodation of public attitudes had become a central part of modern Eighth Amendment law through Chief Justice Warren's "evolving standards of decency" formulation. To be sure, Warren announced that principle at a time when it seemed that U.S. attitudes were evolving inexorably in the direction of greater decency. By 1976, as Justice Stevens observed, it was clear that this evolution had ceased. Still, if one remained true to Warren's formulation, the justices of the late 20th century had no business getting out in front of U.S. public opinion.

Thus, despite the personal reservations of several of the justices who voted to restore the U.S. death penalty in *Gregg*, the Court enabled a swelling tide of death sentences and executions through the 1980s and 1990s. During the peak years of the 1990s, more than 300 death sentences were being imposed annually, while the number of executions started to approach 100 per year.[27]

Did the growing use of capital punishment have any bearing on the mass incarceration phenomenon that is this book's primary focus? At first blush, the answer might seem an obvious *no*. After all, the swelling death row population of the United States accounted for only a tiny portion of the overall imprisonment boom. Even in the peak year of 1996, new death row commitments amounted to less than 0.06 percent of prison admissions. Still, the growing frequency of capital sentences may have contributed in at least three more subtle ways to the development of mass incarceration.

First, the availability of capital punishment in most states altered plea-bargaining dynamics in homicide cases, giving prosecutors much greater leverage and putting much more pressure on defendants to plead guilty. Even defendants with viable defenses would be reluctant to throw the dice when a loss at trial would put their lives in jeopardy. It is probably safe to assume that many homicide defendants in prison today on life or other very long terms would have been able to obtain a better plea deal resulting in a shorter term—or perhaps even an acquittal at trial—had the threat of execution not existed.

Second, as death penalty abolitionists increasingly gave up on the Supreme Court, they turned their attention to state legislatures, often advocating successfully for the adoption of LWOP sentencing alternatives so that juries in capital cases would feel more comfortable declining death. LWOP sentences came to far outnumber death sentences and did contribute in a more direct and measurable way to mass incarceration.

Third, and finally, increased use of capital punishment may have helped to normalize sentences that would have been regarded as extraordinarily harsh in the decade prior to *Gregg*. While death sentences represented only a tiny fraction of the total sentences imposed in the United States, they accounted for a vastly disproportionate number of the sentences that made the headlines. Regular reporting of death sentences may have contributed to an environment in which even multiyear prison terms could seem like a slap on the wrist and a "loss" for the victim of a violent crime.

In sum, although mass incarceration surely would have happened even if *Gregg* had come out differently, *Gregg* and the subsequent surge in capital punishment likely contributed something to the ultimate scale of mass incarceration.

An Eighth Amendment Revival in the New Millennium

Beginning in 2002, the Supreme Court began to regulate capital punishment more aggressively. The key decisions were *Atkins v. Virginia* (2002), which prohibited execution of the intellectually disabled (or, to use the Court's terminology, the mentally retarded); *Roper v. Simmons* (2004), which prohibited the death penalty for crimes committed when the defendant was under the age of 18; and *Kennedy v. Louisiana* (2008), which prohibited the death penalty for the rape of a child. Arguably, these were the most practically significant death penalty restrictions adopted by the Court under the Eighth Amendment in the entire post-*Gregg* era. Moreover, underscoring the extent to which this trilogy of decisions marked a break from the quarter-century following *Gregg*, the first two expressly overturned earlier decisions by the Court—an unusual retreat for the justices from their normal tendency to follow precedent.

In a sense, the Court's movement on capital punishment was predictable. We have seen how public backlash against *Furman* pushed the justices into a more permissive position. By the time of *Atkins* in 2002, however, much evidence pointed to a softening of public support for the death penalty. In opinion polls, support peaked at 80 percent in 1994, and then fell slowly but steadily to 60 percent by 2013.[28] Moreover, as indicated in Figure 6.1, the number of new death sentences and executions fell even more dramatically.[29] Death sentences peaked in 1996, and then fell by more than three-quarters over the next 18 years. Executions peaked in 1999, and then fell by nearly two-thirds over the next 15 years. Some states began to abandon the death penalty entirely. New York led the way in 2004, followed by New Jersey, New Mexico, Illinois, and Connecticut.[30] Other states retaining the death penalty adopted new restrictions on its use. Indeed, the Court made much of these latter trends in *Atkins* and *Roper*, noting that 16 states had recently banned execution of the intellectually disabled and 5 states had recently banned execution for juvenile offenses.[31]

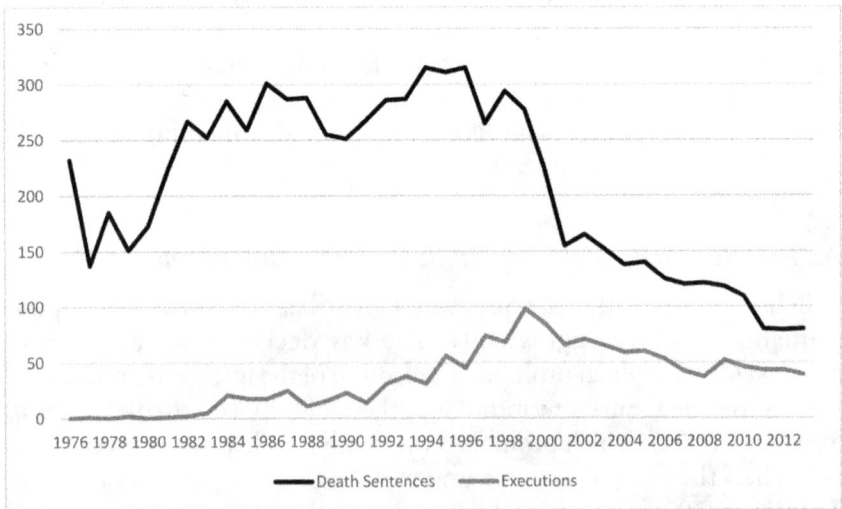

Figure 6.1   Death Sentences and Executions, 1976–2014

Despite this evidence that national standards were once again evolving in the direction of decency, it would be an exaggeration to say that the Court was simply constitutionalizing a new conventional wisdom. In truth, the tea leaves of public opinion were hard to read. Justice Antonin Scalia, an originalist fiercely critical of the new death penalty jurisprudence, was hardly unjustified in his ridicule of the Court's claims that it was following an emerging national consensus: in his *Atkins* dissent, he pointed out that a majority of death penalty states still permitted execution of the intellectually disabled, and cited a study indicating that fully 10 percent of death row inmates fit into this category, even though they were all free to present their limitations as mitigating evidence at sentencing.[32] Public opinion data on the death penalty for juveniles was similarly ambiguous. Scalia's *Roper* dissent noted that most death penalty states permitted execution for juvenile crimes, and such executions were actually being carried out in practice; they accounted for 2.4 percent of executions in the post-*Gregg* era.[33] The numbers were more favorable to the Court's position in *Kennedy*, with only six states authorizing death for child rape—but that number may have been unreliable because of arguments that *Coker* had already banned capital punishment for *any* type of rape back in 1977.[34] Given the prevalence of that broad interpretation of *Coker,* states might have thought it futile to adopt the death penalty for child rape. Indeed, the fact that five states had recently adopted such laws despite uncertainty about their constitutionality might have pointed to an emerging shift in public opinion *away* from the Court's position.

The Court's new death-penalty activism did not happen because the public demanded it. Rather, it is more accurate to say that flagging public enthusiasm for the death penalty finally gave the Court some political room to maneuver that it not had since *Furman,* and a majority of the justices were happy to take advantage of their greater freedom. While the Court is not an elected institution and does not invariably bow to public pressure—the preservation of *Roe v. Wade* and *Brown v. Board of Education* through periods of intense backlash makes that clear—the Court does not often take positions that fly in the face of strongly held majority beliefs, which can imperil the Court's legitimacy if done too frequently. The justices pick their battles, and they seemed, by and large, to have little stomach for a capital punishment fight in the 1980s and 1990s. However, shifts in public opinion after the mid-1990s meant that the political costs of taking on capital punishment were less, especially if the Court proceeded incrementally. Challenging capital punishment in its entirety risked reenergizing public support for death, as *Furman* had done. Instead, the Court took advantage of its enhanced room to maneuver by challenging a limited set of the most troublesome uses of the death penalty. The new rules were meaningful restrictions on capital punishment, but nonetheless left the vast majority of death sentences in place.

Justice Anthony Kennedy stands out as the key figure in the new death penalty jurisprudence. He "flipped" on both the intellectual disability and the juvenile death penalty issues, voting against defendants when the issues were first presented in the 1980s, but then voting the other way in *Atkins* and *Roper*. Indeed, Kennedy provided both the decisive fifth vote in favor of the juvenile death penalty in 1989 and the decisive fifth vote against in 2004. He also provided the key fifth vote against death for child rape in 2008. It was really Kennedy, more than any other justice, who sensed and took advantage of the changed public mood in the new millennium.

Kennedy had filled Lewis Powell's seat on the Court in 1988, and he seemed a fitting successor. Like Powell, Kennedy was a right-leaning moderate who valued judicial restraint, attempting to strike a balance between respecting the Court's precedents and providing greater autonomy for the states. (Although Kennedy often voted with the arch-conservative Scalia, his jurisprudential style contrasted sharply from that of his fellow Reagan appointee, who displayed little reluctance when it came to overturning precedents with which he disagreed.) *Gregg* and the rest of the Supreme Court's highly permissive death penalty cases over the next quarter-century bore Powell's imprint as much as anyone's. Kennedy seemed perfectly content with adhering to Powell's example for his first 14 years in the Court.

What changed? For better or worse, many justices grow more self-confident and bolder about asserting their personal views as they age, and this tendency has seemed especially pronounced as to the death penalty. Most famously, Harry Blackmun, who dissented in *Furman* and then voted to reinstate the death penalty in *Gregg*, declared in a 1994 opinion, "From this day forward, I no longer shall tinker with the machinery of death. ... It is virtually self-evident to me now that no combination of procedural rules or substantive regulations ever can save the death penalty from its inherent constitutional deficiencies."[35] John Paul Stevens, part of the *Gregg* "troika," also became increasingly critical of the death penalty in later years. After his retirement at the end of a long career on the Supreme Court, Stevens identified his affirmance of the Texas death penalty law in

1976 as the single vote he most regretted.[36] Most notable for present purposes, though, was Lewis Powell's conversion. Asked after his retirement what he most regretted, Powell stated that he would have liked to abolish the death penalty altogether and wished he had voted that way even in *Furman*.[37]

The regular review of death penalty appeals gives the justices an intimate familiarity with the unpleasant realities of the U.S. system of capital punishment, which can hardly breed respect for it. Indeed, in 2000, just two years before *Atkins*, the Court overturned a death sentence on Sixth Amendment right-to-counsel grounds in a case that highlighted the poor legal representation provided to so many defendants on death row. With his client's life on the line, Terry Williams's lawyer offered only a cursory, hastily prepared mitigation case at Williams's sentencing hearing, failing to discover, let alone present to the jury, a mountain of available evidence about Williams's horrific, abuse-filled upbringing and cognitive impairments.[38] In a decision that may have foreshadowed his impending shift on the Eighth Amendment, Kennedy voted with the majority to overturn Williams's sentence.

One would have to be hard-hearted indeed not to be troubled by the parade of unfortunates like Terry Williams who trooped before the Court as capital defendants. And, in the end, Justice Kennedy proved no more hard-hearted than Blackmun, Stevens, and Powell. In a much-noted speech delivered in 2003, Kennedy declared that "the prisoner is a person ... he or she is part of the family of humankind. ... A decent and free society, founded in respect for the individual, ought not to run a system with a sign at the entrance for inmates saying, 'Abandon Hope, All Ye Who Enter Here.' "[39] Changing public attitudes toward the death penalty made it easier for Kennedy to bring this sense of compassion to bear in *Atkins*, *Roper*, and *Kennedy*.

At a superficial level, the three decisions employed the same two-part Eighth Amendment proportionality test that had been developed in *Coker* and other earlier cases. First, the Court performed the "objective" analysis of determining whether there was a national consensus against the challenged punishment (e.g., execution of the intellectually disabled). Second, the Court brought to bear its own "independent judgment" as to the proportionality of the punishment.

As Justice Scalia bitterly observed, however, the Court seemed to be applying the objective part of the test much more loosely than it had before. In effect, the Court was elevating its own independent judgment. And that judgment, in turn, rested on a simple proposition: the death penalty should be reserved for the worst of the worst. Although this proposition had its roots in *Gregg*, the post-2000 cases sharpened its articulation and brought greater rigor to its enforcement. As Justice Kennedy put it in his opinion for the Court in *Roper*, "Capital punishment must be limited to those offenders who commit a narrow category of the most serious crimes and whose extreme culpability makes them the most deserving of execution."[40] It seemed that if a defendant could be placed in a category that clearly differentiated his culpability (blameworthiness) from those in the worst category—the killers who freely, deliberately chose to take a human life—then the defendant should be protected from execution. The categorically diminished culpability of the intellectually disabled, of juveniles, and of child rapists (relative to murderers) meant that they could not be put to death. We will see the Court using precisely this type of categorical analysis in its more recent decisions on LWOP.

By 2008, it was clear that the Court—and especially Justice Kennedy, the swing vote in many closely divided cases—had committed itself to a more searching oversight of the U.S. death penalty, whether pursuant to the Eighth Amendment, the Sixth Amendment right to counsel, or one of several other procedural rights guaranteed by the Constitution. Although this has certainly been a notable development, its importance should not be overstated. The Supreme Court has been nibbling around the edges of the death penalty, but has not come close to abolition. The Court has doubtlessly contributed to the declining rate of death sentences and executions depicted in Figure 6.1, but those trends had already emerged before the Court took its activist turn, and would likely have continued with or without the Court's support. States have been abandoning the death penalty not because the Court pushed them to do so, but because a startling tide of DNA-based exonerations raised fears about executing the innocent, because it turned out to be frightfully expensive to maintain a death row and to fight all of the litigation battles that follow a death sentence, and because the increasingly common sentence of LWOP seemed to provide a satisfactory alternative to execution.

It was on LWOP, in fact, that Justice Kennedy next trained his sights.

The Eighth Amendment and Noncapital Sentences

At the start of 2010, the Eighth Amendment jurisprudence on prison sentences looked a lot like the Eighth Amendment jurisprudence on death sentences had looked at the start of 2002, before *Atkins*. In both areas, there was an old case that had embraced the concept of Eighth Amendment limitations, but subsequent decisions by the Court had robbed the precedent of much practical significance.

In the noncapital area, that old precedent was *Solem v. Helm* (1983). Jerry Helm, a South Dakotan with an alcohol problem, accumulated seven nonviolent felony convictions in the 1960s and 1970s. In 1979, as he faced sentencing for the seventh felony—passing a bad $100 check—he was subject to a recidivism statute that made LWOP a possibility. The judge gave him the maximum, reasoning that Helm was "beyond rehabilitation."[41] On appeal all the way to the U.S. Supreme Court, Helm argued that this sentence was unconstitutionally cruel and unusual. In an opinion written by Justice Powell, the Court agreed. Invoking *Robinson* and *Coker*, the Court reiterated that the Eighth Amendment includes a prohibition on disproportionate punishments. As the Court was starting to do in its death penalty cases, the *Solem* majority performed its proportionality analysis by reference both to the "objective evidence" of disproportionality (e.g., whether the defendant could have gotten LWOP for his offense in any other state) and to its own assessment of the defendant's culpability. Finding that "Helm has received the penultimate sentence for relatively minor criminal conduct" and that he would have gotten a lower sentence in at least 48 other states, the Court concluded that the sentence violated the constitutional proportionality rule.[42]

Although *Solem* made clear that the Eighth Amendment regulated the length of prison terms and indicated that the same general considerations should govern the proportionality analysis in both capital and noncapital contexts, *Solem* differed from *Coker* and the other capital cases in that it laid down no bright-line categorical rules, like *Coker*'s ban on the death penalty for adult rape. For instance, the *Solem* Court might have simply declared LWOP off-limits for a nonviolent offense, but it chose not to do so. Instead, the Court offered a case-specific analysis that left many unanswered questions about how rigorously the Court would apply the proportionality rule in future cases. This was, of course, in keeping with Justice Powell's distaste for sweeping pronouncements, especially ones that would significantly impair the autonomy of state officials.

Decided early in the imprisonment boom, *Solem* provided the Court with a jurisprudential tool that it could have used to engage meaningfully with the emerging phenomenon of mass incarceration. However, based on the Court's permissiveness with the death penalty in that era, the betting money was against the Court doing much to challenge long prison sentences, either.

Eight years after *Solem*, the Court confirmed its passive acquiescence to mass incarceration in *Harmelin v. Michigan* (1991), in which
the Court upheld the infamous 650-Lifer law we encountered in
Chapter 2. The statute imposed a mandatory LWOP sentence for the
possession of 650 grams or more of cocaine. Although it was easy to
analogize Ronald Harmelin's life sentence for a nonviolent offense to
Jerry Helm's, the Court nonetheless refused to extend *Solem* beyond
its specific circumstances. By this time, Justice Kennedy had replaced
Powell. Perhaps even more importantly, the centrist David Souter
had replaced the arch-liberal William Brennan, who had been part of
Solem's narrow 5–4 majority. Kennedy and Souter did not want to
throw out *Solem* entirely, as the Court's right wing demanded, but
instead preferred to clarify the earlier decision's proportionality test
so as to ensure that it would only very rarely, if ever, require the invalidation of a prison sentence. They were joined by Justice O'Connor,
who had dissented in *Solem*, but now—consistent with her philosophy
of judicial restraint—declined the opportunity to expressly overturn
the precedent. In effect, O'Connor was playing the same role as had
Powell in *Gregg*, when Powell had passed up an opportunity to formally overturn *Furman*. *Solem* thus survived *Harmelin* in the same
way that *Furman* survived *Gregg*—officially still good law, but so
constricted in its reach as to be not much more than dead letter in
practice.

Kennedy wrote for the centrist troika in *Harmelin*, as Powell had
done 15 years earlier for the *Gregg* troika. While Kennedy's opinion
was not formally a majority opinion—the right-wingers refused to
join—it had all the practical significance of a majority opinion, for it
was clear that the views of Kennedy, Souter, and O'Connor now controlled the Court's Eighth Amendment jurisprudence; lower courts
would follow the troika's reasoning because that would assure their
decisions would not be reversed. Emphasizing the need for the
Supreme Court to defer to state legislative judgments, Kennedy
declared, "The Eighth Amendment does not require strict proportionality between crime and sentence. Rather, it forbids only extreme sentences that are *grossly disproportionate* to the crime."[43] Applying that
standard, as we saw in Chapter 2, Kennedy distinguished drug crime
from Jerry Helm's low-level property offense. Harmelin's "suggestion
that his crime was nonviolent and victimless," Kennedy wrote, "is
false to the point of absurdity."[44] Indeed, given the relationship
between drugs and violence, Kennedy went so far as to analogize drug
dealing to an unintentional killing that occurs during the course of a

robbery.[45] In effect, Kennedy seemed to say that any sentence short of death would be constitutionally acceptable for drug distribution offenses. Indeed, in Kennedy's view, the proportionality of Harmelin's sentence was so clear that it was unnecessary even to consider the sort of objective evidence of disproportionality that had been used in *Solem*.[46]

For those who still hoped that the Court would use the Eighth Amendment to rein in the supersized sentences that became commonplace in the late 20th century, one sliver of hope remained: perhaps *Harmelin* was just a function of the War on Drugs, appearing precisely as public anxiety about drugs was reaching its peak. That hope was dashed 12 years later in *Ewing v. California* (2003), when the Court upheld California's notorious three-strikes law. A hapless thief, Gary Ewing received a life sentence for a low-level property offense that could not be meaningfully distinguished from Jerry Helm's. In 2000, Ewing walked out of the pro shop at a Los Angeles golf course "with three golf clubs, priced at $399 apiece, concealed in his pants leg. A shop employee, whose suspicions were aroused when he observed Ewing limp out of the pro shop, telephoned the police," who arrested Ewing in the parking lot.[47] For this offense, coupled with prior convictions for burglary and robbery, Ewing received a mandatory term of 25 years to life. The Court had no more difficulty affirming this sentence than it had Ronald Harmelin's.

Kennedy and O'Connor again occupied the decisive middle ground, with O'Connor writing the controlling opinion this time. (Souter, consistent with his general leftward drift over the years, now favored the defendant, but the significance of his flip was negated by the arrival of Clarence Thomas, Scalia's partner on the Court's far right, who had replaced the *Harmelin* dissenter Thurgood Marshall; Ewing thus lost by the same 5–4 margin as had Harmelin.) O'Connor reiterated the extreme permissiveness of the *Harmelin* proportionality test. Ewing's (paroleable) life term passed the test because it reflected "a rational legislative judgment, entitled to deference, that offenders who have committed serious or violent felonies and who continue to commit felonies must be incapacitated."[48] As in *Harmelin*, the question was not even close enough to warrant looking at the objective evidence.

Kennedy joined O'Connor's opinion without comment, but it is hard not to suspect that he agonized over this decision. Just one year earlier, he had embraced a more robust view of the Eighth Amendment in *Atkins*. And in only five months, he would deliver his celebrated address to the American Bar Association, in which he urged greater appreciation of the humanity of criminal offenders and, in particular, castigated the use of long mandatory minimums.[49] Perhaps Kennedy was unwilling to make another bold Eighth Amendment move so soon after *Atkins*. Then, too, there was the relatively large number of prisoners who likely would have benefited from a ruling in favor of Ewing: more than 4,000 defendants received life sentences for nonviolent offenses under the three-strikes law.[50] This was many more people than were affected by any of the Court's post-2000 capital punishment decisions. Indeed, the entire U.S. death row population was only about 3,500 at the time that *Ewing* was decided.[51]

Whatever his thinking, Kennedy waited another seven years before extending his new Eighth Amendment approach from capital to noncapital sentencing. In 2010, the case of Terrance Jamar Graham provided him with the platform.

Graham was no altar boy. He and three accomplices first attempted the robbery of a Jacksonville restaurant, during the course of which they beat the restaurant manager with a metal bar.[52] Then, while Graham was out on probation for that crime, he and two accomplices committed a home invasion robbery, holding their victims at gunpoint for half an hour while they ransacked the home. These seemed far more violent offenses than those for which Jerry Helm, Ronald Harmelin, and Gary Ewing received their life terms. Graham got LWOP.

But, if he was no altar boy, he was still . . . a boy—just 16 at the time of the first robbery and 17 at the time of the second. The Court had already ruled in *Roper* that the Eighth Amendment precluded capital punishment for juvenile crimes, that is, crimes committed before the defendant's 18th birthday. How about LWOP?

Not surprisingly, Kennedy was the swing vote and wrote the Court's opinion. He ruled that LWOP may not be used as the punishment for juvenile crimes that fall short of homicide. Although Graham had committed serious violent crimes, he did not take, or attempt to take, anyone's life, which meant that he must be spared the law's penultimate sentence.

Kennedy employed the same two-step analysis that he had been using in his death penalty decisions. As in those cases, his conclusion that the "objective evidence" pointed to a national consensus against the challenged sentence seemed less than compelling. Fully 37 states permitted juvenile LWOP for nonhomicide crimes.[53] Kennedy was forced to rely instead on the infrequency of such sentences in practice. It seemed that Graham was 1 of only about 123 prisoners nationally serving LWOP sentences for nonhomicide offenses committed before they turned 18.[54]

Yet, earlier cases had repeatedly emphasized that law, not practice, was the most reliable of the objective indicators of evolving standards of decency. As Justice Thomas observed in dissent, "That a punishment is rarely imposed demonstrates nothing more than a general consensus that it should be just that—rarely imposed. It is not proof that the punishment is one the Nation abhors."[55] *Graham*, in fact, marked the first time the Court struck down on Eighth Amendment grounds a sentence that was legally permissible in a majority of states. In short, even more than *Atkins*, *Roper*, and *Kennedy*, *Graham* demonstrated that the Court's Eighth Amendment jurisprudence was not actually making a serious effort to follow national consensus, but was instead following the Court's own proportionality judgments—at least insofar as the objective indicators suggested the practical impact would be modest and the risks of backlash accordingly low.

The key to *Graham*, then, was Kennedy's proportionality analysis. In a sense there was almost a mechanical quality to it, putting together the categorical reasoning of *Roper* and *Kennedy*. If the worst punishment (death) should be reserved for the worst offenders, then the second-worst punishment (LWOP) should be reserved for the second-worst class of offenders. *Roper* said that juveniles are categorically at least one step removed from being among the worst. *Kennedy* said, effectively, that offenders who do not kill are also categorically at least one step removed from being among the worst. By extension, juveniles who do not kill must be at least two steps removed from the worst class of offenders, and so cannot be subjected to a sentence (LWOP) that is only one step removed from the worst sentence (death).

But to see *Graham* only in these mechanistic terms is to miss a certain animating spirit in the decision that resonates deeply with the humanitarian sentiments Justice Kennedy displayed in his American Bar Association address. His objections to LWOP are worth quoting at length, for they point to the sort of ethical critique of mass incarceration that has been in short supply through nearly all of the post-2000 reforms considered in this book. Kennedy wrote:

> By denying the defendant the right to reenter the community, the State makes an irrevocable judgment about that person's value and place in society. ...

Life in prison without the possibility of parole gives no chance for fulfillment outside prison walls, no chance for reconciliation with society, no hope. . . .

Terrance Graham's sentence guarantees he will die in prison without any meaningful opportunity to obtain release, no matter what he might do to demonstrate that the bad acts he committed as a teenager are not representative of his true character, even if he spends the next half century attempting to atone for his crimes and learn from his mistakes. The State has denied him any chance to later demonstrate that he is fit to rejoin society based solely on a nonhomicide crime that he committed while he was a child in the eyes of the law. This the Eighth Amendment does not permit.[56]

Two years later, the Court extended *Graham* in *Miller v. Alabama* (2012), barring mandatory LWOP for all juveniles, even those convicted of homicide offenses. As far back as *Gregg* (1975), the Court had prohibited mandatory death sentences; the sentencer always had to be given discretion to weigh aggravating and mitigating circumstances on an individualized basis. Now, the Court extended the same principle to juvenile LWOP, recognizing the unique severity of the sentence as indicated in *Graham*. Notably, though, the decision cast doubt on a much larger number of sentences than the Court's other recent Eighth Amendment decisions, with more than 2,000 prisoners then serving mandatory LWOP sentences for crimes committed before they turned 18.[57] In a sense, then, *Miller* marked the Court's boldest move in the post-2000 reinvigoration of the Eighth Amendment.

Considered collectively, the Court's decisions from *Atkins* through *Miller* seem to mark a revolution of sorts, with the Court—read, Justice Kennedy—finally bringing the Eighth Amendment to bear against some of the penal excesses of the 1980s and 1990s. Yet, the revolution has thus far been a remarkably slow and incremental one. For one thing, the Court has been addressing only very thin slivers of the prison population. Even *Miller*, arguably the boldest decision in the group, directly affected little more than one-tenth of 1 percent of U.S. prisoners. Moreover, several of the decisions practically invited evasion and minimization by state authorities. *Atkins* protected the "mentally retarded" from execution, but left it to the states to establish the legal test for who counted as mentally retarded. Predictably, some states did so in ways that raised a very high bar for defendants to prove their disability.[58] *Graham* and *Miller* imposed limits on the

use of LWOP, but said nothing about how parole must be administered, opening the way for states to use highly restrictive approaches
to the release of life-sentenced juvenile offenders. *Miller* also left open
the possibility that juvenile killers could still be sentenced to LWOP as
long as judges were given some discretion about the use of the
punishment.

Then, too, the Court has been painfully slow to build on its decisions by taking the logical next steps. Consider the LWOP cases.
Today, six years after *Graham*, many natural extensions of that decision's categorical proportionality analysis have yet to be made, including prohibiting nonhomicide LWOP for the intellectually disabled,
LWOP for nonviolent offenses, mandatory LWOP for nonjuvenile
offenders, and very long sentences for juveniles and the intellectually
disabled that are the functional equivalent of LWOP (e.g., a nonpar-
oleable 100-year prison term). Indeed, *Harmelin* and *Ewing* officially
remain good law—that is, binding precedent for the lower courts to
follow—even though they plainly embody a different approach to
the Eighth Amendment than *Graham* and *Miller*.

It is hard not to see the Court's reticence as conditioned by the backlash against *Furman* and the other lightning-rod decisions of the 1960s
and 1970s (*Roe v. Wade, Miranda v. Arizona*, and others). Whether as
a matter of jurisprudential principle, judicial temperament, or practical
politics, the Court has sacrificed analytical coherence in its Eighth
Amendment cases in favor of a cautious incrementalism that sporadi-
cally nudges states away from only a few of their most obvious punitive
excesses. This seems an improvement over the limitless permissiveness
that prevailed before 2000, but hardly a dramatic one. In 1958, Chief
Justice Warren wrote hopefully about the Eighth Amendment as a guarantee that the essential human dignity of offenders would by respected
even as they were being punished, pursuant to evolving standards of
decency. Nearly six decades later, the Eighth Amendment protects dignity only in certain narrowly focused ways, as the Court tries hard not
to outrun standards of decency that remain stubbornly unevolved.

The Constitutionalization of Sentencing Procedure

At the same time that the Court was embarking on its modest
Eighth Amendment revival, it was also modifying Sixth Amendment
law in some notable ways. The Sixth Amendment guarantees a laun-
dry list of procedural rights to criminal defendants. Although the
new millennium's Sixth Amendment revival touched on a number of

rights, the most important for present purposes was the right to a jury trial. Before 2000, the established understanding was that defendants had a constitutional right to a jury trial to determine guilt or innocence, but, once guilt was established, the Sixth Amendment imposed no real limitation on the ability of a judge to determine punishment at a separate sentencing hearing. However, in a series of cases beginning in 2000, the Supreme Court extended jury trial rights to various aspects of sentencing. These procedural decisions had an arcane, technical quality that was difficult for nonlawyers to appreciate, but they were rather more consequential than the relatively clear and accessible Eighth Amendment holdings. Indeed, this may have been no coincidence; perhaps some of the justices were emboldened precisely *because* the risk of public backlash against the Sixth Amendment decisions was so slight.

In order to understand the significance of the recent cases on sentencing procedure, one must know something of a very old precedent, *Williams v. New York*, decided in 1949. A jury convicted Williams of first-degree murder, after which he faced a judge for sentencing. In deciding to impose the death penalty, the judge considered various damaging items of information contained in a probation officer's presentence report, such as Williams's alleged involvement in 30 burglaries for which he had never been convicted.[59] On appeal to the U.S. Supreme Court, Williams argued that the judge's reliance for sentencing purposes on the probation officer's hearsay-riddled report violated his constitutional right to confront and cross-examine his accusers in court. However, the Supreme Court rejected Williams's effort to extend recognized trial rights to the sentencing proceeding. In so doing, the Court relied on the seemingly benevolent character of the informal, individualized sentencing hearings, which had replaced the older system of mandatory penalties. The Court wrote:

> Modern changes in the treatment of offenders make it more necessary now than a century ago for observance of the distinctions in the evidential procedure in the trial and sentencing processes. For indeterminate sentences and probation have resulted in an increase in the discretionary powers exercised in fixing punishments. In general, these modern changes have not resulted in making the lot of offenders harder. On the contrary, a strong motivating force for the changes has been the belief that, by careful study of the lives and personalities of convicted offenders, many could be less severely punished and restored sooner to

complete freedom and useful citizenship. This belief, to a large extent, has been justified.

... We must recognize that most of the information now relied upon by judges to guide them in the intelligent imposition of sentences would be unavailable if information were restricted to that given in open court by witnesses subject to cross-examination.[60]

The *Williams* decision was thus premised on the belief that new information presented to the sentencing judge posttrial would generally be mitigating information beneficial to the defendant (even though this is not what happened to Williams himself). It would indeed be perverse to insist on a rigid observance of defendants' rights when doing so would actually be harmful to most defendants.

The Court's optimism in 1949 about the increasingly humane character of U.S. sentencing was in the same spirit as Chief Justice Warren's comments a few years later about evolving standards of decency. In hindsight, though, we know that U.S. sentencing would take a decisive turn toward greater harshness beginning in the 1970s. New statutes established a multitude of aggravating facts that would increase the defendant's maximum potential sentence, minimum sentence, or both. In these new systems, judges were routinely finding facts that enhanced punishment. The premise of the *Williams* Court that informal procedures at sentencing generally benefited defendants seemed increasingly obsolete.

In 1986, the Court had its first opportunity to update *Williams* in *McMillan v. Pennsylvania*, which dealt with one of the new generation of tough-on-crime sentencing laws. In 1982, Pennsylvania adopted its Mandatory Minimum Sentencing Act, which required a five-year prison term if a sentencing judge found by a preponderance of the evidence that a defendant had visibly possessed a firearm during the commission of a serious felony. On appeal to the Supreme Court, McMillan argued that the law was unconstitutional because it did not require the judge to find visible possession beyond a reasonable doubt, the rigorous standard of proof normally used in criminal trials. Preponderance of the evidence is a lower standard of proof that is satisfied when it is simply more likely than not that a fact exists. In effect, McMillan, like Williams 37 years earlier, was arguing that the special constitutional rules governing criminal trials should also apply to sentencing hearings. Once again, the Court said *no*. In the spirit of its Eighth Amendment decisions of the 1980s and 1990s, the Court emphasized the need to defer to state legislative judgments.[61]

A high point in the Court's permissive line of cases on sentencing procedure was reached in 1998 in *Almendarez-Torres v. United States*. Normally, when a deported alien returns to the United States illegally, he is subject to a maximum prison term of two years. However, the maximum balloons to 20 years if the sentencing judge finds by a preponderance of the evidence that the initial deportation was subsequent to a conviction for an aggravated felony. Almendarez-Torres pled guilty to illegal reentry, with its two-year maximum, but then received a seven-year prison term based on the sentencing judge's fact-finding.[62] Despite the bait-and-switch character of this process, the Supreme Court approved it, citing *McMillan*.

Just two years later, though, the Court would embrace a new approach in *Apprendi v. New Jersey* (2000), ruling that defendants have a right to a jury trial on the facts that increase their punishment.[63] The defendant, Charles Apprendi, fired a gun into the home of an African American family that had just moved into his previously all-white neighborhood. Apprendi was convicted of three weapons offenses. Then, at his sentencing, the prosecutor asked that his maximum sentence be increased by an additional 10 years based on New Jersey's hate crime law. Finding that Apprendi had acted in a racially discriminatory fashion, the judge agreed to the enhancement. However, the Supreme Court overturned this decision because the racial motivation question had not been decided by a jury beyond a reasonable doubt.

The principle would be elaborated and applied more expansively in a series of decisions that have continued more or less to the time of this writing. For present purposes, just two of the post-*Apprendi* decisions merit specific mention: *Blakely v. Washington* (2004) and *Alleyne v. United States* (2013). Among other gaps, *Apprendi* had left open the question of whether the Court's new Sixth Amendment principle applied to presumptive sentencing guidelines, like the federal guidelines discussed in Chapter 5. In most guidelines systems, the sentencing judge must make findings of fact that determine a narrow sentencing range, but all of this process occurs within a statutory maximum sentence. No matter, said the Court in *Blakely*. If a finding of fact would boost the defendant's guidelines sentence, then the defendant has a right to a jury trial on that fact. The very next year, as we have seen, the Court made clear that this ruling applied to the federal guidelines themselves in *United States v. Booker* (2005). *Apprendi* had also left open the question of whether the new Sixth Amendment rule applied to the facts triggering mandatory minimums, like visible possession of a firearm in *McMillan*.

Finally, in *Alleyne*, the Court said *yes*. Henceforth, defendants would have a right to a jury trial on most such minimums.

This line of cases was profoundly, if subtly, consequential. Unlike the Eighth Amendment cases, the Sixth Amendment cases did not categorically preclude states from imposing any particular sentence they wished on any class of offenders. Instead, the cases merely set up a new procedural hoop that states would have to jump through in order to reach the enhanced sentences they desired. Jury trials are more time-consuming and burdensome for prosecutors and judges than informal, *Williams*-style sentencing hearings. That, of course, is a principal reason why prosecutors offer plea deals in most cases—precisely so that they can skip the jury trial and move straight to sentencing. The expansion of Sixth Amendment rights meant that prosecutors would now forego some sentence enhancements they would have otherwise sought, which would, among other effects, tend to reduce prosecutors' plea-bargaining leverage. It was impossible to say precisely how many defendants would benefit and to what extent, but there would surely be a great many who would do at least a little better in the post-*Apprendi* world.

What caused the *Apprendi* revolution? As we have seen, the Court's Eighth Amendment shift in the same time period can be easily attributed to the evolving approach of a single justice, Kennedy, who found the punitive excesses of the tough-on-crime era morally objectionable and who saw just enough of a softening of public attitudes after 2000 to warrant greater constitutional regulation of the harshest penalties. However, the key "flipper" between *Almendarez-Torres* and *Apprendi* was, of all people, Clarence Thomas. Both decisions were 5–4, and it was only Thomas who was in the majority both times. By reputation, Thomas is the hardest of hard-liners and certainly no friend of criminal defendants. Indeed, there is no reason to think that his vote in *Apprendi* and subsequent Sixth Amendment cases reflected underlying concerns about mass incarceration or the feelings of compassion that Kennedy displayed in his Eighth Amendment opinions. Rather, Thomas's position must be understood as an expression of his originalism. In a concurring opinion in *Apprendi*, Thomas canvassed the historical evidence at length and concluded that his new view—one admittedly at odds with his vote in *Almendarez-Torres*—reflected the original meaning of the Sixth Amendment.[64] Indeed, Thomas's fellow originalist, Justice Scalia, had dissented in *Almendarez-Torres* and now joined Thomas in the *Apprendi* majority.

Other surprises abounded in the alignment of the justices. Scalia and Thomas were joined in the majority by John Paul Stevens, Ruth Bader Ginsburg, and David Souter. All were pragmatists who lacked Scalia's and Thomas's devotion to original meaning, but they presumably welcomed the opportunity that originalism afforded to strike a blow at some of the tough-on-crime sentencing laws of the past generation. All three dissented in *Ewing*, indicating their desire to pare back California's three-strikes law; their votes in the *Apprendi* line of cases were predictable and consistent with their Eighth Amendment views. On the other hand, Stephen Breyer—the other left-leaning pragmatist who dissented in *Ewing*—also dissented in *Apprendi*. This probably had something to do with Breyer's biography. As we saw in Chapter 5, Breyer was the principal author of the federal sentencing guidelines, and he recognized the threat *Apprendi* posed to his carefully crafted sentencing system. Although Breyer disliked mandatory minimums, he felt—not unjustifiably—that guidelines represented a fundamentally different and more rational approach to sentencing.[65] He was unwilling to undermine the former at the cost of also undermining the latter. Justice Kennedy, another *Apprendi* dissenter, seems to have had a similar view.[66] Indeed, in his American Bar Association speech that was so critical of mandatory minimums, Kennedy would assert, "In my view, the [federal] guidelines were, and are, necessary."[67]

While the Supreme Court's Sixth Amendment decisions undoubtedly affected a much greater number of cases than the Eighth Amendment decisions, their practical impact should not be overstated. No reduction in the national prison population followed in *Apprendi*'s wake. If its pace of growth at least slowed in the first decade of the new millennium, that undoubtedly had more to do with declining crime rates and a de-escalation of the War on Drugs than it did with any rulings of the Supreme Court. In general, the Sixth Amendment reforms operated quietly on the margins. Indeed, we have already considered in Chapter 5 the long-term impact of *Apprendi* on the federal system. Through *Booker*, *Apprendi* eliminated the mandatory character of the myriad sentence enhancements built into the federal guidelines, but judges retained discretion to reach the same results, and they tended not to stray all that far from what they had been doing pre-*Booker*.

Indeed, as with the Eighth Amendment decisions, the Court blunted the practical impact of the Sixth Amendment decisions by failing to carry them to what struck many as their logical conclusion. First, the Court exempted from the *Apprendi* rule any sentence enhancements based on prior criminal convictions. Oddly, *Almendarez-Torres*—which dealt with just such an enhancement—remains good law, even though it has been repudiated by Justice Thomas, who provided the decisive fifth vote in support of the decision. This is a major gap in *Apprendi*, for recidivism statutes, like the California three-strikes law, are perhaps the most commonly used sentence enhancers. Overruling *Almendarez-Torres* would not, of course, categorically preclude the application of recidivism laws, but the added procedural hoop of a jury trial right could significantly reduce their usage.

Second, and much more importantly, the Court has not extended *Apprendi* to discretionary sentencing systems. As we have seen in the post-*Booker* federal system, for instance, judges remain free to find aggravating facts as long as they also have the power to decide how much weight to give those facts. *Apprendi* itself illustrates the perverse character of this gap. After Charles Apprendi fired that gun into the home of the African American family, he pled guilty to three charges carrying a cumulative maximum sentence of 20 years. At sentencing, his judge found a racist motive, which increased the sentencing exposure to 30 years. However, very few defendants receive the statutory maximum, and Apprendi was no exception—he got 12 years. The Supreme Court threw out the sentence enhancement, of course, but that left the 20-year maximum in place. Upon return to the trial court for resentencing, the judge was free to find a racist motive and to use that motive as a basis for imposing precisely the same 12-year sentence that had been imposed the first time around. Again, there is nothing in the Sixth Amendment cases that bars sentence enhancement based on a judge's finding of facts *within an otherwise-constitutional statutory maximum*. As a result, judges could normally reach the same sentencing results post-*Apprendi* that they had reached in the absence of the new Sixth Amendment "safeguards."

Seen in this light, the Sixth Amendment cases look like many of the other post-2000 sentencing reforms we have considered, with their pervasive emphasis on judicial discretion. Likewise, *Apprendi*, *Blakely*, and *Alleyne* undercut the mandatory punishment trends that were so prevalent in the late 20th century and reinvigorated the central role of the judge in sentencing. However, they do nothing to alter the political pressures on judges. Because those pressures are not so fundamentally different from the pressures facing legislators, we should not expect big changes in outcomes when power over punishment is shifted from legislators to the judiciary.

Conclusion

Constitutional decision making by the Supreme Court is often seen as fundamentally different from, and inherently more problematic than, the policy making that comes from the elected branches of government. The decisions of nine unelected justices seem prone to go against the wishes of a majority of the public, which casts a shadow over the Court's democratic legitimacy. In truth, however, the Court has always been attuned to public sentiment and rarely strays far from the political mainstream. This helps to explain the surprising reality that the Court invariably scores better than Congress and the president in public opinion polls. Perhaps—ironically—freed from the distortions of campaign finance, gerrymandered districts, and organized party politics, the Court may be even better at reading and following public preferences than the elected branches.

In the late 20th century, as the public mood turned increasingly fearful and punitive, some hoped that the Court would serve as a counterweight to the tough-on-crime responses of the politicians. Instead, true to its form as a politically responsive institution in its own right, the Court turned out to be a mostly passive observer to the imprisonment boom. The Court quickly retreated from its initial Eighth Amendment foray in *Solem v. Helm*, and clung doggedly to the outdated, permissive approach to sentencing procedure of *Williams v. New York*.

Since 2000, the same softening of public punitiveness that made possible legislative reforms also enabled greater activism by the Supreme Court, especially in the Eighth Amendment area, where the "evolving standards of decency" test specifically invited the Court to take into account legislative reforms and shifts in public opinion. In some respects, the Court's sentencing decisions in the new millennium have differed fundamentally from the legislative reforms considered in earlier chapters. While the legislative reforms have tended to focus particularly on drug and other nonviolent offenders, the changes to Sixth and Eighth Amendment law have not been so limited. Indeed, by targeting the most severe possible sentences, the Eighth Amendment cases have chiefly benefited truly violent criminals like Terrance Jamar Graham. *Graham* was also notable for its ethically grounded, dignity-based critique of LWOP, which contrasted with the cold utilitarianism of so many of the post-2000 legislative reform efforts. Yet, in its own way, the Court seemed no less diffident than the legislatures. The Sixth and Eighth Amendment "revolutions" unfolded by half-steps over many years, and still remain far short of their potential as moderators of penal excess. Moreover, like the legislatures, the Court has done less to take harsh outcomes off the table than to provide judges and corrections officials with more discretion about those outcomes. As we have seen time and again, such shifts in decision-making power do not guarantee correspondingly big changes in results.

CHAPTER SEVEN

California: Is the Glass Half Empty or Half Full?

California presents the most extraordinary decarceration story of the treading water era. From a high of 175,512 in 2006, the Golden State's prison population fell to 134,534 in 2012—a precipitous drop of nearly one-quarter in just six years.[1] Indeed, even that figure does not do full justice to how steep the imprisonment drop was. The state achieved almost 90 percent of its overall decline in just three years. It seems safe to conclude that no state has ever in any comparable time frame dropped anywhere close to the 37,000 prisoners California shed between 2009 and 2012.

Moreover, despite the dire predictions of many critics, California crime rates did not rise during the decarceration period.[2] To the contrary, California's rate of violent crime dropped every year from 2006 to 2011. Then, after a small uptick in 2012, the rate dropped even further in 2013 and 2014, the most recent year for which data are available. Overall, California's violent crime rate fell by more than one-quarter between 2006 and 2014—almost exactly tracking the drop in the state's imprisonment rate over the same time period.

Nationally, decarceration advocates regularly tout the California experience as proof positive that prison populations can be reduced swiftly without any adverse impact on public safety. Yet, upon closer inspection, California's story may not seem quite so uplifting as it first appears. If the state accomplished unprecedented reductions in imprisonment, that only happened because it had earlier *increased* its prison population at a pace that was extraordinary even by the standards of the national imprisonment boom. The swelling tide of offenders flowing into state institutions produced a corrections crisis. Overcrowding reached epic—indeed, lethal—proportions. Even so, California did not begin to move seriously on decarceration until the state was required to do so by court order—an order that the state fought all the way to the U.S. Supreme Court.

Although the post-2006 imprisonment reductions have diminished the sense of crisis, California's prison system remains overcrowded, with a population about one-third higher than the system was designed to hold.[3] And while California's imprisonment rate has dipped below the overall national average, it remains considerably higher than that of the Northeastern states, which it rivaled just a generation ago.[4]

The prospects for further decarceration in California remain uncertain. Progress has stalled since 2012. Moreover, the legislature has not demonstrated any ability to accomplish meaningful sentencing reform without the threat of an imminent court order hanging over its head. The ballot initiative seems a somewhat more promising route to policy change, but the processes of direct democracy are notoriously expensive and unpredictable. If California has demonstrated the *practical* viability of a fast-decarceration strategy, the *political* viability of the California model for other states is much less clear, absent the pressure of major constitutional litigation.

The California Corrections Crisis

Through the middle decades of the 20th century, California ran one of the nation's most progressive, rehabilitation-focused criminal justice systems.[5] However, the state proved an unusually fertile ground for the new tough-on-crime politics that first appeared in the 1960s and became increasingly prominent throughout the United States over the ensuing decades. Sociologist Vanessa Barker links the triumph of punitive policies in California to the emergence of a new conservative populism in the state, centered on the burgeoning suburbs of Orange County.[6] This conservatism linked distrust of government and academic elites, anger over elevated rates of crime and social disorder, and an ethos of self-reliance and individual responsibility. These various strands of modern conservatism—which seemed to radiate out from southern California to the rest of the nation—ran counter to the idea that rehabilitative treatment was a feasible and desirable response by government to most crime.

Ronald Reagan's landslide gubernatorial election victory in 1966 demonstrated the political force of the new conservatism. As governor, Reagan then began the long process of reorienting California's criminal justice system in a more punitive direction. Most notably—and foreshadowing the state's broader embrace of mandatory minimums in later years—Reagan pushed successfully for the adoption of a minimum sentence of 15 years to life in cases of rape, robbery, and burglary in which the offender inflicted great bodily harm.[7]

Building on Reagan's law-and-order legacy, California went on to adopt more comprehensive sentencing reform in 1976 through its Determinate Sentencing Law (DSL). The DSL ended the possibility of discretionary parole release for most offenses, reduced judicial sentencing discretion, increased sentence lengths for certain offenses and offenders, and explicitly prioritized punishment over rehabilitation.[8]

Although the DSL reflected the punitive attitudes of its day, the law could at least boast a certain philosophical coherence. The new system sought in a systematic way to distinguish more serious crimes from less serious, and to ensure proportionately longer sentences for the former. However, the system's coherence was then undermined through two decades of knee-jerk tough-on-crime law making. This was the era of the "drive by" sentencing law.[9] The state adopted more than 1,000 crime bills between 1984 and 1991. "Virtually none of them reduced sentences and many of them imposed sentence enhancements."[10] Typically, new enhancements responded narrowly to the latest outrage dominating the newspaper headlines—the "crime *du jour.*" Over time, such ad hoc law making wrecked the DSL's system of proportionate punishment.

Complementing the legislature's fractured approach to sentencing policy, California's robust ballot initiative mechanism also resulted in a scattershot series of tough-on-crime enactments. The initiative process allows interest groups to bypass the legislature and submit policy proposals directly to the voters for enactment. The emergence of conservative populism coincided with an explosion of initiative-based law making in California, which profoundly affected public policy in many areas, including criminal justice. Through the ballot initiative process, California voters embraced, among other things, a reinstatement of the death penalty after it had been declared unconstitutional by the state supreme court, an enhancement of murder penalties, and limitations on plea bargaining and bail.[11]

Of course, this trend toward tough-on-crime ballot initiatives reached its climax in the notorious three-strikes law of 1994. Although about half the states adopted three-strikes laws in the 1990s, California's version was the nation's harshest, reaching a much wider proportion of repeat offenders.[12] More specifically, the California law stood out in three respects: (1) it contained a *two*-strikes provision that doubled penalties for qualifying offenses; (2) it counted as strikes convictions for simple burglary, a relatively common offense often considered nonviolent; and (3) *any* felony could count as the third strike. It was the latter provision that led, famously, to life sentences for a number of mundane retail thefts, including thefts of pizza, videocassettes, and (in the case of Gary Ewing, which we considered in Chapter 6) three golf clubs.

All of these *explicit* policy changes encouraged and facilitated corresponding *implicit* policy changes. The steady drumbeat of severe new laws made clear that criminal justice officials might jeopardize their careers through perceived lenience. Indeed, California featured what remains the nation's best-known example of a judge losing office as a result of such perceptions: Chief Justice Rose Bird was unseated in 1986 after a campaign that focused largely on her opposition to capital punishment.[13] Other officials, no doubt, got the message. For instance, despite the retention of a theoretical possibility of discretionary parole release for certain categories of offenders, such release was very rare in practice. One study found that only about 1 percent of parole-eligible, life-sentenced inmates were actually granted parole each year.[14] County-level prosecutors and judges were also said to exercise their discretion in tougher ways.[15] In so doing, they benefited from the extraordinary proliferation of new sentence enhancements.

The various explicit and implicit policy changes led to a rapid expansion of the state prison population, even by the general standards of the national imprisonment boom. Between 1977 and 1998, the 500 percent growth in California's imprisonment rate led all large states.[16] Law professor Jonathan Simon has shown how this growth fundamentally altered how the Golden State fit into the national incarceration picture.[17] For decades, the four traditionally recognized regions of the United States have incarcerated in distinct ways, with the South invariably imprisoning the most, the Northeast the least, and the West and Midwest in between. In 1977, California's imprisonment rate matched that of the Northeast and stood well below that found otherwise in the Western United States. By 2009, however, California's rate had risen *above* Western norms, and more closely matched the incarceration levels found in the South than in the Northeast. Where California had formerly brought down the overall national average, now it was doing the reverse.

In order to house its burgeoning prison population, California embarked on what has been called "the biggest prison building project in the history of the world."[18] In all, the state built 23 major correctional facilities between 1984 and 2005.[19] Yet, even with all of the new construction, California could not keep up with the demand for incarceration. In 1995, the state's prisons held nearly twice as many inmates as they were designed to house.[20] A decade later, this imbalance persisted—essentially unchanged despite all of the new facilities.[21]

Critically for the story that follows, California's prison overcrowding was not simply a matter of discomfort to the inmates, but also a major impediment to the delivery of necessary health services. Inmates responded by filing class action lawsuits. First, in 1990, a group of seriously mentally ill prisoners sued, alleging that the mishandling of their conditions violated the Eighth Amendment Cruel and Unusual Punishments Clause. (The previous chapter considered one line of Eighth Amendment cases dealing with the permissible length of prison terms. Another line, invoked by the California plaintiffs, regulates the conditions of imprisonment, requiring states, among other things, to provide certain minimal levels of health care to inmates.)

In 1995, a federal district court judge ruled in favor of the inmates, finding "overwhelming evidence of the systematic failure to deliver necessary care to mentally ill inmates."[22] The judge concluded that California prisons were "seriously and chronically understaffed," with "no effective method for ensuring ... the competence of their staff."[23] The prisons lacked necessary suicide-prevention procedures, and inmates suffering from mental illness "languished for months, or even years, without access to necessary care."[24]

In 2001, as the prison system struggled to achieve court-ordered improvements in the care of mentally ill inmates, another group of prisoners with serious medical conditions sued. This time, the state actually conceded that it was violating the plaintiffs' constitutional rights and agreed to a remedial plan.[25] However, the state failed to comply with the plan and found itself in court once more. A federal district judge concluded that " 'the California prison medical care system is broken beyond repair,' resulting in an 'unconscionable degree of suffering and death.' "[26] The judge noted, "[I]t is an uncontested fact that, on average, an inmate in one of California's prisons needlessly dies every six to seven days due to constitutional deficiencies in the [California prisons'] medical delivery system."[27] These findings initiated a new round of court orders and charges of noncompliance.

Meanwhile, there were signs that California voters were finally moving beyond the punitive populism that had so dominated the state's politics in the closing decades of the 20th century. Most notably, as we saw in Chapter 2, Proposition 36 passed with an impressive

61 percent of the vote in 2000, mandating treatment instead of incarceration for nonviolent drug possession offenses.

Doubtlessly heartened by the success of Proposition 36, critics of California's three-strikes law decided in 2004 to try the initiative process to achieve reform of the harsh minimum. As noted in Chapter 1, three-strikes laws have had a much smaller impact on the national incarceration rate than is commonly supposed. However, California's version really was an important driver of the state's horrific prison overcrowding. Between 1994 and 2004, about 87,500 people received enhanced sentences under the law (including its "two-strikes" provision, which doubled penalties on a second conviction).[28] By 2004, these inmates accounted for more than one-quarter of California's prison population.

Reformers trumpeted the fiscal burdens caused by the extended sentences imposed on these inmates, often for nonviolent crimes.[29] Their proposed ballot initiative, Proposition 66, did not aim to repeal three-strikes entirely, but did seek to narrow its reach by reducing the number of offenses that could count as strikes. Polls in the summer and early fall of 2004 consistently found that two-thirds or more of California voters favored the proposal.[30]

The prison guards' union, whose members benefited from California's swelling prison population and which had been a leading defender of three-strikes from the time of its adoption, rallied the opposition to Proposition 66.[31] The union collaborated with law enforcement groups, crime victim organizations, and Governor Arnold Schwarzenegger. They waged a fear-mongering campaign that demonstrated that the Willie Horton era had not really ended with the new millennium. Indeed, distinctly reminiscent of the Horton spot, the main television ad of the "No on 66" campaign featured a white rape victim describing what happened to her and warning that the initiative would set her attacker free.[32]

Sociologist Joshua Page contrasts the pro and con campaigns this way:

> Taken together, the "Yes on 66" campaign claimed that California needed a more nuanced, less expensive Three Strikes law. It attempted to reason with voters and appeal to their sense of fairness. The "Yes on 66" campaign's arguments, in other words, were academic, technical, and rational. The "No on 66" campaign's messages were primarily emotional; they targeted voters' guts rather than their minds. Advertisements against the measure did not discuss cost-effectiveness, fairness, or the

relative "smartness" of tinkering with Three Strikes. The commercials' harrowing music, scary images, and simple yet powerful messages communicated that Proposition 66 would create chaos, destroy communities, and lessen public safety.[33]

In the end, Proposition 66 failed, 53 to 47 percent.

With the hope of three-strikes reform now off the table, the California prison system stumbled forward. It was increasingly clear that the system was approaching a crisis point. In 2007, the Little Hoover Commission, an independent, bipartisan state oversight agency, issued a scathing report, bluntly stating, "California's prisons are out of space and running out of time."[34] The commission observed,

> California's correctional system is in a tailspin that threatens public safety and raises the risk of fiscal disaster. . . . For decades, governors and lawmakers fearful of appearing soft on crime have failed to muster the political will to address the looming crisis. . . .
>
> State prisons are packed beyond capacity. Inmates sleep in classrooms, gyms and hallways. . . .
>
> Years of political posturing have taken a good idea—determinate sentencing—and warped it beyond all recognition with a series of laws passed with no thought to their cumulative impact. And these laws have stripped away incentives for offenders to change or improve themselves while incarcerated. Inmates who are willing to improve their education, learn a job skill or kick a drug habit find that programs are few and far between, a result of budget choices and overcrowding. Consequently, offenders are released into California communities with the criminal tendencies and addictions that first led to their incarceration. They are ill-prepared to do more than commit new crimes and create new victims.[35]

The Courts Intervene

Federal district judges have broad powers to order state governments to adopt reforms so as to bring them into compliance with the Constitution. These powers of injunctive relief were best, and most controversially, exemplified by the sweeping school desegregation orders of the 1960s and 1970s, which sometimes included mandatory busing for students. In that same golden age of the "structural injunction," federal judges also asserted authority over many prisons and prison systems in order to rectify ongoing Eighth Amendment violations. Most famously, Judge William Wayne Justice essentially took over the Texas system for nine years in an effort to root out an array of systemic abuses.[36]

In California, the judges handling the mental illness and medical condition cases revived this tradition through the series of remedial orders they issued after finding constitutional violations. However, everything the judges tried was simply overwhelmed by the ever-swelling tide of new inmates entering the California prisons. By the time of the Little Hoover Commission report in 2007, it was clear that the horrific maltreatment of seriously ill prisoners would not end without major reductions in the level of overcrowding. As the legislature continued to dither on sentencing and corrections reform, the federal courts finally reached a breaking point. In order to end the ongoing constitutional violations, the prison population would have to be cut.

But could a federal judge simply order the state to reduce overcrowding? The ramifications were staggering, likely requiring the state either to make massive new investments in prison construction or to release large numbers of prisoners early. Indeed, a Republican Congress had erected special barriers to overcrowding orders in 1996, when it adopted the Prison Litigation Reform Act (PLRA), pursuant to the so-called Contract with America. The PLRA's many provisions restricting prisoner-rights litigation amounted to a generous grab bag of legal protections for put-upon prison administrators.[37] Several of these provisions focused particularly on overcrowding orders.[38] First, no individual judge acting on her own could require a population reduction; rather, the matter would have to be referred to a special three-judge panel. Second, even the three-judge panel could not act without finding by clear and convincing evidence—an unusually high burden of proof—that crowding was the "primary cause" of a violation of a constitutional right and that no other relief would remedy the violation. Finally, the panel also had to show that its order was "narrowly drawn, extends no further than necessary, ... and is the least intrusive means necessary" to remedy the violation.

Undaunted, in late 2006, the plaintiff-inmates in the mental illness and medical condition cases filed motions seeking the appointment of a panel to issue a population-reduction order. Although the judges overseeing the litigation initially delayed ruling on the motions, they did signal their growing impatience with the state's efforts.[39] This finally seemed to prompt some action by state policy makers. In April 2007, with the plaintiffs' motions still pending, the California legislature adopted an overcrowding-reduction plan that relied primarily on the construction of 53,000 new prison and jail beds at a cost of $7.7 billion.[40] The new law also increased funding for rehabilitative programs.

However, the plan quickly fell apart, undone by a state budget crisis, as well as a decision by California attorney general Edmund G. (Jerry) Brown Jr. to take a more aggressive stance in the litigation.[41] (Brown, a Democrat, was working to shed a soft-on-crime reputation he had acquired as governor in the 1970s, when he had appointed the death penalty opponent Rose Bird to the state supreme court. In 2004, for instance, Brown campaigned against Proposition 66, the three-strikes reform. His political strategy paid off, with Brown even gaining the support of the powerful prison guards' union—previously a bitter enemy—in his successful run for governor in 2010.[42])

Unimpressed by the state's response, the judges overseeing the litigation finally granted the motions for a three-judge panel in 2007. The following year, the panel conducted a two-week trial to determine if a population-reduction order was indeed necessary. Finding all of the PLRA's stringent requirements satisfied, the panel issued a 184-page ruling requiring California to reduce its prison population to 137.5 percent of the prison system's design capacity within two years.[43] This would entail the movement of about 46,000 inmates out of prison, assuming, as seemed increasingly clear, that the state's budget crisis precluded any new construction. Attorney General Brown promptly appealed directly to the U.S. Supreme Court. The two-year clock would not start ticking until the high court weighed in.[44]

In 2011, a closely divided Supreme Court affirmed the population-reduction order, five to four. Given his pivotal role in all of the Court's recent Eighth Amendment cases, there should be no surprise that Justice Anthony Kennedy wrote the majority opinion in *Brown v. Plata*. As he had the previous year in *Graham v. Florida*, the juvenile LWOP (life without the possibility of parole) case, Kennedy invoked principles of dignity and decency in the treatment of offenders.[45] He brushed aside the state's rigid interpretations of the PLRA, holding that the statute "should not be interpreted to place undue restrictions on the authority of federal courts to fashion practical remedies" to Eighth Amendment violations.[46] He acknowledged potential public safety risks from the overcrowding-reduction order, but he also noted potential public safety *benefits*. Through poor treatment and overcrowding, he suggested, we may "make people worse."[47] Kennedy thus rejected the implicit premise of the "No on 66" campaign and so much other tough-on-crime rhetoric—that prisoners are more or less uniformly and inherently depraved, and hence that keeping them behind bars as long as possible is the best crime control strategy.

What was most notable about the *Brown* decision, though, was not Kennedy's treatment of abstract questions of law and public policy. Indeed, the decision broke no new ground in Eighth Amendment law. Rather, as Jonathan Simon argues, what stands out was Kennedy's efforts to humanize the prisoners who were enduring unconstitutional prison conditions.[48] For instance, he recounted many specific experiences, such as that of a suicidal inmate held—due to a lack of treatment beds—in a telephone-booth-sized cage without a toilet. After nearly 24 hours in the cage, the inmate was observed "standing in a pool of his own urine, unresponsive and nearly catatonic."[49] Unusually in a Supreme Court opinion, Kennedy also appended photographs to show what it looked like to live in the California prisons. Simon observes, "Pictures and other images of beings in pain intensify the intrinsic human ability to empathize, to connect to emotions of sympathy and outrage."[50] More than anything else, such humanizing gestures in Kennedy's opinion served to link *Brown* to the compassion for prisoners that animated *Graham*.

In any event, whatever the ethical grounding of *Brown*, the Supreme Court's decision meant that the two-year clock on the overcrowding order would soon start ticking. California had bought some time for itself by fighting the order upto the Supreme Court; however, the state's financial picture in 2011 looked no more favorable for a new wave of prison construction than it had in 2007. (As a result of a chronic underfunding of public pensions and other factors, the Golden State's finances had been particularly hard hit by the Great Recession.[51]) Somehow, California would have to figure out a way to reduce its prison population by tens of thousands of inmates.

Realignment: California Responds to the Overcrowding Crisis

To their credit, state policy makers did not wait for the Supreme Court decision before resuming their efforts to bring down the prison population. For instance, the legislature adopted the Community Corrections Performance Incentives Act in 2009, hoping that improved probation systems at the county level would help keep probationers from returning to prison. Probation failures had been a significant contributor to the California corrections crisis. Each year, about 19,000 offenders were being revoked to prison for failure to comply with the terms of their probation, with an annual $1 billion price tag for the state.[52] California's revocation rate was higher than the national average and reflected both a chronic underfunding of probation services and the state's unusual system for managing probation, in which supervision was a wholly county responsibility without any state financial support. In many counties, probation resources were spread far too thinly to provide needed treatment or other assistance in an effective manner. Local officials, moreover, had a clear fiscal incentive to revoke promptly at the first sign of trouble: revocation let the county off the hook and made the state financially responsible for the offender.

The 2009 law, however, changed the fiscal picture, creating a new system of performance-based state funding for local probation services. In essence, counties that were able to do a better job of keeping their probationers out of trouble and out of prison would get to keep a portion of the state budgetary savings. Over time, counties would not only have an incentive to provide better support for probationers, but also a growing financial capacity to do so. The vision of a "virtuous circle" of self-sustaining criminal justice reform paralleled the dream of justice reinvestment, which was becoming increasingly prominent nationally at the same time.

Probation reform in California resulted from years of study and advocacy in the state. The reforms drew inspiration from national work supported by the Pew Center on the States (a leader in the national Justice Reinvestment Initiative), and from a similar law that had been recently adopted in Arizona.[53] Earlier California juvenile justice legislation also provided a model.[54] In the early 2000s, poor conditions in California's juvenile detention facilities had prompted a class action lawsuit. Unlike the contemporaneous adult prison litigation, however, the juvenile litigation had resulted in a relatively quick settlement through which the state agreed to make dramatic cuts in its number of inmates.[55] Pursuant to this agreement, California adopted its Juvenile Justice Realignment Act in 2007. In essence, the act transferred responsibility for all but the most serious juvenile offenders from the state to the counties. By 2010, the number of juveniles in state-level incarceration had fallen by 80 percent, with savings to the state of more than $100 million. Moreover, researchers found that "realignment" had given many juveniles better living conditions, improved treatment, and easier access to their families.[56]

The perceived success of juvenile realignment helped to inspire the probation reforms by demonstrating the ability of local officials to

achieve better correctional outcomes if given proper incentives and resources. Success with juveniles also encouraged policy makers finally
to make long-discussed reforms to parole in California.

Parole revocations were an even bigger source of prison admissions
than probation revocations, accounting for nearly 70,000 in 2008.[57]
California's 2009 Corrections Reform Bill aimed to staunch this flow.
The law relied on a new risk-assessment instrument to help the
Department of Corrections and Rehabilitation do a better job of
focusing its limited supervision resources on the highest-risk offenders.
Other, lower-risk offenders would not be actively supervised and
would be protected from revocation for purely technical violations of
parole. Moreover, when parolees were rearrested, new guidelines
would prioritize community-based sanctions for less serious violations.[58] The parole reform bill also increased good-time credits for
nonviolent, nonsex offenders and required that certain low-level
"wobbler" offenses, which can be prosecuted as felonies, be handled
as misdemeanors, instead.[59]

Thus, by 2011, when the Supreme Court's *Brown v. Plata* decision
set the clock ticking on court-ordered population reduction, California
had already developed considerable reform momentum. Changes to
the juvenile system and to adult probation and parole pointed the way
to the even more sweeping changes the state would soon make. The
established pattern of reform was to shift greater responsibility for
offenders to local officials and to make a greater effort to keep those
on probation or parole in the community and out of prison.

Newly elected as governor, and in the shadow of the Supreme Court
litigation, Jerry Brown negotiated an extraordinarily ambitious new
reform plan with a handful of key organizations, including those representing law enforcement agencies and county governments.[60] The
resulting 2011 Public Safety Realignment Act featured two key components.[61] First, most low-level felons could no longer be sentenced
to state prison terms. Offenders convicted only of nonserious, nonviolent, nonsex-registerable felonies ("triple-nons," to use the new short-
hand) would generally remain under county jurisdiction, either in jail
or on community supervision. Second, starting on October 1, 2011,
triple-non-type offenders released from prison would be supervised
by county probation offices, not the state parole agency, and they
could be returned to state prison only for the commission of a new
felony.

Realignment partially ended what the criminologists Franklin
Zimring and Gordon Hawkins have called the "correctional free

lunch."[62] They refer to the odd division of responsibility for imprisonment found throughout the United States: local officials (police, prosecutors, judges) make the key decisions about which felons go to prison and for how long, while state governments provide the prisons and foot the bill. Like "free" goods in many other contexts, imprisonment is probably overconsumed by local decision makers. However, realignment meant that incarceration for the triple-nons would no longer be a free good at the local level in California. Incarceration would not mean a state prison, but a local jail maintained at local expense. In theory, the localization of financial responsibility should lead to fewer and shorter sentences of incarceration, and the development of more effective alternatives to incarceration. Realignment might thus help to reduce prison overcrowding at two different levels. First, it would immediately divert the triple-nons from prison and into county programs. Second, the improved county programs might reduce recidivism and help to ensure that the triple-nons did not later graduate to imprisonable offenses.

The theory had appeal, but there were also some significant concerns. For one thing, notwithstanding the rejiggered fiscal picture, prosecutors and judges might adhere to their established practices because of risk-aversion or simple inertia. Of course, if the triple-nons continued to get the same sentences of incarceration, those sentences would now be served in jail instead of prison. This would still help the state deal with the immediate pressures created by *Brown*, but potentially at the cost of new problems with jail overcrowding. Moreover, as we saw in our consideration of North Carolina's recent movement of misdemeanants from prisons to jails, local penal facilities are normally set up for short-term inmates and typically offer little programming.[63] It was far from clear that California's jails would be able to deal effectively with an influx of longer-term inmates, who might get little assistance behind bars and leave with poor prospects for staying out.

To the extent that sentencing practices *did* change and come to rely less on incarceration, a spike in crime seemed a distinct possibility. Assuming that recidivism rates remain constant, more offenders getting out earlier—or perhaps never even going *in*—will inevitably precipitate more crime. California's recidivism rates, among the nation's highest,[64] would have to come down. That, in turn, seemed to necessitate big, rapid improvements in the availability and quality of rehabilitative programming. Fortunately, the reform plan did contemplate a massive, $2 billion infusion of state money to the counties to help them carry out their new correctional responsibilities,[65] but it was possible that most of the money would simply go into building new jail space. If so, there seemed little hope of major advances on the programming front.

Despite the risks, California may not have had any other options for dealing with the *Brown* overcrowding mandate—or at least none that were both financially and politically feasible in 2011, another extremely challenging budget year for the state. The legislature adopted realignment in April, and it went into effect on a short timeline in October.

The initial results were remarkably positive. At the end of 2012, about 15 months into realignment, California's prisons held a little more than 119,000 prisoners—down about 43,000 from the 2006 peak, and a little under 150 percent of the system's design capacity.[66] Indeed, California's one-quarter reduction in imprisonment was on par with the reductions achieved by the nation's decarceration champions up to then, New York and New Jersey, but achieved in even less time. Moreover, contrary to the dire predictions of the *Brown* dissenters in the Supreme Court, California did not experience any perceptible increase in major crime. Its rate of violent crime actually *fell* 10 percent between 2010, the last full year before realignment, and 2014. More sophisticated multivariate regression analyses have found no statistically significant impact of realignment on violent crime, and only a modest adverse effect on property crime.[67] California became—and remains— Exhibit A in arguments that the United States could dramatically reduce imprisonment without large public safety costs.

Still, as impressively as realignment performed, it did not do quite well enough. *Brown* required the prison population to drop all the way to 137.5 percent of capacity, but California's progress stalled at 150 percent. By early 2013, with the two-year deadline looming later that year, limitations in the original realignment legislation were becoming increasingly clear. For one thing, like so many other states that have adopted reforms since 2000, California discovered that it could get only so far by trying to move low-level, nonviolent offenders out of prison. For another, there was the issue of retroactivity. Realignment directed *new* triple-non offenders to county systems, but it did not apply retroactively to triple-non offenders who were already imprisoned by the state. Under realignment, no one who was already in prison moved out of prison, no matter how clearly excessive the sentence.

Additionally, while this did not directly contribute to the stalled imprisonment figures, many reformers were disappointed by the extent to which many judges continued to order substantial terms of incarceration for the triple-nons—different now only inasmuch as the terms were being served in local jails. The patterns varied dramatically by county. At one extreme, local officials in San Francisco responded to realignment by strengthening and encouraging use of alternatives to incarceration. The district attorney even created an Alternative Sentencing Planner position to support the use of new approaches by line prosecutors.[68] A year and a half into realignment, San Francisco judges were relying heavily on "split" jail sentences, which converted some of the jail term into a period of community supervision. As a result, the county's jail population actually *declined* under realignment.[69] By contrast, judges in Los Angeles were making very little use of split sentences.[70] Consequently, just one year into realignment, the jail population had increased by 3,489, or nearly one-quarter.[71]

Consistent with the San Francisco/Los Angeles contrast, one study of realignment implementation found a stark divide among the counties in the way that new state funds were spent.[72] The group of "enforcement-focused" counties allocated more than four times as much of their funds to the sheriff, jails, and law enforcement than did the contrasting "reentry-focused" counties. Meanwhile, the reentry-focused counties allocated about twice as many resources to programs and services for offenders than did the enforcement-focused counties.

In early 2013, with prison numbers stalled at about 150 percent of capacity, the state tried to convince the three-judge panel overseeing compliance with the overcrowding order that no further reductions in the prison population were necessary.[73] The panel refused to let the state off the hook entirely, but did extend the deadline an extra six months. Governor Brown and the legislature used that time to hammer out a new strategy to supplement realignment. Now, with California's budgetary situation considerably more favorable than it had been two years earlier, the state's main strategy became increasing imprisonment capacity, rather than reducing the number of prisoners. Legislation in September 2013 set aside $315 million for contracts with out-of-state and in-state private facilities.[74] The state also asked the three-judge panel for a further extension of time in order to hit the 137.5 percent target.

The panel granted an extension until 2016, but its order exacted a price.[75] California would not be permitted to reach the target prison population by shipping more inmates out of state. Rather, the state's negotiators had to agree to certain population-reduction measures, including increased good-time credits for some nonviolent inmates, parole eligibility for nonviolent second-strikers as soon as they served half of their sentences, expedited release for inmates already granted parole, and expanded compassionate release for elderly and ill inmates. The panel's order thus expanded California's reforms into the existing inmate population, including potentially to some inmates convicted of violent and other serious crimes.

Progress toward the 137.5 percent target resumed, boosted by a large increase in the use of in-state contract beds.[76] Indeed, California hit its overcrowding target in early 2015, more than a year before the revised court deadline.[77] By then, the state had adopted yet another set of reforms, this time through the initiative process.

The Voters Speak: New Ballot Initiatives after Realignment

For many years, criminal justice ballot initiatives in California almost invariably resulted in a ratcheting up of toughness. Then, in 2000, the success of the drug initiative, Proposition 36, showed that direct democracy might go the other way. However, the failure of Proposition 66 (three-strikes reform) four years later served as a reminder that fear-mongering could still be a powerful force in initiative campaigns. Finally, in the wake of *Brown*, the state fiscal crisis, and realignment, voters again proved willing to adopt imprisonment-reducing proposals.

First, in 2012, came the long-awaited, much-contested reform of three-strikes. The NAACP Legal Defense Fund renewed the reform push, engaging the assistance of Stanford Law School's Three Strikes Project, which was providing legal assistance to three-strikers.[78] Together, these organizations worked with a pollster to determine how much change Californians could swallow. Certainly not a full repeal of three-strikes, they found out, and probably not even as much as Proposition 66 had attempted. However, their survey research found much greater support for more modest reform. The 2004 initiative had proposed a straightforward change to bring California's version of three-strikes in line with similar laws adopted elsewhere. Recall that California's version required the first two strikes to be violent or serious offenses, but permitted any felony to serve as the third strike. Proposition 66 would have required the third strike to be serious or violent, too, but voters apparently would not tolerate giving a break to an offender who had already committed two major crimes simply because the third one was less serious. So, the new proposal, while also seeking to raise the bar for the third strike, specifically carved out any offenders who at any time had previously been convicted of rape, murder, or child molesting. In the words of the authors, "This was intended to preclude Willie Horton-type ads that had been so effective against Prop. 66."[79]

The authors were unhappy about this concession to political reality, and about another important decision: simple residential burglary, a relatively common crime, would continue to count as a serious offense for three-strikes purposes.[80] On the other hand, the proposal would provide a retroactive benefit to most of the 4,000 inmates who were serving life sentences for nonviolent, nonserious third strikes.[81] Although these offenders would not automatically get reduced prison terms, judges were instructed to grant resentencing requests unless doing so "would pose an unreasonable risk of danger to public safety."

The final proposal—numbered Proposition 36, like the drug initiative of 12 years earlier—gained widespread support, including from a number of prominent law enforcement leaders.[82] For instance, Los Angeles County district attorney Steve Cooley emphasized the state's fiscal crisis and the pressures created by the *Brown* court order for imprisonment reduction.[83] He asserted hopefully that Proposition 36 would forestall more radical reform of three-strikes.

Other arguments in favor of Proposition 36 likewise focused on cost-savings and public safety. Supporters asserted the following:

- Precious financial and law enforcement resources should not be improperly diverted to impose life sentences for some non-violent offenses. Prop. 36 will assure that violent repeat offenders are punished and not released early.
- Taxpayers could save over $100 million per year—money that can be used to fund schools, fight crime and reduce the state's deficit. The Three Strikes law will continue to punish dangerous career criminals who commit serious violent crimes—keeping them off the streets for 25 years to life.
- Prop. 36 will help stop clogging overcrowded prisons with non-violent offenders, so we have room to keep violent felons off the streets.[84]

Such arguments carried the day, as Proposition 36 gained nearly 70 percent of the vote.

Perhaps most impressive was the voters' acceptance of the retroactivity provision, which did not aid hypothetical future offenders, but flesh-and-blood prisoners currently serving life sentences. Afterward, supporters claimed, "Prop. 36 is the first voter initiative since the Civil

War, and perhaps the first in U.S. history, that retroactively shortens the sentences of inmates currently in prison."[85] Indeed, the year before, Governor Brown had specifically designed realignment so as to avoid any such reductions and the political resistance they might spark. However, Proposition 36 showed that retroactivity would not necessarily doom sentencing reform. Moreover, although the initiative gave judges discretion to deny resentencing in the name of public safety, most of the eligible inmates actually did get reduced terms. As of February 2015, more than 2,000 inmates had been released under the retroactivity provision, with hundreds more petitions still awaiting decision.[86] Only a tiny portion (4.7 percent) had been returned to prison for committing new crimes, which was about one-tenth of the overall recidivism rate for released California inmates over the same time period.

Buoyed by the success of Proposition 36, reformers launched another sentence-reducing ballot initiative in 2014. Known as Proposition 47, this proposal aimed to fix one of the most visible problems with realignment: the triple-nons were now being diverted from prison, but their sentences were not necessarily any shorter. As a result, the jails were becoming increasingly overcrowded. In order to address this problem, Proposition 47 sought to cap the sentences in many of the low-level cases by reclassifying several wobbler property offenses as misdemeanors. (An unusual feature of California criminal law, "wobblers" could be prosecuted as either felonies or misdemeanors.) The affected wobblers included low-dollar thefts, shoplifting, and bad-check offenses. Additionally, Proposition 47 reclassified simple possession of cocaine, heroin, and other drugs as a misdemeanor. Like Proposition 36, the new initiative included a retroactivity provision, with murderers, rapists, and child molesters excepted. Unlike Proposition 36, the new proposal earmarked the state's savings for various social services, including mental health and drug abuse treatment intended to reduce recidivism.

The arguments for Proposition 47 echoed those made for Proposition 36, emphasizing savings for taxpayers and the public safety benefits of ensuring adequate incarceration space for the most dangerous offenders.[87] Once again, these arguments carried the day by a wide margin, with nearly 60 percent of the electorate voting *yes*.

Proposition 47 had an even bigger impact than Proposition 36. By early 2016, nearly 4,500 prison inmates had been released under the later initiative's retroactivity provision.[88] Going forward, the Department of Corrections and Rehabilitation estimates that the prison population will remain about 3,500 less than it would have been without Proposition 47.[89] And California's jail population dropped even more sharply in the wake of Proposition 47, falling by nearly 12 percent in just one year.[90] For the 2016–2017 fiscal year, $68 million in savings were being credited to Proposition 47 and allocated to the initiative's designated social services.[91]

Between them, Propositions 36 and 47 seemed to indicate a real change in the California electorate. Where the initiative process had formerly seemed to favor only toughness, now it was being used an instrument for imprisonment reduction. What caused the shift? In part, the new direction of direct democracy likely reflected underlying changes in California's demographics and political culture. Since the time of three-strikes in 1994, California—the home of Ronald Reagan—had turned deep blue, with persistent Democratic dominance of state government. While Democratic politicians were hardly immune to tough-on-crime tendencies—recall, for instance, Jerry Brown's outspoken opposition to three-strikes reform in 2004— California's political realignment indicated that the conservative populism that reshaped all aspects of the state's government in the late 20th century had lost much of its force. Although this development was probably not enough in itself to produce new criminal justice policies, it did create a political environment that was more open to decarceration reforms.

At the same time, quite apart from any underlying changes in the electorate, it must be appreciated that the "Yes" campaigns on 36 and 47 were very sophisticated, well-financed political operations that could get their messages out more effectively than the opposition. "Yes on 36" raised $2.7 million, while "No" had less than $120,000.[92] George Soros, the biggest "Yes" contributor, donated $1 million to the cause by himself. (The billionaire financier was also one of the main backers of the first Proposition 36 and other drug-related initiatives discussed in Chapter 2.) Meanwhile, "Yes on 47" raised nearly $11 million, in comparison to $551,800 for "No."[93] Soros's Open Society Policy Center contributed nearly $1.5 million to the "Yes" war chest.

Additionally, Propositions 36 and 47 benefited from the overcrowding crisis and a fear that more radical reforms might follow if the initiatives failed. As a result, the law enforcement interests that normally back tough-on-crime policies were divided. Thus, the lead public faces of Propositions 36 included the district attorneys of Los Angeles, San Francisco, and Santa Clara, and the Los Angeles police chief. The San Francisco district attorney also fronted Proposition 47, as did a former San Diego police chief. For its part, the prison guards' union—the catalyst for opposition to three-strikes reform in 2004—sat out the later initiative campaigns. A softening in the union's traditionally punitive stance reflected a generational change in its leadership, as well as the threat of more radical reform posed by the *Brown* litigation and a growing public perception that the union bore much responsibility for the corrections crisis.[94]

In short, Propositions 36 and 47 may have owed less to a profound, durable change in voter attitudes toward crime and punishment than to a particular confluence of circumstances, especially the *Brown* litigation and an epic economic collapse that severely limited California's options in responding to the three-judge panel's overcrowding order. Indeed, background fears of predatory recidivism still seemed strong. The propositions were carefully drafted so as to exclude the most Willie Horton–like offenders. Arguments for the propositions then centered on the need to preserve adequate prison space for the truly dangerous. If anything, the proposition campaigns may have reinforced, rather than challenged, prevailing beliefs about the need for long-term incapacitation of large numbers of offenders.

The California "Miracle": Looking Forward

California has achieved a remarkable reduction in imprisonment since 2006. To be sure, some of the reduction was deceptive, especially in the immediate aftermath of realignment, because part of the prison population was effectively transferred to local jails. Some inmates may prefer to do their time in jails closer to home, but others may favor the greater stability and availability of programming at the state institutions designed for long-term inmates. On balance, there would be little reason to applaud if imprisonment dropped, but incarceration (that is, the sum total of prison and jail inmates) remained constant. Fortunately, that is not what happened in California. Some counties responded to realignment by jailing more, but others did not. Over time, the net effect was a genuine, impressive drop in *both* imprisonment and overall incarceration. Figure 7.1 compares the prison and jail figures for 2006 and 2014, the most recent year for which data are available, showing an overall drop in incarceration of nearly 19 percent. While imprisonment declined far more dramatically than jail incarceration, the latter figure also went down a little. Moreover, Proposition 47 was not adopted until 2014, meaning that more recent data will almost certainly show significant further reductions in imprisonment and incarceration.

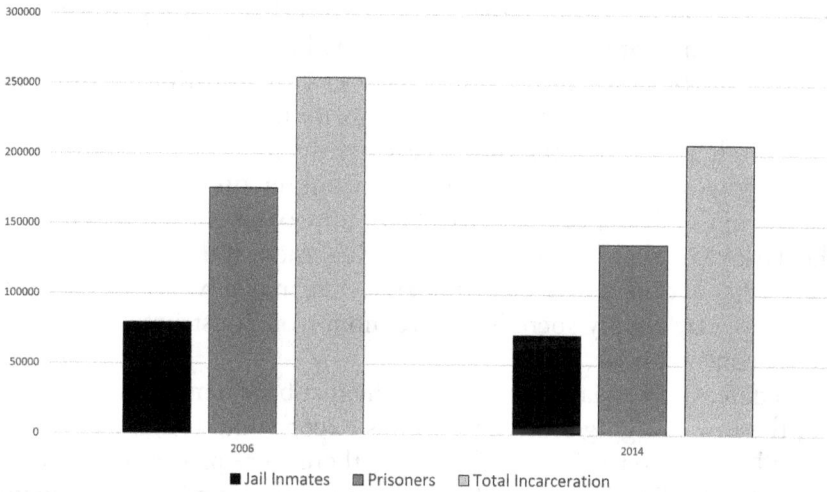

Figure 7.1   Jail and Prison Populations in California, 2006 and 2014 (The prison figures are the year-end, total jurisdiction counts from the Bureau of Justice Statistics' on-line prisoner data tool: http://www.bjs.gov/index.cfm? ty=nps. The jail figures come from Todd D. Minton et al., Census of Jails: Population Changes, 1999–2013 (Washington, D.C.: Bureau of Justice Statistics, 2015), 9; Danielle Kaeble et al., Correctional Populations in the United States, 2014 (Washington, D.C.: Bureau of Justice Statistics, 2016), 17.)

In the context of this book, which has highlighted one disappointing reform story after another, the success indicated by Figure 7.1 begs the question: Has California figured it out—is it truly on track to bringing its era of mass incarceration to an end? There are both cautionary and hopeful notes to sound. It is not clear to me which notes deserve greater emphasis, so I will present the case both ways and let the reader decide whether California is truly poised to break the treading water mold.

The Pessimistic Take: A Future of Stalled Decarceration

Nearly all of the decarceration that has occurred in California can be attributed to the *Brown* litigation and the historic overcrowding levels that the Supreme Court found so disturbing. The state's prison population remains well above the system's design capacity, if no longer to such an exceptional degree. At the end of 2014, at least five states had more overcrowded prisons than California, and at least two others were just a little less.[95] As we saw in Chapter 6, the

Supreme Court tends to move cautiously and is unlikely to support further rounds of judicial intervention as long as California avoids significant backsliding. Even in this era of Eighth Amendment renaissance, the Supreme Court has mostly limited itself to restricting harsh punishments that are outside the U.S. mainstream. Overcrowding in California may no longer qualify. Moreover, California's fiscal circumstances have improved considerably since the dark years that followed the Great Recession. If the courts do push for further action on overcrowding, the state may now be in a position to comply by simply spending more money on construction or additional contract beds.

To date, California's gains have really just been a matter of harvesting the low-hanging fruit. The state's exceptional toughness in the years leading up to *Brown* meant that there were plenty of prisoners who clearly did not belong behind bars. Only in a state that went badly overboard during the imprisonment boom would there be enough triple-nons and technical parole violators in prison such that moving them out would make a real difference. Rearranging sentencing laws so as to accomplish these things should have posed no great practical or political difficulties, and California's success in this regard provides little assurance that the state will be able to make much progress with the double-nons.

California has now cut deeply enough that further progress will require significantly greater courage and imagination. By late 2015, more than 93 percent of California's prisoners had at least one serious or violent conviction on their records.[96] Nearly 30 percent were serving life terms, including the three-strikers. Another quarter were serving two-strikes sentences, meaning that they had at least two convictions for serious or violent offenses. Fewer than 5 percent had been imprisoned for drug offenses, and fewer than 12 percent for property crimes. With the prison population looking increasingly dangerous, further decarceration will require hard choices. The fact that, after realignment, so many California counties simply jailed the low-level offenders for whom they were now responsible hardly bodes well for the potential decarceration of higher-level offenders.

It is important to note that California's decarceration to date has been boosted by an extraordinary, long-term decline in the state's rate of violent crime, as indicated in Figure 7.2. Between 1992 and 2014, California's violence rate dropped by nearly 65 percent. Indeed, given this historic drop, it is surprising that California has not managed even larger decreases in imprisonment—fewer violent criminals should lead

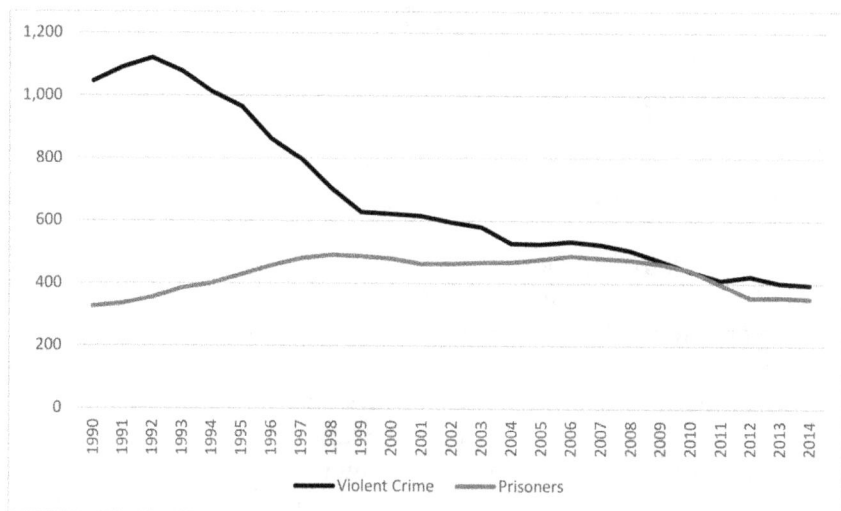

Figure 7.2   California Violent Crime and Imprisonment Rate, per 100,000 Residents

directly to fewer prisoners. In any event, while crime rates are notoriously difficult to predict, it seems highly unlikely that California's rate will continue to drop for another two decades. A distinct flattening in the trendline has already become apparent since 2011. If crime declines end—and even more so if they are reversed, as seems almost certain at some point—then the challenge of further decarceration will only grow more difficult.

Importantly, tough-on-crime political dynamics are still apparent in California, and have consistently thwarted reform efforts in the legislature. For instance, though Proposition 47 did eventually reduce drug possession to a misdemeanor, this happened only after earlier efforts to reduce drug possession sentences through the regular legislative process had been defeated by stiff opposition from the district attorneys', sheriffs', and police chiefs' associations.[97] Indeed, in recent years, Republicans in the legislature have doubled down on toughness. Not one of them voted for realignment, and they have vigorously publicized the reform's occasional failures—violent crimes committed by felons who were on community supervision as a result of realignment.[98] While the GOP remains a minority party in California, its consistently punitive stance discourages Democrats from supporting reform, as they fear being labeled soft-on-crime by their electoral opponents. This dynamic, coupled with the opposition of law enforcement groups, has time and again stymied proposals for California to create a sentencing commission—even a 2009 proposal that had the support of Democratic legislative leaders and then-governor Arnold Schwarzenegger.[99]

To be sure, the success of Propositions 36 and 47 demonstrates the potential for direct democracy to break the legislative logjam and push decarceration measures into law. Yet, it is possible to read too much into these initiative victories. The reforms were narrowly targeted on particular segments of the offender population and, with a wary eye on the potential for Willie Horton–type ads, carefully excluded those with the most troubling prior convictions. Moreover, two of the three features that made California's three-strikes law uniquely harsh remain fully intact.[100] As the low-hanging decarceration fruit disappears from the prison population, it is not clear how much more can be accomplished through direct democracy. The Proposition 36 and 47 campaigns were themselves presented to the voting public as ways to ensure adequate prison space for violent criminals. The fate of Proposition 34 in 2012—a proposal to end the death penalty—demonstrated continued voter resistance to giving any sort of break to the highest-level offenders. Despite a multimillion-dollar "Yes" campaign that outraised the opposition by a nearly 19:1 ratio, Proposition 34 went down to defeat, 48 to 52 percent.[101] A renewed effort to ban capital punishment in 2016 was also defeated, this time by a slightly larger margin.[102]

The Optimistic Take: Structural Reform Sets the Stage for Ongoing Decarceration

Realignment was a genuine game changer. Building on the probation, parole, and juvenile reforms of the late Schwarzenegger years, realignment represents a fundamental philosophical shift in California's approach to sentencing and corrections. From a crude system of incapacitation and deterrence, California has shifted to an emphasis on community supervision and rehabilitative treatment.

True, some counties were slow to embrace the potential for reform and responded to realignment simply by sending more offenders to jail. Local officials needed time to adapt to the new realities. Moreover, as a result of a poorly designed formula for distributing state financial support for realignment, the traditionally more punitive counties were effectively rewarded for their past practices and empowered to continue them in the short run.[103]

Over time, however, the logic of realignment will assert itself. The correctional free lunch is a thing of the past. Fiscal pressures will force counties to build up their alternatives to incarceration and their treatment infrastructure. The faster-moving counties are showing the way. Their innovations will spread to other counties as the value of the new programs becomes increasingly clear. (Preliminary research already indicates that counties focusing their realignment funds on reentry services are reducing recidivism rates more effectively than the counties that prioritized enforcement.[104])

Generally cautious and risk-averse, judges and prosecutors will slowly become more comfortable with new sentencing options and approaches, and incorporate them into day-to-day practice. The resulting fiscal savings can be reinvested so as to make community supervision even more effective and attractive. Moreover, while realignment only forces the diversion of triple-nons from prison, the systematic improvement of community corrections and the growing comfort of judges and prosecutors with alternatives to incarceration will inevitably also lead to changes in the way that offenders with more serious records are handled.

Put differently, as grim as prospects may appear for the adoption of new decarceration policies by the state legislature, realignment diminishes the importance of top–down reform and creates a structure in which decarceration may proceed in a bottom–up fashion. Notably, for instance, in contrast to the repeatedly stalled efforts to create a statewide sentencing commission, San Francisco has established its own *local* sentencing commission as part of its implementation of realignment.[105]

Finally, while much of the rhetoric surrounding recent California reforms seems to accept and reinforce the belief that individuals who have been convicted of violent crimes are inherently different from the rest of us and more or less permanently dangerous, there have also been a few implicit suggestions that a more flexible and hopeful attitude may be starting to take hold. Consider, for instance, the retroactivity provisions of Propositions 36 and 47, which did apply to some inmates with a history of violence.

Perhaps most notable, though, were some developments on the parole front. Under the Determinate Sentencing Law, most of California's prisoners were not even eligible for discretionary parole release. For those offenders who did theoretically qualify, such as the three-strikers with their sentences of 25 years to life, the parole process was notoriously stingy. This resulted, in part, from a 1988 reform that gave the governor a veto over the release of murderers and an ability to send other parole decisions back to the parole board for reconsideration.[106] For instance, Governor Gray Davis (1999–2003) vetoed nearly every parole grant, while his successor Arnold Schwarzenegger (2003–2011) vetoed about 80 percent.[107]

In 2013, however, the legislature established a new Youth Offender Parole Program, which required the parole board to consider the release of inmates who committed their offenses before the age of 18, giving "great weight to the diminished culpability of juveniles as compared to adults, the hallmark features of youth, and any subsequent growth and increased maturity of the prisoner."[108] The legislature clearly intended to put a thumb on the scale in favor of release, and made this favorable process available to those with both determinate and indeterminate sentences. Although there were a variety of significant restrictions on the program, there was no categorical exclusion for those convicted of violent crimes. Then, in 2015, the legislature expanded the program to cover inmates who were serving time for crimes they committed before the age of 23.[109] By early 2016, 250 inmates had been released under the program, most of whom had been convicted of violent crimes.[110]

Meanwhile, Governor Jerry Brown was proving far more receptive to regular parole applicants than had his predecessors. He had approved parole for 2,300 murderers and 450 other lifers.[111]

Resoundingly reelected in 2014 and term-limited from running again, Brown confirmed his support for more flexible release policies by proposing and financially supporting Proposition 57, which was approved by voters in November 2016. Proposition 57 provides parole eligibility and the possibility of early release to thousands of prisoners.[112] Those currently serving sentences for violent crimes are excluded, but earlier convictions for violence are not disqualifying. The initiative also authorizes the Department of Corrections and Rehabilitation to award credits to inmates for good behavior and rehabilitative accomplishments, with no exclusion for violent crimes, and shifts from prosecutors to judges the power to decide whether juvenile offenders will be tried in adult court. The actual impact of Proposition 57 will not be clear for many years, and will depend on the exercise of discretion by parole and corrections officials, but the initiative seems to provide further evidence that California's voters are increasingly open to reducing the prison terms of some offenders with violence in their past—a necessary predicate for California to build on the extraordinary decarceration it has already achieved.

CHAPTER EIGHT

Conclusion: Looking Back, Looking Ahead

With few exceptions, the sentencing legislation of the 1980s and 1990s pointed in one direction: greater use of incarceration. Then, beginning in about 2000, the basic thrust of new sentencing laws changed. The reforms of the new millennium varied widely from state to state and year to year, but they generally reflected a belief that some group of offenders being sent to prison should be kept in the community, or that some group of inmates should be given an opportunity for early release. To be sure, legislatures have also continued to pass tough-on-crime laws since 2000, but these punitive outbursts seem more episodic than systematic. Instead, the new era has been typified by the Justice Reinvestment Initiative (JRI), which has been formally embraced by more than half of the states and which establishes a structured process for identifying groups of incarcerated offenders who can be more cost-effectively managed in other ways. Other states, not officially part of the JRI movement, have nonetheless been influenced by it and adopted reforms in the same spirit.

Yet, despite all of this legislative activity, imprisonment has hardly budged. Indeed, the national prison population continued to grow in the new millennium, albeit at a slower pace. Eventually, imprisonment did start to drop, but only marginally. If California is excluded, national decarceration has been virtually nonexistent. Although a handful of other states have also achieved notable reductions in imprisonment, their gains have been offset by continued *increases* elsewhere. For years, commentators have been heralding a "new politics of sentencing"—I myself used that as an article title in 2002[1]—but mass incarceration remained the on-the-ground reality at the end of the Barack Obama administration no less than it had been at the end of the Bill Clinton administration.

Why has all of the legislative activity not had a greater impact? This final chapter synthesizes the main themes of the narrative up to this point, and then concludes with some thoughts on what might be necessary for the next decade of reform to have a greater impact than the last.

Looking Back: The Treading Water Era

The post-2000 reforms have been blunted by certain recurring flaws in their design. These flaws, in turn, reflect both underlying institutional dynamics and the persistence of many of the basic ideas about crime and punishment that prevailed in the era of the imprisonment boom.

Design Flaws

For all of their diversity, the basic thrust of the post-2000 reforms might be boiled down to simply this: *nonviolent* offenders should be either diverted from prison entirely or moved out of prison more quickly once there. This ideal seems unobjectionable enough, but it was incapable of bringing the national imprisonment rate down to earlier U.S. or current international norms. For one thing, more than half of state prisoners are serving their time for violent offenses.[2] Indeed, if weapons violations and driving under the influence are included—two types of offenses that many like to characterize as violent because of their tendency to cause death or severe injury—then the proportion of "violent" inmates would approach 60 percent. If we add burglary offenses—property invasions that can lead to dangerous confrontations and that are also sometimes classified as violent—then we get to about 70 percent violent offenders in our state prisons. And even that figure does not fully reflect all of those in prison who might be characterized as "violent" using the most expansive definitions of the term. For instance, as we saw in Chapter 2, the federal drug court law excludes as "violent" those drug offenders who either possessed a gun—whether or not the gun was ever used in any way —or who have any *past* convictions for violent offenses. With such definitions, there may be a few jurisdictions that could achieve significant decarceration by keeping nonviolent offenders out of prison, but the nation as a whole cannot; there just are just too few prisoners who belong in the wholly nonviolent category.

Calls to end mass incarceration by emptying the prisons of nonviolent offenders typically rest on mistaken assumptions about the importance of the War on Drugs in driving the imprisonment boom. Many Americans are now strongly predisposed to view the War on Drugs in negative terms and thus too quick to assign it the primary blame for mass incarceration. There is an ironic echo here. In the mid- and late 20th century, many Americans were strongly predisposed to view drug distribution in negative terms and thus too quick to assign it the primary blame for the nation's increasing crime rates. Drug *enforcement* is now scapegoated as drug *distribution* once was. In any event, whatever the other failings of the War on Drugs, it did not fill the nation's prisons with plainly nonviolent drug offenders.

In addition to the exclusion of violent offenders from diversion and early release opportunities, a second major design flaw of the post-2000 reforms has been to rely on enhanced official discretion to achieve decarceration. Mandatory minimums have been softened or eliminated, but reforms do not normally *require* reduced punishment; judges have mostly been free to continue to impose the same sentences as they had prereform. Similarly, many reforms have given parole boards and other corrections officials the power to release inmates earlier, but such reforms do not mean that any inmate will actually be freed. For instance, as we saw in Chapter 3, many states have adopted theoretically expansive compassionate release laws, permitting corrections officials to release elderly and disabled inmates, but the actual numbers let go have been almost negligible in practice.

The federal system offers a striking example of this sort of inertia. For years, judges complained bitterly about the harshness and inflexibility of the federal sentencing guidelines. Then, as a result of the Supreme Court's *Booker* decision in 2005, the guidelines lost their binding character overnight; judges were broadly empowered to impose the sentences they thought best. Yet, most judges simply continued with business as usual. Without a prosecutor's support, judges proved very reluctant to impose sentences outside the guidelines, and, indeed, average sentence lengths actually *increased* slightly after *Booker*.

It is a mistake to assume that frontline criminal justice actors—police, prosecutors, judges, parole boards, probation officers, and the like—are necessarily, or even typically, more lenient than the lawmakers who established the tough-on-crime laws of the boom era. Many of these officials have to face the same voters as the lawmakers, and all of them operate in a politicized environment that can make lenience dangerous to one's career prospects. Indeed, these officials tend to operate without an important constraint that may help to rein in legislative excesses; the state lawmakers who pass tough-on-crime bills are also responsible for paying for the prison system, but the frontline officials tend not to have such fiscal disincentives against the overuse of incarceration.

As with the focus on nonviolent drug offenders, it is understandable why many reformers have thought discretion alone could achieve large-scale decarceration. It is widely understood that lawmakers reduced official discretion during the boom era through such highly publicized enactments as three-strikes, truth in sentencing, and life without the possibility of parole. As so often happens, people assume that correlation implies causation—that the concurrence of reduced discretion with mass incarceration means that the former caused the latter. However, as we saw in Chapter 1, the story is considerably more complicated than that. *Implicit* policy changes—that is, changes adopted by frontline actors through their day-to-day exercises of discretion—played a possibly even more important role than explicit policy changes in driving the imprisonment boom. Thus, in and of itself, discretion assures no decarceration; it all depends on how the incentives and disincentives are lined up for the officials who get to make the important choices.

Although my narrative has especially emphasized the importance of violence exclusions and official discretion in undermining reforms, a variety of other design issues are also apparent. Another difficulty we have encountered is what I might call the community supervision trap. In many diversion-from-incarceration initiatives—think of drug treatment courts as a paradigmatic example—there is a basic trade-off: the offender gets to stay in the community, but not simply in a conventional probation arrangement. The offender will get more treatment, but will also be subject to more conditions and closer monitoring. However, more conditions inevitably mean more violations, and closer monitoring inevitably means a greater percentage of violations are discovered. As a result, an initiative that starts as a diversion from incarceration can actually lead to a surge in revocations and *increased* incarceration. To some extent, these unfortunate tendencies can be constrained through a well-designed system of graduated sanctions, but few initiatives have gone so far as to entirely abandon incarceration as a potential response even to purely technical violations of community supervision. Officials have proven loathe to surrender their ultimate source of power over the offenders in their charge.

The incarceration-increasing potential of enhanced community supervision may be exacerbated by two recurring problems we have seen in earlier chapters. First, although effective rehabilitative programming could theoretically defeat the community supervision trap—that is, programming might permit more offenders to be placed on supervision without a corresponding increase in violations and revocations—programming tends to be underfunded. For instance, we have seen criticisms that "reinvestment" has been the weak link in the JRI, and even to the extent that new funding has been put into justice systems, the funding has been directed more to police and probation officers than to treatment providers. Second, many diversion programs have suffered from "net-widening," that is, the tendency for such programs to draw in very low-level offenders who were not likely to be incarcerated anyway, but who now may face significant risks of incarceration through the rigorous systems of monitoring and sanctions that go with diversion. For instance, before a drug court is implemented in a jurisdiction, police and prosecutors might tend to ignore simple drug possession offenses by addicts, but, after the drug court is in place, those same offenders might be seen as good candidates for the diversion—even though it would not really be a "diversion" as to them. Once in drug court, they are likely to spend some time behind bars as a response to the normal struggles that addicts experience in treatment.

Reformers typically frame community supervision as an *alternative* to incarceration, but this is misleading. In truth, community supervision also functions as a *back door* to incarceration. Offenders on community supervision routinely violate their conditions of release. (Many conditions are unrealistic from the start.) A violation or three will not necessarily land an offender behind bars, but at some point an attention-getting sanction will seem necessary—perhaps just a "quick dip" in jail, to use the North Carolina nomenclature, or a full-blown revocation. One way or another, putting more offenders on community supervision seems inevitably to lead to more back-door incarceration. Likewise, increasing the demands of supervision or the intensity of monitoring will eventually send more offenders behind bars. On balance, more extensive or rigorous community supervision may be good policy, but it is not a very effective decarceration strategy, at least if not coupled with strict constraints on use of the back door (as in California's Proposition 36 diversion program for drug offenders) and major new investments in rehabilitative programming.

One more recurring design flaw merits note here. We have seen time and again that reforms are adopted in legislative packages that also include tough-on-crime measures. For instance, the 2002 Michigan law that eliminated quantity-based drug mandatory minimums also ratcheted up the severity of the state's sentencing guidelines. The North Carolina JRI law created a new sentence enhancement for habitual breaking and entering. The federal Fair Sentencing Act of 2010 decreased statutory crack penalties, but increased the guidelines sentences for cases involving violence. Many other examples could be given. In general, the incarceration-increasing provisions of the reform packages we have considered seem outweighed by the incarceration-decreasing measures. Still, these gestures toward greater severity diminish, in ways small or large, the overall decarceration potential of reforms.

Deeper Explanations

Why have the post-2000 reforms been designed in these problematic ways? As I have already suggested, part of the story was naivety and misunderstanding about the real cause of the imprisonment boom. However, other forces have also been at play. They can be divided into two categories: institutional inertia and self-interest and the stubborn persistence of key beliefs and social values that underlay the imprisonment boom.

If we think in terms of narrow economic or political self-interest, the big players in the criminal justice system have little reason to favor large-scale decarceration. Corrections departments, for instance, are likely to see their budgets shrink—an unhappy development in the life of any bureaucratic agency. (In states that contract with private prisons or have unions representing prison workers, those organizations will also have significant economic interests in maintaining mass incarceration.) Meanwhile, the local-level officials—police, prosecutors, judges, jailers, and, in some states, probation officers—appreciate having a capacious state prison system where troublesome offenders can be sent and maintained at state expense. (This is the "correctional free lunch" that California partially eliminated through realignment.) Decarceration complicates the work of local officials, especially if it means a large, abrupt increase in the number of convicted felons in the community—bearing in mind that local officials are the ones most politically accountable for public safety.

Additionally, and quite apart from the budgetary and political risks of decarceration, there is the inevitable resistance to change that exists in any large organization. Indeed, state and local criminal justice agencies are high-volume businesses with complex, well-established bureaucratic processes for managing offenders from arrest through punishment; reform inevitably disrupts these processes, produces a multitude of unintended consequences, and creates more work for busy officials at least through a transition period. It is easy to understand why these officials would resist change.

Resistance has an impact at two levels. First, at the level of policy development, key institutional actors are likely to oppose the adoption of really meaningful imprisonment-reducing reforms. We have seen many illustrations of this, most prominently in the California story. For instance, the correctional officers' union played a central role in defeating three-strikes reform in 2004. For an example outside of California, recall the revolt of federal prosecutors against the statutory reform agenda favored by their nominal boss, Attorney General Holder. The opposition of correctional officers, police, and prosecutors can be a major political obstacle to reform because these frontline officials are often seen by the public as having special knowledge about how to handle offenders and protect public safety. Thus, proponents of reform often work hard to obtain the support of law enforcement officers. There are good political reasons why prosecutors and police officials were listed as the lead sponsors of Propositions 36 and 47, the recent successful reform initiatives in California. Likewise, in the JRI, the prescribed policy-development process engages criminal justice agencies and officials from the start. Coopting these actors seems good politics, but the strategy can come with a big price tag. The authors of Proposition 36, for instance, have described making compromises that narrowed the reform in order to maintain the support of law enforcement.[3] Similarly, as we saw in Chapter 4, the JRI has been sharply criticized for doing more to empower corrections officials than to achieve decarceration, and for making nearly all of its "reinvestments" in established criminal justice agencies.

Second, at the level of policy implementation, all of the discretion built into so many of the reforms gives resistant institutional actors an opportunity to undermine or minimize the practical impact of new policies. Indeed, the prominent role of official discretion in these reforms is doubtlessly a further reflection of the political clout of the key actors and their influence over the reform process.

Ideology complements these institutional dynamics. Survey research shows some decline in punitive sentiment in the United States since the 1990s, but tough-on-crime attitudes remain widespread and at higher levels than in the years before the imprisonment boom.[4] For instance, in one recent survey, 54 percent of respondents said that society is better served by harsher punishment of criminals, as opposed to 46 percent who favored greater efforts to rehabilitate.[5] Additionally, despite sharp, sustained reductions in crime since the 1990s, most Americans still believe that crime is getting worse each year.[6]

Or consider my own recent research on public opinion in Wisconsin, a partisan battleground state that lies near the nation's political center of gravity. My colleagues and I found the following:

- 62 percent of registered voters believe that the courts are too lenient with criminals;
- 84 percent support tougher sentences for repeat offenders;
- only 34 percent say that the justice system is doing a good job of ensuring that people who commit crimes receive the punishment they deserve;
- only 27 percent agree that many of the people locked up in prison do not deserve to be there; and
- only 37 percent agree that many prisoners could be safely released.[7]

Such public beliefs help to explain why the post-2000 reforms have not had a greater impact. For one thing, these beliefs give the important institutional actors greater leverage in their efforts to derail or undermine reform. For another, they have encouraged some politicians to adhere to the same tough-on-crime rhetoric and policy positions that predominated in the late 20th century. This seems most common in the Republican Party. Although a few prominent Republicans have embraced the decarceration agenda, there has been stiff resistance by several congressional Republicans to reform on the federal level. We have also noted the consistent, outspoken opposition by Republican lawmakers to almost all of the recent reforms in California. My survey research in Wisconsin similarly finds large, statistically significant differences in the attitudes of Republican and Democratic voters toward punishment and rehabilitation.[8] Even when the unreconstructed Republicans are not in the legislative majority, their opposition to reform can make other lawmakers skittish, raising the specter of harsh attack ads on crime policy and discouraging bold new initiatives. These partisan dynamics may particularly condition the reliance of lawmakers on discretion-based reforms, which provide them with some political insulation—in the event of a Willie Horton–like catastrophe, the finger of blame can be directed to the responsible frontline official and away from those who adopted the underlying policy.

Given the persistence of punitive attitudes, it may seem surprising that reforms happened at all. By and large, however, the post-2000 reforms have not presented a direct challenge to the beliefs and attitudes that underlay the imprisonment boom. The main arguments for reform have been: (1) incarceration is expensive and current fiscal pressures demand greater restraint in its use, and (2) nonviolent offenders should be kept out of prison so as to reserve limited incarceration space for more dangerous offenders. Compare these points, for instance, with the key premises of the Willie Horton ad that were highlighted in Chapter 1:

- predatory violent and sexual crime is the nation's preeminent crime problem;
- many or most criminals are beyond rehabilitation and deserve only minimal care and support from society;
- criminal justice officials should emphasize rigorous physical control of criminals;
- officials who fail to incapacitate offenders to the maximum extent can be rightfully blamed for repeat offenses; and
- any lenience or consideration shown to criminals presents not only a threat to the physical safety of others, but also a symbolic repudiation of crime victims.

The arguments for the post-2000 reforms do not call into question the belief that our society is full of violent predators who must be incapacitated; to the contrary, the arguments *reinforce* that belief by emphasizing the importance of reserving adequate prison space for violent offenders. If there is anything subtly new in what seems the dominant belief system of the treading water era, it would be an acknowledgment of fiscal constraints on the use of imprisonment and a greater confidence in the ability of officials to manage the risks posed by certain limited categories of offenders in the community. However, even as to the latter—essentially, the nonviolent drug offenders—the post-2000 reforms hardly embody a spirit of compassion or forgiveness. Drug treatment courts—now a favorite of the JRI movement—remain the paradigmatic model of community supervision in the treading water era; as we saw in Chapter 2, these courts emphasize physical control of the offender through regular drug tests, court appearances, and "motivational jail."

On occasion, we have seen hints of a different, more ethically based model of reform. There are Justice Kennedy's opinions in *Graham v.*

Florida and *Brown v. Plata,* for instance, or some of the observations of President Obama and Attorney General Holder about the racial discrimination and structural socioeconomic disadvantage baked into our system of mass incarceration. These ways of conceptualizing reform more directly challenge the beliefs and values that drove the imprisonment boom. However, the dominant approach today emphasizes economic, not ethical, imperatives. We remain far from the views of humane, reintegration-focused punishment that prevail in western Europe, as noted in Chapter 3.

Reforms happened in the United States because the state fiscal crises of the early 21st century made change necessary; it was simply inconceivable that state budget makers would continue to pay for new prison construction indefinitely as they had in the 1990s. The institutional actors had to accept *some* reform. In the end, their interests converged reasonably well with the priorities of the liberals who had fought for years against mandatory minimums, the War on Drugs, truth in sentencing, three-strikes, and so forth. Liberals were delighted to see a repudiation of these symbolically powerful manifestations of tough-on-crime politics, while corrections officials, judges, and prosecutors were pleased to retain, or even expand, their own discretion through the same reforms. For their part, at least some conservatives were mollified by efforts to wrap reform in the mantle of fiscal responsibility; by reassurances that the most dangerous offenders would be kept in prison, perhaps even longer in some cases; and by promises that community supervision would be made more rigorous. The peculiar shape of the post-2000 reforms was no accident, but instead embodied trade-offs that were intended to gain the acceptance of diverse groups of institutional stakeholders and political leaders. Reform did not necessarily require universal legislative agreement—although in some states this was nearly achieved—but, in a political environment in which public punitiveness remained strong, it often seemed important to gain at least some support from law enforcement and across partisan lines. It remains an open question, though, whether the push for least-common-denominator reform went so far in some jurisdictions as to deprive the resulting changes of any net value.

Looking Ahead: What Might Make for More Meaningful Decarceration?

If future policy changes are to have more of an impact on imprisonment rates, reformers must address what I have outlined as the deeper causes of the treading water phenomenon. Let us consider institutional interests first, and then ideology.

Restructuring Institutional Interests

Local officials benefit from the "correctional free lunch"—the ability to ship their troublemakers out of the community for extended periods of time at state expense—but this fiscal structure warps incentives. The realignment experience in California points to the potential benefits of restructuring correctional responsibilities and funding: sharp reductions in incarceration with little or no impact on public safety. When realignment took away the ability of local officials to send low-level offenders to state prison, local officials responded with new programs and sentencing practices. Although some of the "triple-non" offenders were simply diverted to jail, most were not. Better practices had been possible all along, but it took a fundamental restructuring of state–local responsibilities to unleash local innovation.

The realignment model is not the only, or even necessarily the best, strategy for restructuring state–local relations. The neighboring states of Minnesota and Wisconsin make for an illuminating comparison. In the 1970s, the two states had very similar crime and imprisonment rates.[9] Since then, their crime rates have continued to move in sync, but their imprisonment rates have diverged sharply, with Wisconsin growing its prison population at a far more rapid pace. Since the early 1980s, Wisconsin's imprisonment rate has consistently been about twice as high as Minnesota's. One cause for Minnesota's relative restraint was its Community Corrections Act of 1973, which offered state subsidies to counties to manage their own community supervision programs. With the combination of local control and state funding of community corrections, probation looked more appealing than prison to local officials for a relatively wide range of cases. State sentencing guidelines, designed with an eye to holding imprisonment growth under control, also pushed local officials to exercise restraint. By contrast, in Wisconsin, the state handled all probation supervision. Local officials, who had no control over the way supervision was administered, tended to be skeptical of it and were much quicker than their Minnesota counterparts to take advantage of the imprisonment free lunch. (Wisconsin also lacked anything like Minnesota's presumptive sentencing guidelines.) As a result, while Wisconsin's prison population is twice the size of Minnesota's, the probation numbers are almost exactly flipped: Wisconsin's probation population is half the size of Minnesota's.[10] Again, with closely parallel long-term crime trends in the two states, there is no reason to think that public safety has suffered in Minnesota for its dramatically greater reliance on community supervision over imprisonment.

Wisconsin itself offers another illustration of the potential decarceration benefits of local responsibility and control. While the Badger State never adopted a Community Corrections Act for *adult* offenders, it does have one for *juveniles*. In general, Wisconsin's counties are financially responsible for the costs of responding to juvenile delinquency, with the exception of those categorized as serious juvenile offenders.[11] The state provides a grant to counties to help cover the costs, but counties have substantial freedom to decide how to use the state money. The state also charges counties for the care of nonserious offenders sent to state correctional facilities, which encourages local officials to utilize alternatives to incarceration. With this system, Wisconsin achieved an extraordinary two-thirds reduction in the number of individuals held in its state juvenile correctional facilities between 1996 and 2012.[12] Over the same time period, Wisconsin's adult prison population *increased* by more than 70 percent.

There are, in short, several different models for restructuring local incentives that have shown promising results. We also saw another in Chapter 7, in the form of California's 2009 Community Corrections Performance Incentives Act, which financially rewarded counties for reducing their revocation rates. The point here is not so much to push for one particular model, but to highlight the basic idea that a combination of targeted state subsidies and local control can promote the development and wider utilization of alternatives to incarceration on the local level. (This point might recall Susan Tucker and Eric Cadora's plea for localization, a central component of their original vision for justice reinvestment that was mostly ignored in practice.) The decarceration potential of this strategy can be supported through appropriately designed, presumptive sentencing guidelines like Minnesota's. While controversial, "chargebacks" to counties for the unnecessary use of state institutions—as Wisconsin does in its juvenile program—also warrant consideration. There may also be merit to categorically closing the state prisons to certain types of lower-level offenders, as was done in realignment, although other states might have to go beyond the "triple-nons" in order to have a real impact on imprisonment rates.

In seeking to restructure the incentives of local officials, state policy makers have at their disposal both carrots (subsidies, performance grants) and sticks (sentencing guidelines, chargebacks, categorical exclusions on imprisonment). New carrots are unlikely to provoke local opposition, but may have to be quite large and expensive for the state to overcome local-level inertia on a scale that would make a real dent in imprisonment rates.

In theory, as justice-reinvestment proponents have been saying for years, the carrots could be paid for through the savings achieved through reduced imprisonment, but there are at least two major impediments to realizing this ideal. First, there is the timing problem: subsidies paid out today for enhanced alternatives to imprisonment may not generate any real savings on the back end for many years (if ever). New programs take time to build and prove themselves. Then, even when the flow of offenders into prison is slowed, the state still does not realize any substantial savings until a certain decarceration tipping point is reached—a facility must be closed. With the exception of very sick or very dangerous inmates, the marginal cost of each prisoner to the state is relatively low; the big savings come only when the high fixed costs of maintaining an entire facility are eliminated. To the policy maker today, that must seem a distant and uncertain prospect—hardly a reassuring basis on which to make a major fiscal commitment to the decarceration carrots. Second, there is the political problem: reallocating money from the state prison system to local criminal justice officials will provoke resistance from the state corrections bureaucracy and allied interests (private prisons and other corporate contractors, the correctional officers' union, and the mostly rural host communities that welcomed new prisons in the 1980s and 1990s as a source of economic development). Between the timing and political problems, policy makers may struggle to cobble together the funding for really compelling positive incentives, suggesting the need for some "sticks," too. It is the sticks, however, that arouse local opposition.

Absent some extreme, external pressure—like the court order that drove realignment in California—it is not likely that reformers will be able to make big changes in the state–local corrections relationship without a political battle. In general, as we have seen, reformers in the treading water era have tried to avoid these fights with the major institutional interests in the criminal justice system. Arguably, indeed, this has been a necessary reform strategy in a political environment in which punitive attitudes remain widely prevalent among voters. System insiders, especially those wearing a badge, have a great deal of credibility with the public and seem quite capable of rallying opposition to reform with tough-on-crime rhetoric and fear-mongering, as the correctional officers did in defeating Proposition 66. In short, for all its seeming promise, restructuring the incentives of local officials may not be capable of achieving large-scale decarceration without significant changes first in social attitudes toward crime and punishment. Before turning to the possibility of ideological change, though, let us consider the possibility of restructuring incentives at a different level of government.

State correctional bureaucracies have had a complex relationship with recent reform efforts. No one likes to work in a badly overcrowded prison, which, among other drawbacks, can put staff in greater physical danger. Thus, when fiscally pressed state legislatures put the brake on new prison construction, if not even before, many corrections officials became genuinely interested in reforms that would restrain the growth in their prison populations. Many, indeed, had a deep-rooted professional commitment to the ideal of rehabilitation and welcomed the new-found interest among policy makers in evidence-based programming for offenders. Not surprisingly, corrections officials have often participated actively and deeply in some reform efforts, perhaps most notably in those sponsored by the JRI. At the same time, officials have seemed particularly intent in these contexts on preserving their budgets and maximizing their discretion—an agenda that is clearly apparent in many of the JRI reforms. Additionally, corrections officials have often been quite hesitant to use what new or expanded early-release authority they have been given, doubtlessly fearful of a political backlash over controversial decisions or Willie Horton–like failures.

It is one thing to ask corrections officials and other mass incarceration stakeholders—contractors, unions, host communities—to live within the existing capacity constraints, but quite another to get their support for measures intended to close prisons and cut prison-related spending and employment. As with the local officials, it would help if the incentives of some or all of these stakeholders could be restructured so as to engage greater support—or at least less resistance—from them for meaningful decarceration.

Law professor Avlana Eisenberg has recently suggested some promising ways of altering the incentives.[13] She notes, for instance, that Michigan successfully minimized union resistance to prison closures through a multiyear strategy of reducing prison workforces by natural attrition and shifting prison employees into new jobs in the corrections department, including community supervision jobs. (More generally, corrections employees and leaders alike may be mollified if prison closures simply result in a corresponding shift of budget dollars and jobs into the community supervision units of the same state corrections department; however, this strategy would cut against the ideal of increased funding and responsibility for locally controlled community supervision agencies.) Eisenberg also suggests performance-based compensation systems, in which payment levels are tied to outcomes like reduced recidivism and reincarceration. She particularly has in mind privately run prisons in this regard, although there might be some potential in the public sector, too. (In the 1990s, for instance, California had some success with an experiment that provided increased funding for units in the state parole supervision bureaucracy that reduced their revocation rates.[14]) Eisenberg also suggests that private contractors might be enticed by the potential for new business opportunities in the expanding field of community corrections.

In the end, though, something more dramatic is probably necessary. Once again, California provides an intriguing model. The courts imposed a firm, numerical limit on overcrowding, which effectively dictated a clear decarceration target in a specific period of time. Despite all of the state's doomsaying during the litigation, once the target was set, state leaders proved boldly innovative and ultimately succeeded in reaching the goal. Similarly, if corrections departments elsewhere were simply told they had to reduce their prison populations by, say, a quarter in six years (California's achievement), they would probably also rise to the occasion.

Unfortunately, the courts are not likely to push other states with lower overcrowding levels to the same extent that they pushed California. Could a similar target be imposed by other means? One might imagine, for instance, a ballot initiative in which the voters adopt a clear, significant decarceration goal. In 1978, California voters famously adopted Proposition 13, which rolled back and capped property tax rates, forcing dramatic readjustments in the provision of government services.[15] Why not a Proposition 13 for mass incarceration? A safety valve might be included to permit delays in achieving the goal if significant, good-faith efforts are being made (much as the three-judge panel in California extended its initial decarceration deadline). Additionally, there might be assurances of no layoffs for prison employees willing to take other state employment, which might soften some of their opposition. Even so, would this be politically feasible in any state? The odds would seem very long indeed in the absence of some fundamental rethinking about crime and punishment in U.S. society.

Ideological Change

Real decarceration requires real change in the attitudes of the U.S. public. Fortunately, although punitiveness remains widespread, attitudes do seem to be changing. Using various measures, researchers find that punitiveness peaked in about the mid-1990s and has been slowly, but fairly steadily, falling since then.[16] In Chapter 6, for instance, we saw that support for the death penalty—one punitiveness proxy commonly used by social scientists—fell from 80 percent in 1994 to 60 percent in 2013. Still, this figure remained well above the 42 percent recorded in 1966. If public attitudes toward crime and punishment do not move further toward what they were in the 1960s, then it seems unlikely that the clock will be turned back on incarceration rates, either.

What are the prospects for further attitudinal movement in that direction, and how might reformers be able to nudge it along? Let us consider once again the set of beliefs and values reflected in the Willie Horton ad; a rejection or softening of these might make possible much bolder and more effective policy change than we have seen in the treading water era.

First, the ad—and the imprisonment boom more generally—rests in large part on an acute fear of crime, especially violent crime. Fear of crime seems deeply intertwined with public punitiveness. Although punitiveness is a complex phenomenon that draws its strength from a number of sources, multivariate regression analyses do find a statistically significant correlation between changes in the one and changes in the other.[17] With crime rates in long-term decline, this correlation is good news for reformers. Better informing the public that crime rates are at a 40-year low would seem a promising strategy for shifting opinion more decisively against mass incarceration.

Additionally, the risks of criminal victimization should be put into comparative perspective. Figure 8.1, for instance, depicts the risks of death by homicide compared with other leading causes of death.[18] The risks of accidental death, for instance, are eight times as great—including twice as great a risk of dying in a car accident—and the risks of suicide approach three times as great.

Of course, other types of violent crime are more common than homicide, but these, too, should be considered comparatively. In the most recent year for which data are available, about 0.77 percent of Americans over the age of 12 experienced a serious violent crime.[19] By contrast, for instance, nearly 9 percent of Americans went to the

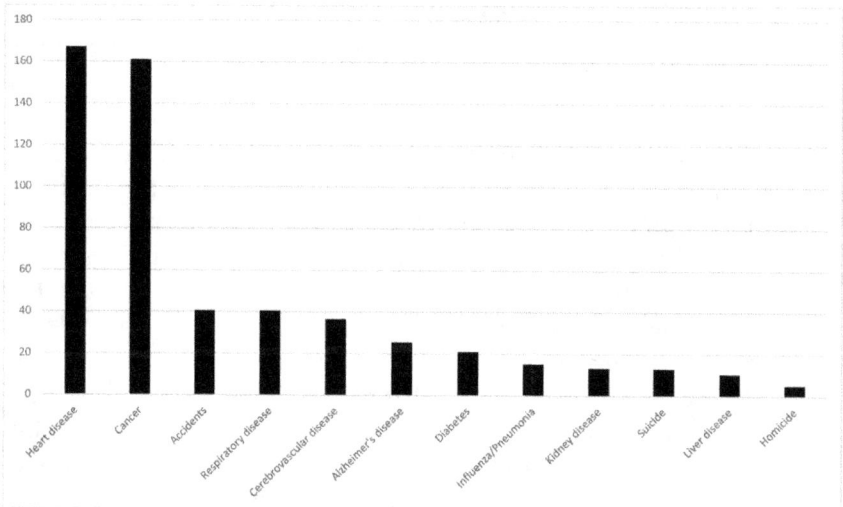

Figure 8.1   Rates of Selected Causes of Death, per 100,000 Population

emergency room for an accidental injury, while nearly 13 percent of adults suffered from diabetes, 12 percent from heart disease, 6 percent from cancer, and 3 percent from stroke.[20] Moreover, among the cases of serious violent crime, only about one-third resulted in an injury, and fewer than half involved a stranger. In short, the average person's risk of being injured from a predatory violent crime is far overshadowed by many other health risks.

It may be difficult, however, to break through entrenched views that crime is getting worse. Despite the sharp, sustained drop in crime for a quarter-century, more than 60 percent of Americans still report each year that crime is up from the previous year.[21] One likely cause of this disjunction is the distorted picture of crime created by the media, especially local television news. Research verifies the familiar adage, "If it bleeds it leads." Crime reporting dominates the local evening news, with violent crime being the particular favorite.[22] Other research indicates that the public mostly forms its opinions about crime from media coverage, and that exposure to stories about violent crime increases the fear of victimization.[23] Reformers might need to develop strategies to counter these tendencies. There may be some potential to disrupt the dynamics as traditional media are increasingly displaced by social media and other online resources. For instance, Web sites, blogs, Twitter, and the like can be used to disseminate more complete information about crime trends and to provide context for the disturbing crime stories that grab the headlines. Additionally, reformers might work to educate those who work in traditional media. As one group of researchers puts it, "Often the way the media handle a crime story is less a function of news values than of lack of familiarity with the criminal justice system; crime reports are seldom written by reporters who specialize in criminal justice. ... Media personnel are prone to the same misunderstandings about crime and punishment as the lay-person, and their reporting will reflect these misunderstandings."[24]

Second, the imprisonment boom also rested on a perception that criminals are mostly beyond rehabilitation, necessitating crude deter-rent threats and long-term incapacitation as the only workable public safety strategies. The post-2000 reforms pushed a more hopeful atti-tude toward the "nonviolent," but mostly left unchallenged harshly negative views of violent offenders. Further progress requires move-ment beyond the simplistic nonviolent/violent distinction.

For instance, reformers may focus on the decarceration of certain subcategories of offenders who most clearly do not fit the model of inherent depravity and dangerousness. Two obvious targets are the young and the old. The Supreme Court's decision in *Graham v. Florida*, barring life without parole (LWOP) for most juvenile offend-ers, establishes an appealing template for talking about youth crime. For a variety of good reasons, grounded in both science and common experience, it is appropriate to view juveniles as more amenable to rehabilitation than adults. Although the Supreme Court is unlikely to show bold leadership in enhancing the constitutional restrictions on juvenile sentencing, there may be greater potential for legislative re-form. As we saw in Chapter 7, for instance, California moved more swiftly to reform its juvenile than its adult sentencing. More generally, there has been a remarkable, if quiet, decarceration trend nationally for juveniles, with the number of delinquents committed to youth detention facilities dropping by more than half between 2001 and 2013.[25] This suggests a real openness in the political system to viewing juvenile offenders in more hopeful ways.

From the standpoint of decarceration in the adult system, the chal-lenge is to build on the current juvenile trends in two directions. First, reformers might seek greater restraint in the punishment of those juveniles committing the most serious crimes that typically lead to pros-ecution in adult court and imprisonment in adult institutions. For in-stance, the Supreme Court's decision in *Miller v. Alabama* prohibited mandatory LWOP even in cases of murder committed by juveniles. Legislatures could build on that by also prohibiting *discretionary*

LWOP and other very long sentences in juvenile homicide cases. Second, the category of young offenders treated in more rehabilitation-oriented ways could be extended above the traditional juvenile cut-off age of 18. The brain science relied on in *Graham* shows continuing maturation into the twenties. To some extent, our laws already reflect this reality, perhaps most visibly in the national drinking age of 21. Our criminal justice policies also ought to recognize the real differences between 20-year-old offenders and 30- or 40-year-old offenders. One thoughtful proposal, for instance, would raise the age of juvenile court jurisdiction to 21, with additional, diminishing protections for young defendants up to the age of about 25.[26]

Reformers might also focus on the old. As we saw in Chapter 3, most offenders age out of crime. Contrary to stereotypes about the inherent, permanent depravity of criminals, recidivism rates tend to be quite low for prisoners released in their fifties or later. This should support much stricter limitations on the use of life and multi-decade sentences. It might also support more robust forms of compassionate release for older prisoners. In practice, compassionate release programs tend to rely on the discretion of risk-averse corrections officials, which undermines their effectiveness. Release might instead be made presumptive for some prisoners, for instance, those over the age of 60 who have served at least five years.

Focusing attention on the distinctive characteristics of the young and the old might help reformers to break down the violent/nonviolent dichotomy and achieve greater decarceration of those convicted of violent crimes who nonetheless pose little ongoing threat to public safety. There is a risk, though, that a strategy of emphasizing the relatively lower dangerousness of certain subcategories of offenders may inadvertently reinforce perceptions that the rest continue to present an unacceptable threat. An alternative or supplemental strategy would be to emphasize progress that has been made in treating offenders more broadly. In the early years of the imprisonment boom, much publicized research cast doubt on the ability of correctional programming inside or outside prison to reduce recidivism rates. Since then, new treatment approaches have been developed, extensively studied, and refined over time. Cognitive-behavioral therapy, in particular, has proven its value, and seems capable of reducing recidivism rates by about 25 to 50 percent.[27] Better informing the public about such advances in rehabilitative treatment might help to undermine perceptions of generalized, inherent depravity.

Yet, a recidivism reduction of 25 to 50 percent still leaves quite a bit of repeat crime. For instance, studies find that about two-thirds of released prisoners are rearrested for a new crime within three years.[28] If that figure could be reduced to one-third, would that really make the public more willing to take a chance on earlier releases? Should it?

Thus far, we have considered *empirical* beliefs that helped to fuel the imprisonment boom—perceptions of reality relating to the risk of victimization, the likelihood that offenders will recidivate, and the effectiveness of rehabilitative programming. In some important respects, these empirical beliefs are either wrong or at least much exaggerated. In principle, it should be possible to correct misunderstandings of reality with a good dose of public education. However, these empirical beliefs are deeply intertwined with a set of *normative* beliefs—ideas about social values that defy objective proof or disproof. Again, we can see these normative beliefs exemplified by the Willie Horton ad. Most centrally, there are the complementary beliefs that the well-being of offenders should not matter to society and that penal policies should symbolically affirm the worth of victims over offenders. These beliefs establish a moral framework within which empirical information about crime and punishment is evaluated. For instance, research may establish that 60-year-old prisoners have only a 5 percent recidivism rate. Should they be released to community supervision as a matter of course? That becomes a hard case to make if we do not think their well-being matters at all, and if we see their release as an implicit repudiation of innocent victims. Viewed in that ethical light, the net fiscal benefits relative to the residual recidivism risk would have to be quite compelling indeed to justify release. Put differently, science can tell us what risk is presented by any given offender, but it cannot tell us how much risk is too much—that is a social value judgment.

It is difficult to imagine an end to mass incarceration without widespread, fundamental changes in the way that Americans make these sorts of value judgments. Troublingly, harsh views about the moral worth of offenders seem bound up with entrenched attitudes of racial resentment. Punitiveness may correlate with fear of crime, but research suggests that it may correlate even more powerfully with certain views of race, like the view that blacks just need to work harder in order to be as well off as whites.[29] Research also shows that Americans consistently overestimate the percentage of crime committed by blacks and Latinos, rate blacks and Latinos as more prone to violence than whites, and associate images of black people with guns and danger.[30] As two leading scholars put it, "when [many Americans] think about crime, the picture in their head illuminates a young, angry, black, inner-city male who offends with little remorse."[31]

Punitiveness also seems linked to feelings of economic insecurity, especially among white males.[32] It is possible that the pleasure that comes from the punishment of others may provide a sort of "compensatory satisfaction" for those who experience chronic frustration in other aspects of their lives.[33] (Neurological research shows that the imposition of punishment stimulates the reward centers of the brain.[34]) In any event, there has been no shortage of economic insecurity for most Americans, especially those without college degrees, over the past generation. The disappearance of well-paying manufacturing jobs from the United States and the related long-term growth in economic inequality may be contributing to the perpetuation of harshly negative attitudes toward offenders. It is probably no coincidence that the surprising success of law and order presidential candidate Donald Trump in 2016 was based on the support of working-class whites.

There is hope, but no certainty, of more empathetic attitudes toward offenders. For instance, to the extent that punitiveness is rooted in the racial resentments of many white voters, there is a possibility that the increasing diversity of the U.S. electorate may eventually help to marginalize those views. Also, in the wake of a 2016 presidential election in which both sides emphasized help for the working class, it is possible that new policies—or at least continued economic growth and low unemployment in the United States—will alleviate some of the economic insecurity that may contribute to punitiveness.

Savvy reformers may also be able to nudge the empathy-building process along by working to humanize offenders, as Justice Kennedy did so powerfully in *Brown*, the California overcrowding case. Or consider the role of the story of Gary Fannon, Jr., in drawing attention to the injustices of 650-Lifer in Michigan or the importance of the heart-rending experiences of cancer and AIDS patients in driving support for medical marijuana laws.

Most Americans form their impressions of offenders through the media, but news coverage of crime rarely contextualizes the offense. Viewers are left with little or no sense of who the perpetrators are, what led them to commit their crimes, and what happens to them in the criminal justice system. These can be compelling stories. As a law professor, I have often led groups of students into prisons, where they have had opportunities to speak with inmates and learn about their lives. Invariably, students express discomfort, even some fear, about these encounters beforehand, but afterward indicate surprise at how "normal" the offenders seemed. In the same spirit, President Obama reacted to his visit with federal prisoners at El Reno by expressing his sense that the mistakes they had made were not so terribly different from the mistakes that he and many others had made in their own lives. If offenders are themselves engaged in the reform process and given an opportunity to tell their stories, then it may be possible to mitigate the "othering" of offenders that is so prevalent in our media coverage and political discourse.

For many offenders, an important part of the story would be the effort they make to turn their lives around and become contributing members of society. Often, this includes support for other offenders, too. In July 2015, for instance, the *New York Times Magazine* included an extraordinary story of two former California inmates (both convicted of serious violent crimes) who regularly drive for hours to meet newly released prisoners who lack other sources of support. Carlos and Roby will "spend all day with the guy (so far they've picked up only men), taking him to eat, buying him some clothes, advising him, swapping stories, dialing his family on their cellphones or astonishing him by magically calling up Facebook pictures of nieces and nephews he's never met—or just sitting quietly, to let him depressurize."[35] In Milwaukee, a group called Table of the Saints, formed and led by ex-cons, hosts a weekly meeting for offenders reentering the community, providing them with a support network and referrals to social services. In Las Vegas, a former prisoner named Jon Ponder leads Hope for Prisoners, a nationally recognized nonprofit that links returning offenders with mentors who provide support for a year; at the end of that time, the ex-cons are then invited to undergo training to become mentors themselves.

In a federal prison in Pennsylvania, a client of mine, Adam Bentley Clausen, has worked with corrections officials to develop and run cutting-edge programs to help prepare his fellow inmates for reentry. Clausen himself presents a compelling story of redemption. Convicted at age 24 of a series of armed robberies and sentenced to 213 years in prison—effectively a life term—Clausen sought some way of using his time behind bars productively. He focused initially on physical fitness, studying the subject intensely and becoming a guru for other inmates on diet and exercise. Over time, he came to realize that he had real leadership abilities and could improve life in his institution in other ways, too. His prison has become a model for reentry preparation in the federal system, with Clausen playing a key role. Today, he dreams of gaining release through executive clemency and starting a nonprofit in Philadelphia to work with "returning citizens" (as he insists they be called).

Stories like Clausen's belie the stereotype of offenders as wholly self-centered. Notably, research indicates that punitive attitudes are correlated with the perception that offenders are lacking in "warmth" (kindness, good-naturedness, trustworthiness).[36]

Punitive attitudes may also be countered by involving offenders' families in reform efforts and telling their stories. In the overwhelming focus on the "offender versus victim" conflict, offenders' families have become almost invisible in the public conversation over sentencing policy. Yet, harsh sentences can have a devastating impact on innocent family members. Incarceration often entails a loss of income; thousands of dollars of court-related expenses for attorneys, fines, and fees; and the burden of maintaining contact with a family member held in a faraway institution. With most offenders coming from disadvantaged backgrounds, the economic costs alone not infrequently add up to a full year's worth of household income.[37] Incarceration also damages familial relationships, often hitting children the hardest. Contrary to common beliefs, parents who have committed crimes are not necessarily disinterested or ineffective parents. For instance, among incarcerated fathers, 42 percent lived with their children prior to their punishment, and many others had regular visitation.[38] Research establishes that the incarceration of a father is associated with increased aggression and delinquency and poorer grades among children.[39] Parental incarceration is also associated with depression, physical health problems including asthma and migraines, and a variety of long-term, later-in-life problems including lower incomes and higher rates of homelessness.[40] Conveying such family effects and experiences may cause sentencing policy to be seen in a different ethical light.

In encouraging the development of more positive, hopeful attitudes toward offenders, reformers may be able to draw on religiously based ideals and make common cause with faith-based organizations. Mercy, forgiveness, reconciliation, the existence of a spark of the divine in all people, the humble recognition that we are all sinners who should be slow to cast the first stone at others—these concepts find powerful expression in religious scripture and resonate with the deeply held beliefs of many Americans. To be sure, some conservative Christians helped to promote punitive attitudes in the late 20th century, drawing their inspiration from "eye for an eye" conceptions of justice that also find expression in scripture.[41] More recently, religiously inspired voices seem more prominent on the other side of policy debates. One high point was the enactment of the federal Second

Chance Act of 2007, which passed with the outspoken support of Christian groups like Prison Fellowship and the Salvation Army.[42] As we saw in Chapter 5, President George W. Bush's support of the law seemed connected to his own religious beliefs. Similarly, then-senator Sam Brownback of Kansas, another leading supporter, declared in a committee hearing that Americans must recognize "that every person is a beautiful, unique soul, a child of a living God, regardless of whether they are in prison or not."[43] Such views dictate a very different ethical framework for considering sentencing reform than the efficiency-based arguments that have seemed more common in recent years.

An important and uncertain question is whether reformers should emphasize racial justice as a central argument for decarceration. There can be no serious dispute that the burdens of mass incarceration have fallen disproportionately on communities of color and serve, inadvertently or otherwise, to reinforce long-standing patterns of disadvantage in U.S. society. Whatever implicit biases they may hold, most Americans seem at least superficially committed to the ideal of equal opportunity regardless of color. If mass incarceration were widely seen as racist, that would undoubtedly transform the ethical character of debates over sentencing policy. However, Americans have widely differing views about what constitutes racism, and it is not clear that most would accept the contention that current racial disparities in imprisonment are unjustified. An analogy may be drawn to debates over racial profiling by the police. Although there seems broad agreement that racial profiling is unacceptable, there are sharp disagreements over what actions constitute racial profiling.[44] Similarly, if reformers in the imprisonment context press racial disparity concerns, the public conversation may become bogged down in questions about whether disparities are warranted by different levels of crime commission. Additionally, disparity-based arguments may reinforce the unfortunate tendency of many Americans to think of the generic offender as dark-skinned.

One particularly constructive focal point for reformers might be changes in felon-disenfranchisement laws. Twelve states restrict the voting rights of offenders even after they have fully served their sentences, while an additional 22 states take away the ability of those on community supervision to vote.[45] Only two states, Vermont and Maine, permit prisoners to vote. In recent years, though, organizations like the Sentencing Project have pressed for liberalization. They had notable successes in 2016 in Maryland and Virginia.[46] Although enhancing offenders' voting rights does not directly produce any reduction in imprisonment, the effort to achieve such reform may be helpful in at least two respects. Most obviously, success means the addition of many new voters to the electorate who are unlikely to hold reflexively negative views about the moral worth of offenders. Perhaps more importantly, though, the public conversation surrounding felon disenfranchisement does not turn on the fiscal and recidivism-reduction considerations that have dominated sentencing reform debates in the treading water era, but instead focuses attention on more fundamental questions about what sort of political community we want to have, to what extent the commission of a serious crime should alter a person's status in the community, and whether it is tolerable to relegate a sizable share of our population to second-class citizenship on a permanent or near-permanent basis. In addition to felon enfranchisement, an array of other potential reforms may also help to affirm the ideal that we hope and expect offenders eventually to become regular, contributing members of society, including easier "expungement" of past convictions, the creation of official certificates of recovery or rehabilitation, and the prohibition of certain forms of discrimination based on criminal history. Such reforms are politically viable; by one count, 43 states changed their laws in these or similar ways between 2008 and 2014.[47]

In the effort to humanize offenders, Eighth Amendment litigation may play an especially important role. There are, to be sure, real limits on how far the courts will push the political system; large-scale decarceration is unlikely to happen through a courts-only strategy. There may be some worthwhile victories to be had through the courts, as in *Graham*, *Miller*, and *Brown*, but the greatest value of litigation may lie in its potential to mobilize prisoners and former prisoners, and to connect them with other activists and reform organizations. Additionally, litigation provides a public platform for telling offender stories, draws public attention to the worst aspects of tough-on-crime policies, and may help to validate a dignity-centered, as opposed to an efficiency-centered, discourse on sentencing policy.

Changing entrenched social attitudes may sound like an impossibly daunting task. However, a broad consensus in support of fundamentally new approaches is not necessary; a shift in the center of gravity of social attitudes may suffice. With two decades of slow, steady change already accomplished, a tipping point may be near.

None of this is to suggest that offenders should be given a free pass or even that the interests of offenders and their families should be given a greater weight than those of anyone else. Rather, the point is that these interests should be given *some* weight. When one's generic image of the criminal is a remorseless predator—especially when one comes from the dominant social group, and the generic criminal belongs to a racial or ethnic minority group—then it is all too easy to discount the needs and wishes of offenders entirely. However, if offenders are recognized as one of us—as fellow human beings, and, even more than that, as members of the same political community—then the costs and benefits of reform proposals must be evaluated differently. This change of ethical frame would establish a foundation for real decarceration and an end to the era of treading water.

Notes

Introduction

1. Figures are based on the year-end number of prisoners who have a sentence of one year or greater and who are under the jurisdiction of the federal government or a state government. These numbers are collected and reported annually by the Bureau of Justice Statistics of the U.S. Department of Justice, which also has a convenient online tool for data going back to 1978: http://www.bjs.gov/index.cfm?ty=nps. For older imprisonment data, see Bureau of Justice Statistics, *Prisoners 1925–1991* (Washington, DC: Government Printing Office, 1982), 2. In this book, I will use the terms "imprisonment" and "incarceration" slightly differently. "Incarceration" is the broader term, including not only those offenders serving time in the state and federal penal institutions, but also those being held in local jails, generally for much shorter periods of time.

2. Michael M. O'Hear, "The New Politics of Sentencing," *Federal Sentencing Reporter* 15, no. 1 (2002): 3.

3. Michael M. O'Hear, "Beyond Rehabilitation: A New Theory of Indeterminate Sentencing," *American Criminal Law Review* 48, no. 3 (2011): 1248.

4. See, for example, Nancy LaVigne et al., *Justice Reinvestment Initiative State Assessment Report* (Washington, DC: Urban Institute, 2014).

5. The national prison population dropped by 46,757 from year-end 2008 to year-end 2014, while California's dropped by 37,582.

6. "Reported violent crime" refers to the reported rates of the violent "index" crimes: nonnegligent homicide, rape, robbery, and aggravated assault. These figures are collected and reported annually by the Federal Bureau of Investigation, which now makes the data available through a convenient online tool at http://www.ucrdatatool.gov/index.cfm. For an explanation of imprisonment figures, see note 1 above.

7. More sophisticated multivariate regression analysis of U.S. crime and imprisonment data indicates that increased imprisonment can reduce crime if the starting point is a very low imprisonment rate, but that further imprisonment has diminishing marginal returns. Thus, it appears that U.S. imprisonment increases in the 1970s may have had a beneficial effect in restraining crime increases, but further imprisonment increases after 1980 had reduced benefits. "Since approximately 1990, the effectiveness of increased incarceration on bringing down crime has been essentially zero." Oliver Roeder, Lauren-Brooke Eisen, and Julia Bowling, *What Caused the Crime Decline?* (New York: Brennan Center for Justice at New York University School of Law, 2015), 23.

8. The issues are thoroughly covered in a recent report issued by the National Research Council of the National Academy of Science. Committee on Causes and Consequences of High Rates of Incarceration, *The Growth of Incarceration in the United States: Exploring Causes and Consequences* (Washington, DC: National Academies Press, 2014).

9. Ibid., 314–315.

10. Ibid., 92.

11. Ibid., 36.

12. Ibid., 155–156.

13. Ibid., 221–227, 247.

14. Ibid., 156.

15. Ibid., 279.

16. Faye S. Taxman, April Pattavina, and Michael Caudy, "Justice Reinvestment in the United States: An Empirical Assessment of the Potential Impact of Increased Correctional Programming on Recidivism," *Victims and Offenders* 9 (2014): 55.

Chapter 1

1. Francis X. Clines, "For No. 83-A-6607, Added Years for .35 Ounces; 20 Years after Law Mandating Prison Terms, Few of Targeted Kingpins Fill Cells," *New York Times*, March 23, 1993, http://www.nytimes.com/1993/03/23/nyregion/for-no-83-6607-added-years-for-.35-ounces-20-years-after-law-mandating-prison.html.

2. Lisa R. Nakdai, "Are New York's Rockefeller Drug Laws Killing the Messenger for the Sake of the Message?" *Hofstra Law Review* 30 (2001): 574.

3. McMillan v. Pennsylvania, 477 US 79, 81 (1986); Justin Brooks, "The Politics of Prisons," *Michigan Bar Journal* 77 (1998): 155.

4. National Criminal Justice Association, *A Guide to State Controlled Substances Acts* (Washington, DC: National Criminal Justice Association, 1999).

5. 1993 Wis. Act 97, §§14–15 (1994).

6. 1993 Wis. Act 98, §137m (1994).

7. Franklin E. Zimring, Gordon Hawkins, and Sam Kamin, *Punishment and Democracy: Three Strikes and You Are Out in California* (New York: Oxford University Press, 2001), 4.

8. Daniel W. Stiller, "Initiative 593: Washington's Voters Go Down Swinging," *Gonzaga Law Review* 30 (1995): 434.

9. Zimring, Hawkins, and Kamin, *Punishment and Democracy*, ix.

10. David Mills and Michael Romano, "The Passage and Implementation of the Three Strikes Reform Act of 2012 (Proposition 36)," *Federal Sentencing Reporter* 25 (2013): 265.

11. United States Sentencing Commission, *Fifteen Years of Guidelines Sentencing: An Assessment of How Well the Federal Criminal Justice System Is Achieving the Goals of Sentencing Reform* (Washington, DC: Government Printing Office, 2004), 46.

12. William Spelman, "Crime, Cash, and Limited Options: Explaining the Prison Boom," *Criminology & Public Policy* 8 (2009): 57.

13. Michael Tonry, "Sentencing in America, 1975–2025," *Crime and Justice* 42 (2013): 155.

14. Joan Petersilia, "Parole and Prisoner Reentry in the United States," in *Prisons*, ed. Michael Tonry and Joan Petersilia (Chicago: University of Chicago Press, 1999), 496.

15. Ashley Nellis, *Life Goes On: The Historic Rise of Life Sentences in America* (Washington, DC: The Sentencing Project, 2013), 3.

16. Ashley Nellis, "Throwing Away the Key: The Expansion of Life without Parole Sentences in the United States," *Federal Sentencing Reporter* 23 (2010): 28.

17. Nellis, *Life Goes On*, 13.

18. Matt Taibbi, "Cruel and Unusual Punishment: The Shame of Three Strikes Laws," *Rolling Stone*, March 27, 2013, http://www.rollingstone.com/politics/news/cruel-and-unusual-punishment-the-shame-of-three-strikes-laws-20130327.

19. Walter Dickey and Pam Stiebs Hollenhorst, *Three Strikes Laws: Five Years Later* (Washington, DC: Center for Effective Public Policy, 1998), 4–5.

20. Spelman, "Crime, Cash, and Limited Options," 57, 59.

21. Aaron D. Wilson, *Rockefeller Drug Laws Information Sheet* (New York: Partnership for Responsible Drug Information, 2000), http://www.prdi.org/rocklawfact.html.

22. Al Baker, "Time Eases Tough Drug Laws, but Fight Goes On," *New York Times*, April 16, 2004, http://www.nytimes.com/2004/04/16/nyregion/time-eases-tough-drug-laws-but-fight-goes-on.html.

23. Marie Gottschalk, "Sentenced to Life: Penal Reform and the Most Severe Sanctions," *Annual Review of Law and Social Sciences* 9 (2013): 361, n. 7.

24. United States Sentencing Commission, *Report to Congress: Mandatory Minimum Penalties in the Federal Criminal Justice System* (Washington, DC: Government Printing Office, 2011), xxix.

25. Spelman, "Crime, Cash, and Limited Options," 57, 59.

26. Kevin R. Reitz, "Don't Blame Determinacy: U.S. Incarceration Growth Has Been Driven by Other Forces," *Texas Law Review* 84 (2006): 1795–1799.

27. Nellis, *Life Goes On*, 1.

28. Wisconsin Sentencing Commission, *All Drug Offenses Committed on or after January 31, 1990, to June 30, 1992 and Sentenced after January 31, 1990 to June 30, 1992* (Madison, WI: Wisconsin Sentencing Commission, 1992), 5.

29. John F. Pfaff, "The Micro and Macro Causes of Prison Growth," *Georgia State University Law Review* 28 (2012): 1239.

30. Michael Tonry, *Thinking about Crime: Sense and Sensibility in American Penal Culture* (New York: Oxford University Press, 2004), 37.

31. United States Department of Justice, Bureau of Justice Statistics, *Felony Defendants in Large Urban Counties, 2000* (Washington, DC: Government Printing Office, 2003); United States Department of Justice, Bureau of Justice Statistics, *Felony Defendants in Large Urban Counties, 1990* (Washington, DC: Government Printing Office, 1993).

32. Quite the contrary, the data point to some consistency in the criminal history of murderers: in 1990, 68 percent of the murder defendants had a prior arrest, while in 2000 the figure was nearly identical at 67 percent.

33. David C. Anderson, *Crime and the Politics of Hysteria* (New York: Random House, 1995), 91, 108–110.

34. Ibid., 231.

35. Kathleen Hall Jamieson, *Dirty Politics: Deception, Distraction, and Democracy* (New York: Oxford University Press, 1992), 17.

36. Anderson, *Crime and the Politics of Hysteria*, 233.

37. Ibid.

38. Michael O'Hear, *Wisconsin Sentencing in the Tough-on-Crime Era: How Judges Kept Power and Why Mass Incarceration Happened Anyway* (Madison, WI: University of Wisconsin Press, 2017).

39. John J. Donohue III and Justin Wolfers, "Uses and Abuses of Empirical Evidence in the Death Penalty Debate," *Stanford Law Review* 58 (2005): 791.

40. President's Commission on Law Enforcement and Administration of Justice, *The Challenge of Crime in a Free Society* (Washington, DC: Government Printing Office, 1967), 3–6.

41. Ibid., 14.

42. Ibid., 17.

43. Ibid., 6.

44. Michelle Alexander, *The New Jim Crow: Mass Incarceration in the Age of Colorblindness* (New York: New Press, 2012).

45. Michael M. O'Hear, "Punishment, Democracy, and Victims," *Federal Sentencing Reporter* 19, no. 1 (2006): 1–2.

46. David Garland, *The Culture of Control: Crime and Social Order in Contemporary Society* (Chicago: University of Chicago Press, 2001).

Chapter 2

1. Marc Mauer, *Race to Incarcerate* (New York: New Press, 2006), 21–23.

2. Michael Javen Fortner, *Black Silent Majority: The Rockefeller Drug Laws and the Politics of Punishment* (Cambridge, MA: Harvard University Press, 2015).

3. Michael Javen Fortner, "The Real Roots of '70s Drug Laws," *New York Times*, September 28, 2015, http://www.nytimes.com/2015/09/28/opinion/the-real-roots-of-70s-drug-laws.html. However, some historians believe that Fortner has overstated the extent to which urban blacks were committed to a tough-on-crime agenda. Khalil Gibran Muhammad, " 'Black Silent Majority,' by Michael Javen Fortner," *New York Times*, September 21, 2015, http://www.nytimes.com/2015/09/27/books/review/black-silent-majority-by-michael-javen-fortner.html.

4. William J. Stuntz, *The Collapse of American Criminal Justice* (Cambridge, MA: Harvard University Press, 2011), 267–274.

5. Ted Gest, *Crime & Politics: Big Government's Erratic Campaign for Law and Order* (New York: Oxford University Press, 2001), 110.

6. Harmelin v. Michigan, 501 U.S. 957 (1991).

7. David F. Musto, ed., *Drugs in America: A Documentary History* (New York: NYU Press, 2002), 276–277.

8. U.S. Department of Justice, Bureau of Justice Statistics, *Felony Defendants in Large Urban Counties, 2000* (Washington, DC: Government Printing Office, 2003), 30, 32.

9. Allen J. Beck and Paige M. Harrison, *Prisoners in 2000* (Washington, DC: Government Printing Office, 2001), 11.

10. John S. Goldkamp, "The Origin of the Drug Treatment Court in Miami," in *The Early Drug Courts: Case Studies in Judicial Innovation*, ed. W. Clinton Terry, III (Thousand Oaks, CA: Sage Publications, 1999).

11. Ibid., 22.

12. Ibid., 37.

13. Ibid., 22.

14. Michael M. O'Hear, "Federalism and Drug Control," *Vanderbilt Law Review* 57 (2004): 825.

15. U.S. Department of Justice, Office of Justice Programs, *Drug Courts* (2015), https://www.ncjrs.gov/pdffiles1/nij/238527.pdf.

16. U.S. Department of Justice, Bureau of Justice Assistance, *Defining Drug Courts: The Key Components* (Washington DC: Bureau of Justice Assistance, 2004).

17. Michael M. O'Hear, "Drug Treatment Courts as Communicative Punishment," in *Retributivism Has a Past, Has It a Future?*, ed. Michael Tonry (New York: Oxford University Press, 2011), 237–238.

18. http://www.nadcp.org/learn/do-drug-courts-work.

19. Data in this paragraph reflect combined federal and state totals. Allen J. Beck and Darrell K. Gilliard, *Prisoners in 1994* (Washington, DC: Bureau of Justice Statistics, 1995), 10–11.

20. West Huddleston and Douglas B. Marlowe, *Painting the Picture: A National Report on Drug Courts and Other Problem-Solving Court Programs in the United States* (Alexandria, VA: National Drug Court Institute, 2011), 6.

21. Heather C. West, William J. Sabol, and Sarah J. Greenman, *Prisoners in 2009* (Washington, DC: Bureau of Justice Statistics, 2010), 29; E. Ann Carson, *Prisoners in 2013* (Washington, DC: Bureau of Justice Statistics, 2014), 17.

22. Kit R. Van Stelle, Janae Goodrich, and Stephanie Kroll, *Treatment Alternatives and Diversion (TAD) Program: Participant Outcome Evaluation and Cost-Benefit Report* (Madison, WI: University of Wisconsin Population Health Institute, 2014), 5.

23. This number is calculated from the biannual information papers on adult corrections that are produced by the Wisconsin Legislative Fiscal Bureau.

24. 42 U.S.C. § 3797u-1.

25. 42 U.S.C. § 3797u-2(a)(1).

26. 42 U.S.C. § 3797u-2(a)(2).

27. National Association of Criminal Defense Lawyers, *America's Problem-Solving Courts: The Criminal Costs of Treatment and the Case for Reform* (Washington, DC: National Association of Criminal Defense Lawyers, 2009), 22. In general, "misdemeanors" are defined as crimes involving a maximum punishment of one year or less of incarceration, a length of time that would normally be served in a local jail, rather than a state prison.

28. National Association of Criminal Defense Lawyers, *America's Problem-Solving Courts*, 22.

29. Eric L. Sevigny, Harold A. Pollack, and Peter Reuter, "Can Drug Courts Help to Reduce Prison and Jail Populations?" *Annals of the American Academy of Political and Social Science* 647 (2013): 203.

30. Ibid., 206–207.

31. National Association of Criminal Defense Lawyers, *America's Problem-Solving Courts*, 22.

32. Jimmy Steyee, *Program Performance Report: Implementation Grantees of the Adult Drug Court Discretionary Grant Program, October 2012–March 2013* (Washington, DC: Bureau of Justice Assistance, 2013), 4.

33. Ibid., 3.

34. Sevigny, Pollack, and Reuter, "Can Drug Courts Help to Reduce Prison and Jail Populations?" 194.

35. Steyee, *Program Performance Report,* 12–17.

36. Sevigny, Pollack, and Reuter, "Can Drug Courts Help to Reduce Prison and Jail Populations?" 204.

37. Steyee, *Program Performance Report,* 5.

38. Terance D. Miethe, Hong Lu, and Erin Reese, "Reintegrative Shaming and Recidivism Risks in Drug Court: Explanations for Some Unexpected Findings," *Crime & Delinquency* 46 (2000): 536.

39. U.S. Department of Justice, Bureau of Justice Assistance, *Defining Drug Courts,* 11.

40. Michael M. O'Hear, "Rethinking Drug Courts: Restorative Justice as a Response to Racial Injustice," *Stanford Law & Policy Review* 20 (2009): 480–481.

41. Steyee, *Program Performance Report,* 7.

42. O'Hear, "Rethinking Drug Courts," 480; Steyee, *Program Performance Report,* 6.

43. O'Hear, "Rethinking Drug Courts," 481.

44. Mark R. Fondacaro and Megan J. O'Toole, "American Punitiveness and Mass Incarceration: Psychological Perspectives on Retributive and Consequentialist Responses to Crime," *New Criminal Law Review* 18, no. 4 (2015): 500.

45. Edward J. Latessa and Angela K. Reitler, "What Works in Reducing Recidivism and How Does It Relate to Drug Courts?," *Ohio Northern University Law Review* 41 (2015): 767–775.

46. Ibid., 779.

47. Ibid., 776–778.

48. Morris B. Hoffman, "The Denver Drug Court and Its Unintended Consequences," in *Drug Courts in Theory and Practice,* ed. James L. Nolan, Jr. (New York: Aldine de Gruyter, 2002), 70–71.

49. Latessa and Reitler, "What Works in Reducing Recidivism," 759.

50. Hoffman, "The Denver Drug Court," 76.

51. Princeton Survey Research Associates International, *The NSCS Sentencing Attitudes Survey: A Report on the Findings* (Williamsburg, VA: National Center for State Courts, 2006), 13.

52. Curtis J. VanderWaal et al., "State Drug Policy Reform Movement: The Use of Ballot Initiatives and Legislation to Promote Diversion to Drug Treatment," *Journal of Drug Issues* 36 (2006): 621.

53. Cal. Penal Code §§ 1210, 1210.1.

54. Gerald F. Uelmen and Alex Kreit, "Sentencing Alternatives," in *Drug Abuse and the Law Sourcebook,* ed. Uelmen and Haddox (Eagan, MN: Thomson Reuters 2015), § 14.6.

55. Michael M. O'Hear, "When Voters Choose the Sentence: The Drug Policy Initiatives in Arizona, California, Ohio, and Michigan," *Federal Sentencing Reporter* 14 (2002): 337.

56. Alex Ricciardulli, "Getting to the Roots of Judges' Opposition to Drug Treatment Initiatives," *Whittier Law Review* 25 (2003): 356.

57. Ibid., 355–356.

58. Ibid., 358–359.

59. Andrea Lofgren, "A Sign of Things to Come? Drug Policy Reforms in Arizona, California, and New York," *NYU Journal of Legislation and Public Policy* 14 (2011): 789–790.

60. VanderWaal et al., "State Drug Policy Reform Movement," 624.

61. Ibid., 625.

62. Ibid., 631.

63. Ibid., 635.

64. Gardner v. Schwarzenegger, 178 Cal. App. 4th 1366 (2009).

65. "2008 California Criminal Law Ballot Initiatives," *Berkeley Journal of Criminal Law* 14 (2009): 173.

66. Elizabeth Evans et al., "Comparative Effectiveness of California's Proposition 36 and Drug Court Programs before and after Propensity Score Matching," *Crime & Delinquency* 60 (2014): 909.

67. Scott Ehlers and Jason Ziedenberg, *Proposition 36: Five Years Later* (Washington, DC: Justice Policy Institute, 2006).

68. Cal. Penal Code § 1210.1(b).

69. Christine Gardiner, " 'An Absolute Revolving Door': An Evaluation of Police Perception and Response to Proposition 36," *Criminal Justice Policy Review* 23 (2011): 279.

70. Uelmen and Kreit, "Sentencing Alternatives," § 14.6; Gardiner, " 'An Absolute Revolving Door,' " 287.

71. People v. Canty, 32 Cal. 4th 1266 (2004).

72. Uelmen and Kreit, "Sentencing Alternatives," § 14.6.

73. Uelmen and Kreit, "Sentencing Alternatives," § 14.6; Darren Urada et al., *Evaluation of Proposition 36: The Substance Abuse and Crime Prevention Act of 2000, 2009 Report* (Los Angeles: University Of California, Los Angeles Integrated Substance Abuse Programs, 2009): Chapter 2, http://www.uclaisap.org/Prop36/documents/2009%20SACPA%20Report%20Final%2011242009.pdf.

74. Urada et al., *Evaluation of Proposition 36*, 19.

75. Ibid., 19.

76. Evans et al., "Comparative Effectiveness of California's Proposition 36 and Drug Court Programs."

77. Uelmen and Kreit, "Sentencing Alternatives," § 14.6.

78. Urada et al., *Evaluation of Proposition 36*, 296.

79. Gardiner, " 'An Absolute Revolving Door,' " 290.

80. Ram Subramanian and Ruth Delaney, *Playbook for Change? States Reconsider Mandatory Sentences* (New York: Vera Institute of Justice, 2014).

81. Ibid., 13.

82. Mike Sager, "The Case of Gary Fannon," *Rolling Stone*, September 3, 1992, http://www.maryellenmark.com/text/magazines/rolling%20stone/920S-000-007.html.

83. Laura Sager, "Advocating for Change in Mandatory Minimum Sentencing," *Thomas M. Cooley Law Review* 16 (1999): 33.

84. Gary Fannon Jr., "I Am Free," *Rolling Stone*, September 19, 1996, http://www.maryellenmark.com/text/magazines/rolling%20stone/920S-000-013.html.

85. Avis Thomas-Lester, "Brother's Drug Sentence Ignited Woman's Crusade," *Washington Post*, November 20, 2007, http://www.washingtonpost.com/wp-dyn/content/article/2007/11/19/AR2007111901698.html.

86. Sager, "Advocating for Change in Mandatory Minimum Sentencing," 34.

87. Ibid., 29.

88. Ibid., 32.

89. Justin Brooks, "The Politics of Prisons," *Michigan Bar Journal* 77 (1998): 156.

90. Ibid., 157.

91. Elizabeth Alexander, *Michigan Breaks the Political Logjam: A New Model for Reducing Prison Populations* (New York: American Civil Liberties Union, 2009), 7.

92. Vincent Schiraldi, "Digging Out: As U.S. States Begin to Reduce Prison Use, Can America Turn the Corner on Its Imprisonment Binge," *Pace Law Review* 24 (2004): 571.

93. Ann Frost, "The Politics of Punishment in the War on Drugs: Race and Racial Language in Policy Shifts" (PhD diss., University of Washington, 2014), 185.

94. Families against Mandatory Minimums, *FAMM's Guide to the Michigan Sentencing Reforms* (Washington, DC: Families against Mandatory Minimums, 2003).

95. Sue Stutzky, *Eliminate Mandatory Minimums for Drug Sentences* (Lansing, MI: House Fiscal Agency, 2002).

96. Patrick Affholter and Bethany Wicksall, *Eliminating Michigan's Mandatory Minimum Sentences for Drug Offenses* (Lansing, MI: Senate Fiscal Agency, 2002), 6.

97. Stutzky, *Eliminate Mandatory Minimums for Drug Sentences*, 9.

98. Judith Greene and Marc Mauer, *Downscaling Prisons: Lessons from Four States* (Washington, DC: Sentencing Project, 2010), 31.

99. Ibid., 30.

100. Alexander, *Michigan Breaks the Political Logjam*, 11.

101. Al Baker, "Time Eases Tough Drug Laws, But Fight Goes On," *New York Times*, April 16, 2004.

102. Aaron D. Wilson, *Rockefeller Drug Laws Information Sheet* (New York: Partnership for Responsible Drug Information, 2000), 2.

103. Greene and Mauer, *Downscaling Prisons*, 32.

104. Beck and Harrison, *Prisoners in 2000*, 11.

105. Wilson, *Rockefeller Drug Laws Information Sheet*, 2.

106. Jim Parsons et al., *End of an Era? The Impact of Drug Law Reform in New York City* (New York: Vera Institute of Justice, 2015), 5, http://www.vera.org/sites/default/files/resources/downloads/drug-law-reform-new-york-city-summary-01.pdf.

107. Greene and Mauer, *Downscaling Prisons*, 9.

108. Ibid., 8.

109. Ibid., 9.

110. Ibid., 16–17.

111. Ibid., 17–18.

112. Ibid., 18.

113. Parsons et al., *End of an Era?*, 7.

114. Greene and Mauer, *Downscaling Prisons*, 25.

115. Leslie Kellam and Leigh Bates, *2009 Drug Law Changes: 2014 Update* (Albany, NY: New York Division of Criminal Justice Services, 2014), 5, http://www.criminaljustice.ny.gov/drug-law-reform/documents/dlr-update-report-may-2014.pdf.

116. The data come from Kellam and Bates, *2009 Drug Law Changes: 2014 Update*, 5.

117. Greene and Mauer, *Downscaling Prisons*, 8; Kellam and Bates, *2009 Drug Law Changes: 2014 Update*, 7.

118. Kellam and Bates, *2009 Drug Law Changes: 2014 Update*, 14.

119. Ibid., 12.

120. Parsons et al., *End of an Era?*, 16.

121. National Conference of State Legislatures, *State Medical Marijuana Laws*, http://www.ncsl.org/research/health/state-medical-marijuana-laws.aspx.

122. O'Hear, "Federalism and Drug Control," 830–831; Drug Policy Alliance, *Our Victories*, http://www.drugpolicy.org/our-victories.

123. Michael Vitiello, "Proposition 215: De Facto Decriminalization of Pot and the Shortcomings of Direct Democracy," *University of Michigan Journal of Law Reform* 31 (1998): 715.

124. Ibid., 717.

125. "State Medical Marijuana Laws," National Conference of State Legislatures, http://www.ncsl.org/research/health/state-medical-marijuana-laws.aspx.

126. Jonathan P. Caulkins et al., *Considering Marijuana Legalization: Insights for Vermont and Other Jurisdictions* (Santa Monica, CA: RAND Corporation, 2015), 2.

127. Ibid., 1.

128. O'Hear, "Federalism and Drug Control," 836.

129. Pew Research Center, *In Debate over Legalizing Marijuana, Disagreement over Drug's Dangers* (Washington, DC: Pew Research Center, 2015), http://www.people-press.org/2015/04/14/in-debate-over-legalizing-marijuana-disagreement-over-drugs-dangers/.

130. Seth Motel, "Six Facts about Marijuana," *Fact Tank* (blog), *Pew Research Center,* April 14, 2015, http://www.pewresearch.org/fact-tank/2015/04/14/6-facts-about-marijuana/.

131. Ibid.

132. Caulkins et al., *Considering Marijuana Legalization,* 3.

133. Ibid.

134. Motel, "Six Facts about Marijuana."

135. Washington Office of Secretary of State, *2012 General Election Voters' Guide,* https://wei.sos.wa.gov/agency/osos/en/press_and_research/PreviousElections/2012/General-Election/Pages/Online-Voters-Guide.aspx.

136. Jonathan P. Caulkins, et al., *Marijuana Legalization: What Everyone Needs to Know* (New York: Oxford University Press, 2012), 50.

137. Ryan S. King and Marc Mauer, *The War on Marijuana: The Transformation of the War on Drugs in the 1990s* (Washington, DC: Sentencing Project, 2005), 27.

138. Data come from the annual *Prisoners* reports by the U.S. Bureau of Justice Statistics.

139. *Results from the 2014 National Survey on Drug Use and Health: Detailed Tables* (Rockville, MD: Substance Abuse and Mental Health Services Administration, 2015), Table 7.15B.

140. Franklin E. Zimring, *The City That Became Safe: New York's Lessons for Urban Crime and Its Control* (New York: Oxford University Press, 2012), 114.

141. Greene and Mauer, *Downsizing Prisons,* 8–9.

142. Zimring, *City That Became Safe,* 99.

143. Ibid., 116.

Chapter 3

1. William Spelman, "Crime, Cash, and Limited Options: Explaining the Prison Boom," *Criminology & Public Policy* 8 (2009): 57, 59.

2. Jesse J. Norris, "The Earned Release Revolution: Early Assessments and State-Level Strategies," *Marquette Law Review* 95 (2012): 1583, n. 149.

3. Tina Maschi, Alexandra Kalmanofsky, Kimberly Westcott, and Lauren Pappacena, *An Analysis of United States Compassionate and Geriatric Release Laws: Towards a Rights-Based Response for Diverse Elders and Their Families and Communities* (New York: Fordham University Be the Evidence Press, 2015), 6, https://www.researchgate.net/publication/275652571_An_Analysis_of_United_States_Compassionate_and_Geriatric_Release_Laws_Towards_a_Rights-Based_Response_for_Diverse_Elders_and_Their_Families_and_Communities 2/14/16.

4. Ibid., 6, 8, 14–18.

5. American Civil Liberties Union, *At America's Expense: The Mass Incarceration of the Elderly* (New York: American Civil Liberties Union, 2012), i.

6. Ibid., ii.

7. Ibid., 28.

8. Ron Hillerman, "Older Prisoners: Is There Life after "Life" Sentencing? A White Paper," in *Policy and Program Planning for Older Adults*, ed. Elaine Theresa Jurkowski (New York: Springer, 2007), quoted in Nicole M. Murphy, "Dying to Be Free: An Analysis of Wisconsin's Restructured Compassionate Release Statute," *Marquette Law Review 95* (2012): 1693.

9. American Civil Liberties Union, *At America's Expense*, 22.

10. Ibid., 23–24.

11. Murphy, "Dying to Be Free," 1697.

12. Ibid., 1701.

13. Michael O'Hear and Darren Wheelock, "Imprisonment Inertia and Public Attitudes toward 'Truth in Sentencing,' " *Brigham Young University Law Review* (2015): 271–272.

14. Murphy, "Dying to Be Free," 1706.

15. Michael O'Hear, *Wisconsin Sentencing in the Tough-on-Crime Era: How Judges Retained Power and Why Mass Incarceration Happened Anyway* (Madison, WI: University of Wisconsin Press, 2017), chapter 7.

16. Ibid.

17. Rachael Bedard, "When Dying Alone in Prison Is Too Harsh a Sentence," *New York Times*, December 28, 2015.

18. Jeffrey Benzing, "Prison Release Rarely an Option for Dying State Inmates," *PublicSource*, June 14, 2015, http://publicsource.org/investigations/prison-release-rarely-option-for-dying-state-inmates#.VubeH_krIdU.

19. Louis Hansen, "Uncommon Freedom: Geriatric Release from Prison Rare," *The Virginian-Pilot*, December 28, 2013, http://pilotonline.com/news/local/crime/uncommon-freedom-geriatric-release-from-prison-rare/article_e41dd00b-bfb9-5478-9e1c-ff77f84ad732.html.

20. Maschi et al., *Analysis of United States Compassionate and Geriatric Release Laws*.

21. Michael M. O'Hear, "Good Conduct Time for Prisoners: Why (and How) Wisconsin Should Provide Credits toward Early Release," *Marquette Law Review* 98, no. 1 (2014): 493.

22. Ibid., 495.

23. Michael M. O'Hear, "Beyond Rehabilitation: A New Theory of Indeterminate Sentencing," *American Criminal Law Review* 48, no. 3 (2011): 1288–1292. I include in this number states that adopted "earned-time" programs, which are explained later in the text.

24. O'Hear, "Good Conduct Time," 538–542.

25. Dan Bernstein and E. Michele Staley, *Merit Time Program Summary: October 1997–December 2006* (Albany, NY: New York Department of Corrections Services, 2007), 1.

26. Ibid., 15.

27. Ibid., iii.

28. Ibid., i.

29. Ibid., 25.

30. O'Hear, "Good Conduct Time," 534.

31. Malcolm C. Young, *White Paper: Good Conduct Credit in Illinois* (2012), 1–2, http://perma.cc/M2TR-WXUJ.

32. Ibid., 2.

33. Ibid., 3.

34. Ibid., 4.

35. Patrick Yeagle, "Illinois Starts Giving Prison Inmates Release Credits: IDOC Adopts Reformed Program to Lower Prison Population," *Illinois Times*, February 28, 2013, http://illinoistimes.com/article-11086-illinois-starts-giving-prison-inmates-release-credits.html, *archived at* http://perma.cc/U32Q-A362.

36. O'Hear, "Good Conduct Time," 536.

37. E. K. Drake, R. Barnoski, and S. Aos, *Increased Earned Release from Prison: Impacts of a 2003 Law in Recidivism and Crime Costs, Revised* (Olympia, WA: Washington State Institute for Public Policy, 2009).

38. O'Hear, "Good Conduct Time," 505–507.

39. I develop an ethical argument along these lines in much more depth in Michael M. O'Hear, "Solving the Good-Time Puzzle: Why Following the Rules Should Get You out of Prison Early," *Wisconsin Law Review* (2012): 195–236.

40. Peggy B. Burke, "The Future of Sentencing: Parole Discretion and Risk Reduction," *Federal Sentencing Reporter* 28, no. 2 (2015): 88.

41. Marc Mauer, "State Sentencing Reforms: Is the 'Get-Tough' Era Coming to a Close?" *Federal Sentencing Reform* 15, no. 1 (2002): 50.

42. O'Hear, "Beyond Rehabilitation," 1288–1292. I exclude from this number those states whose only parole reforms were in the area of compassionate release.

43. Joel M. Caplan, "What Factors Affect Parole," *Federal Probation* 71 (June 2007): 17.

44. Judith Greene and Marc Mauer, *Downscaling Prisons: Lessons from Four States* (Washington, DC: Sentencing Project, 2010), 42–43.

45. Hawker v. Consovoy, 198 F.R.D. 619 (D.N.J. 2001).

46. Greene and Mauer, *Downscaling Prisons*, 43.

47. Hawker v. Consovoy, 198 F.R.D. at 630.

48. New Jersey State Parole Board, *Annual Report 2003* (Trenton: New Jersey State Parole Board, 2004), 15.

49. Beth Schwartzapfel, "Parole Boards: Problems and Promise," *Federal Sentencing Reporter* 28, no. 2 (2015): 82–83.

50. Ibid., 83.

51. Barbara Hanson Treen, *Geranium Justice: The Other Side of the Table* (Portsmouth, NH: RiverRun Bookstore, 2014), 150, quoted in Schwartzapfel, "Parole Boards," 80–81.

52. Schwartzapfel, "Parole Boards," 81.

53. Ibid.

54. Emily Lawler, "Michigan Criminal Justice Reforms, Shelved in 2015, Are on the Radar for First Half of Next Year," MLive.com, December 28, 2015.

55. Gus Burns, "AG Bill Schuette Rallies against Parole Reform, Proposes More Privatization," MLive.com, October 12, 2015.

56. James Q. Whitman, *Harsh Justice: Criminal Punishment and the Widening Divide between America and Europe* (New York: Oxford University Press, 2003), 8.

57. Ram Subramanian and Alison Shames, *Sentencing and Prison Practices in Germany and the Netherlands: Implications for the United States* (New York: Vera Institute of Justice, 2013), 7.

Chapter 4

1. See Table 4.1.

2. Jennifer Gonnerman, "Million-Dollar Blocks," *Village Voice*, November 9, 2004, http://www.villagevoice.com/news/million-dollar-blocks-6398537.

3. "About Us," Justice Mapping Center, http://www.justicemapping.org/about-us/.

4. Susan B. Tucker and Eric Cadora, *Justice Reinvestment: To Invest in Public Safety by Reallocating Justice Dollars to Refinance Education, Housing, Healthcare, and Jobs* (New York: Open Society Institute, 2003), https://www.opensocietyfoundations.org/sites/default/files/ideas_reinvestment.pdf.

5. Gonnerman, "Million-Dollar Blocks."

6. Ibid.

7. Council of State Governments Justice Center, *Joint Informational Hearing, Judiciary and Appropriations Committees*, April 22, 2014, https://csgjusticecenter.org/wp-content/uploads/2014/04/CT-Justice-Reinvestment -Informational.pdf.

8. James Austin et al., *Ending Mass Incarceration: Charting a New Justice Reinvestment* (2013), 6, http://sentencingproject.org/wp-content/ uploads/2015/12/Ending-Mass-Incarceration-Charting-a-New-Justice -Reinvestment.pdf.

9. Public Opinion Strategies and Benenson Strategy Group, *National Research of Public Attitudes on Crime and Punishment* (Philadelphia: Pew Center on the States, 2010), 3.

10. Nancy LaVigne et al., *Justice Reinvestment Initiative State Assessment Report* (Washington, DC: Urban Institute, 2014), 6.

11. Ibid.

12. Todd R. Clear, "A Private-Sector, Incentives-Based Model for Justice Reinvestment," *Criminology & Public Policy* 10, no. 3 (2011): 585–586.

13. LaVigne et al., *Justice Reinvestment Initiative State Assessment*, 6.

14. Ibid., 13–17.

15. These numbers are compiled from Austin et al., *Ending Mass Incarceration*, 1, n. 1; LaVigne et al., *Justice Reinvestment Initiative State Assessment*, Appendix A; and the JR Web site maintained by the Bureau of Justice Assistance: https://www.bja.gov/programs/justicereinvestment/JR _sites.html.

16. Ross Homel, "Justice Reinvestment as a Global Phenomenon," *Victims and Offenders* 9 (2014): 6–7.

17. LaVigne et al., *Justice Reinvestment Initiative State Assessment*, 3.

18. Ibid., 3–4.

19. Austin et al., *Ending Mass Incarceration*, 1, 3.

20. Ibid., 3.

21. Ronald F. Wright, "Counting the Costs of Sentencing in North Carolina, 1980–2000," *Crime & Justice* 29 (2005): 39.

22. Council of State Governments Justice Center, *Justice Reinvestment in North Carolina: Analysis and Policy Framework to Reduce Spending on Corrections and Reinvest in Strategies to Increase Public Safety* (New York: Council of State Governments Justice Center, 2011).

23. Ibid., 2.

24. Ibid., 1.

25. Ibid., 13–18.

26. Ibid., 5, 19.

27. Ibid., 7.

28. Ibid., 16.

29. Brian Freskos, "N.C. Legislators Look at Overhauling State's Criminal Justice System," *StarNews Online*, April 14, 2011.

30. N.C. Session Law 2011-192, § 7(a).

31. Gary D. Robertson, "Bipartisan NC Justice Overhaul Keeps Good Marks," *Charlotte Observer*, November 16, 2014.

32. Council of State Governments Justice Center, *Justice Reinvestment in North Carolina: Three Years Later* (New York: Council of State Governments Justice Center, 2014).

33. Prisoner totals in this paragraph are derived from the online Corrections Statistical Analysis Tool maintained by the federal Bureau of Justice Statistics.

34. North Carolina Sentencing and Policy Advisory Commission, *Justice Reinvestment Act Implementation Evaluation Report* (Raleigh: North Carolina Sentencing and Policy Advisory Commission, 2015), 37.

35. The Justice Center reported that technical revocations typically resulted in a seven-month stint in prison pre-JR. Council of State Governments Justice Center, *Justice Reinvestment in North Carolina: Analysis and Policy Framework*, 20. To be precise with the terminology, technical violations under the JR law were not handled through "revocation," but through "Confinement in Response to Violation."

36. The effective (not literal) transfer of inmates from prisons to jails occurred primarily through two complementary mechanisms in the new law. First, misdemeanants sentenced to terms of incarceration greater than 90 days were now serving those terms in jails instead of prisons. (Under the JR bill as originally adopted, misdemeanants sentenced to more than 180 days were still sent to prison, but a later amendment rejected this limitation.) Second, probation misdemeanants who committed technical violations faced potential revocation and commitment to prison pre-JR; post-JR, though, these offenders would normally be incarcerated in jail for terms of no more than 90 days through the new Confinement in Response to Violation program. North Carolina Sentencing and Policy Advisory Commission, *Justice Reinvestment Act Implementation Evaluation Report*, 6–7, 14.

37. North Carolina Sentencing and Policy Advisory Commission, *Justice Reinvestment Act Implementation Evaluation Report*, 17–18.

38. M. Claire Donnelly, "The Laws Are A-Changin': A Look into the North Carolina's Statewide Misdemeanant Program," Charlotte School of Law Civil Rights Clinic Blog, March 10, 2015, https://cslcivilrights.com/2015/03/10/the-laws-are-a-changin-a-look-into-the-north-carolinas-statewide-misdemeanant-confinement-program/.

39. Arrests for major violent crimes (homicide, rape, robbery, and aggravated assault) fell each year after 2011, from 19,735 to 16,763 in 2014. The data come from the FBI's annual *Crime in the United States* reports.

40. North Carolina Sentencing and Policy Advisory Commission, *Justice Reinvestment Act Implementation Evaluation Report*, 20.

41. Ibid., 20–21.

42. Robertson, "Bipartisan NC Justice."

43. North Carolina Sentencing and Policy Advisory Commission, *Justice Reinvestment Act Implementation Evaluation Report*, 17.

44. Ibid., 39.

45. North Carolina Sentencing and Policy Advisory Commission, *Justice Reinvestment Act Implementation Evaluation Report*, 21, 33.

46. Ibid., 49.

47. Gary D. Robertson, "NC Lawmakers Look at New Crimes, Tougher Penalties," *Charlotte Observer*, June 22, 2014.

48. This offense is now codified at N.C.G.S.A. § 14-258.1(g).

49. This offense is now codified at N.C.G.S.A. § 95-111.13(j).

50. Except as indicated through other specific citations, the information in this section on JR reforms adopted in other states is drawn from LaVigne et al., *Justice Reinvestment Initiative State Assessment*, Appendix A.

51. Stephanie A. Duriez, Francis T. Cullen, and Sarah M. Manchak, "Is Project HOPE Creating a False Sense of Hope? A Case Study in Correctional Popularity," *Federal Probation* 78 (September 2014): 58.

52. Ibid., 60.

53. These were Arkansas, Kentucky, and South Dakota.

54. Duriez et al., "Project HOPE," 64–65.

55. Mason L. Boling, "That Was the Easy Part: The Development of Arkansas's Public Safety Improvement Act of 2011, and Why the Biggest Obstacle to Prison Reform Remains Intact," *Arkansas Law Review* 66 (2013): 1115–1116.

56. Ibid., 1114–1115.

57. The Sentencing Project, *The State of Sentencing in 2015: Developments in Policy and Practice* (Washington, DC: Sentencing Project, 2016), 9.

58. Pew Center on the States, *South Carolina's Public Safety Reform: Legislation Enacts Research-Based Strategies to Cut Prison Growth and Costs* (Philadelphia: Pew Center on the States, 2010), 6; Yvonne Wenger, "New Law Changes Criminal Sentencing," *Post and Courier*, June 3, 2010, http://www.postandcourier.com/article/20100603/PC1602/306039980.

59. Council of State Governments Justice Center, *Idaho's Justice Reinvestment Approach: Strengthening Probation and Parole, Structuring Parole Decision Making, and Measuring Recidivism-Reduction Efforts* (New York: Council of State Governments Justice Center, 2014), 3.

60. Pew Center on the States, *South Carolina's Public Safety Reform*, 7.

61. Council of State Governments Justice Center, *Idaho's Justice Reinvestment Approach*, 3.

62. Pew Center on the States, *South Carolina's Public Safety Reform*, 8.

63. Donald Gilliland, "Pennsylvania's Attempt at Justice Reinvestment Prison Reform Becomes Law; Savings May Take a While to Meet Estimates," *PennLive*, October 25, 2012.

64. LaVigne et al., *Justice Reinvestment Initiative State Assessment*, 59.

65. These included Delaware, Louisiana, and West Virginia. Ibid., Appendix A.

66. Council of State Governments Justice Center, *Justice Reinvestment in North Carolina: Analysis and Policy Framework*, 19.

67. LaVigne et al., *Justice Reinvestment Initiative State Assessment*, 90.

68. Council of State Governments Justice Center, *Justice Reinvestment in North Carolina: Analysis and Policy Framework*, 19.

69. These numbers were calculated from the Bureau of Justice Statistics online Corrections Statistical Analysis Tool. They reflect year-end jurisdiction-total prison populations.

70. Sonja B. Starr, "The New Profiling: Why Punishing Based on Poverty and Identity Is Unconstitutional and Wrong," *Federal Sentencing Reporter*, 27, no. 4 (2015): 229.

71. Bernard E. Harcourt, "Risk as a Proxy for Race: The Dangers of Risk Assessment," *Federal Sentencing Reporter*, 27, no. 4 (2015): 237.

72. Ibid.

Chapter 5

1. Peter Baker, "Obama, in Oklahoma, Will Focus on Overhaul of Criminal Justice System," *New York Times*, July 16, 2015.

2. Barack Obama, Remarks by the President after Visit at El Reno Federal Correctional Institution, July 16, 2015, https://www.whitehouse .gov/the-press-office/2015/07/16/remarks-president-after-visit-el-reno-federal -correctional-institution.

3. E. Ann Carson, *Prisoners in 2014* (Washington, DC: Bureau of Justice Statistics, 2015), 2.

4. Lawrence M. Friedman, *Crime and Punishment in American History* (New York: Basic Books, 1993), 261–273.

5. Michael O'Hear, *Wisconsin Sentencing in the Tough-on-Crime Era: How Judges Retained Power and Why Mass Incarceration Happened Anyway* (Madison, WI: University of Wisconsin Press, 2016), chapter 7.

6. Hindelang Criminal Justice Research Center, *Sourcebook of Criminal Justice Statistics 2003* (Albany, NY: University at Albany), Table 1.104.

7. Ibid., Table 1.85; *Sourcebook of Criminal Justice Statistics Online* Table 1.79.2010, http://www.albany.edu/sourcebook/pdf/t1792010.pdf.

8. Lynn Bauer, *Justice Expenditure and Employment in the United States, 2001* (Washington, DC: Bureau of Justice Statistics, 2004), 4; Executive Office of the President of the United States, *Budget of the United States Government* (Washington, DC: Government Printing Office, 2000), 2.

9. Michael M. O'Hear, "The Original Intent of Uniformity in Federal Sentencing," *University of Cincinnati Law Review*, 74, no. 3 (2006): 769–777.

10. Kate Stith and José A. Cabranes, *Fear of Judging: Sentencing Guidelines in the Federal Courts* (Chicago: University of Chicago Press, 1998), 58.

11. O'Hear, "Original Intent," 780–784.

12. Stith and Cabranes, *Fear of Judging*, 60–61.

13. Michael M. O'Hear, "Remorse, Cooperation, and 'Acceptance of Responsibility': The Structure, Implementation, and Reform of Section 3E1.1 of the Federal Sentencing Guidelines," *Northwestern University Law Review* 91, no. 4 (1997): 1512–1521, 1534–1539.

14. United States Sentencing Guidelines § 5K1.1.

15. O'Hear, *Wisconsin Sentencing*, Chapter 7.

16. Ted Gest, *Crime and Politics: Big Government's Erratic Campaign for Law and Order* (New York: Oxford University Press, 2001), 120–121.

17. I derive this list from United States Sentencing Commission, *Report to Congress: Mandatory Minimum Penalties in the Federal Criminal Justice System* (Washington, DC: United States Sentencing Commission, 2010), 22–29.

18. Ibid., 32–36.

19. United States Sentencing Commission, *Special Report to the Congress: Cocaine and Federal Sentencing Policy* (Washington, DC: United States Sentencing Commission, 1995), ii–xiv.

20. Ibid., xi.

21. Ibid., xii.

22. United States Sentencing Commission, *Special Report to the Congress*, 1.

23. Marc Mauer, *Race to Incarcerate* (New York: New Press, 2006), 69.

24. Ibid., 152.

25. Ibid., 87–88.

26. The Ashcroft Memorandum of September 22, 2003, is reprinted in the *Federal Sentencing Reporter* 16, no. 2 (2003): 129–133. The Ashcroft Memorandum of July 28, 2003, is reprinted in the *Federal Sentencing Reporter* 15, no. 6 (2003): 375–377.

27. Frank O. Bowman, III, "The Sarbanes-Oxley Act and What Came After," *Federal Sentencing Reporter* 15, no. 4 (2003): 232–233.

28. "Senate Judiciary Committee, Criminal Justice Oversight Subcommittee Hearing on 'Oversight of the United States Sentencing Commission: Are the Guidelines Being Followed?' October 13, 2000," *Federal Sentencing Reporter* 15, no. 5 (2003): 320–322.

29. Various representative statements are reprinted in the *Federal Sentencing Reporter* 5, no. 5 (2003).

30. Alan Vinegrad, "The New Federal Sentencing Law," *Federal Sentencing Reporter* 15, no. 5 (2003): 310.

31. Various representative statements are reprinted in the *Federal Sentencing Reporter* 5, no. 5 (2003). In the interest of full disclosure,

I coauthored the letter from 70 criminal law professors in opposition to the Feeney Amendment.

32. United States Sentencing Commission, *Fifteen Years of Guidelines Sentencing: An Assessment of How Well the Federal Criminal Justice System Is Achieving the Goals of Sentencing Reform* (Washington, DC: United States Sentencing Commission, 2004), vi.

33. Ibid.

34. Ibid.

35. Ibid.

36. Ibid., 52–53.

37. Ibid., xiv.

38. Ibid.

39. Ibid., xv.

40. The data reflect year-end jurisdiction populations, as reported through the Bureau of Justice Statistics' online Corrections Statistical Analysis Tool, http://www.bjs.gov/index.cfm?ty=nps.

41. The data come from the Bureau of Justice Statistics' online tool, Federal Criminal Case Processing Statistics, http://www.bjs.gov/fjsrc/var .cfm?ttype=one_variable&agency=BOP&db_type=Prisoners&saf=STK.

42. Paige M. Harrison and Allen J. Beck, *Prisoners in 2005* (Washington, DC: Bureau of Justice Statistics, 2006), 9, http://www.bjs.gov/content/pub/ pdf/p05.pdf.

43. United States Sentencing Commission, *Fifteen Years of Guidelines Sentencing*, 99.

44. Ibid., 101–102.

45. Ibid., xii.

46. Ibid., 131.

47. Ibid., 132.

48. Erik Luna and Barton Poulson, "Restorative Justice in Federal Sentencing: An Unexpected Benefit of *Booker*?," *McGeorge Law Review* 37, no. 4 (2006): 787.

49. Dan Eggen, "Ashcroft Defends Tough Policies: Attorney General Says 'Expansions of Freedom' Halted Terrorists," *Washington Post*, February 2, 2005, A2, http://www.washingtonpost.com/wp-dyn/articles/ A55388-2005Feb1.html.

50. Amy Baron-Evans and Anne E. Blanchard, "The Occasion to Overrule *Harris*," *Federal Sentencing Reporter* 18, no. 4 (2006): 255.

51. Alliance for Justice, *The State of the Judiciary: Judicial Selection During the 113th Congress* (Washington, DC: Alliance for Justice, 2014), 11, http://www.afj.org/wp-content/uploads/2014/06/AFJ-State-of-the -Judiciary-Report-June-2014.pdf.

52. Mauer, *Race to Incarcerate*, 85.

53. Michael M. O'Hear, "The Second Chance Act and the Future of Reentry Reform," *Federal Sentencing Reporter* 20, no. 2 (2007): 75–76.

54. Bush pled guilty to a driving under the influence charge in 1976. Laurie Kellman, "Bush Once Pleaded Guilty to DUI," *Washington Post*, November 3, 2000.

55. Beth A. Colgan, "The Presidential Politics of Prisoner Reentry Reform," *Federal Sentencing Reporter* 20, no. 2 (2007): 110–113.

56. United States Sentencing Commission, *Report on the Continuing Impact of* United States v. Booker *on Federal Sentencing* (Washington, DC: United States Sentencing Commission, 2012), Part C, 19.

57. Nancy Gertner, "Judicial Discretion in Federal Sentencing—Real or Imagined?," *Federal Sentencing Reporter* 28, no. 3 (2016): 166.

58. Jason Hernandez, "Presumptions for Guidelines Sentences after *Booker*, *Federal Sentencing Reporter* 18, no. 4 (2006): 252.

59. Michael M. O'Hear, "Explaining Sentences," *Florida State Law Review* 36, no. 3 (2009): 463.

60. Ibid., 474.

61. Kimbrough v. United States, 552 U.S. 85, n. 4 (2007).

62. Marvin Frankel, *Criminal Sentences: Law without Order* (New York: Hill and Wang, 1973).

63. Hernandez, "Presumptions for Guidelines Sentences," 253.

64. 552 U.S. 85 (2007).

65. 552 U.S. 38 (2007).

66. Robert Pratt, "The Discretion to Sentence," *Federal Sentencing Reporter* 28, no. 3 (2016): 162.

67. United States Sentencing Commission, *Report on the Continuing Impact of* United States v. Booker, Part B, 38.

68. Ibid., Part C, 19.

69. Gertner, "Judicial Discretion in Federal Sentencing," 165.

70. United States Sentencing Commission, *2007 Sourcebook of Federal Sentencing Statistics* (Washington, DC: United States Sentencing Commission, 2008), Table 37.

71. Ibid., Tables 39, 40.

72. Douglas A. Berman, "The Varied Challenges of Undoing Past Sentencing Injustices," *Federal Sentencing Reporter* 20, no. 4 (2008): 223.

73. David Yellen, "The Sentencing Commission Takes on Crack, Again," *Federal Sentencing Reporter* 20, no. 4 (2008): 227.

74. Berman, "Varied Challenges of Undoing Past Sentencing Injustices," 224.

75. "Statement of Gretchen C. F. Shappert before the United States House of Representatives Committee on the Judiciary Subcommittee on Crime, Terrorism, and Homeland Security," *Federal Sentencing Reporter* 20, no. 4 (2008): 255–256.

76. Berman, "Varied Challenges of Undoing Past Sentencing Injustices," 224–225.

77. United States Sentencing Commission, *Preliminary Crack Cocaine Retroactivity Data Report* (Washington, DC: United States Sentencing Commission, 2011), Table 1.

78. Ibid., Table 5.

79. Ibid., Table 8.

80. United States Sentencing Commission, *Recidivism among Offenders Receiving Retroactive Sentence Reductions: The 2007 Crack Cocaine Amendment* (Washington, DC: United States Sentencing Commission, 2014), 3.

81. United States Sentencing Commission, *2007 Sourcebook*, Table 43.

82. Frank O. Bowman, III, "The Sounds of Silence: American Criminal Justice Policy in Election Year 2008," *Federal Sentencing Reporter* 20, no. 5 (2008): 289.

83. Remarks of Senator Barack Obama: Howard University Convocation, Washington, DC, September 28, 2007, http://www.procon.org/sourcefiles/Obama20070928.pdf.

84. Ibid.

85. Ibid.

86. Douglas A. Berman, "The Many (Opaque) Echoes of Compromise Crack Sentencing Reform," *Federal Sentencing Reporter* 23, no. 3 (2011): 167.

87. Statement of Lanny A. Breuer, Assistant Attorney General, Criminal Division, United States Department of Justice, Before the United States Senate Committee on the Judiciary Subcommittee on Crime and Drugs Hearing Entitled "Restoring Fairness to Federal Sentencing: Addressing the Crack-Powder Disparity," April 29, 2009, https://www.justice.gov/sites/default/files/testimonies/witnesses/attachments/2009/04/29/2009-04-29-crm-breuer-crack-powder.pdf.

88. The text of the Fair Sentencing Act is reproduced in the *Federal Sentencing Reporter* 23, no. 3 (2011): 171–174.

89. "Floor Statement of Rep. Lamar Smith (R-Tex.) on the Fair Sentencing Act of 2010, July 28, 2010," *Federal Sentencing Reporter* 23, no. 2 (2010): 108–109.

90. Ibid., 109.

91. Ibid.

92. Remarks of Senator Barack Obama: Howard University Convocation.

93. Holder's early life is described in Javier C. Hernandez, "Holder, High Achiever Poised to Scale New Heights," *New York Times*, November 30, 2008.

94. Helene Cooper, "Attorney General Chided for Language on Race," *New York Times*, March 7, 2009, A26.

95. Eric Holder, "Remarks at the Annual Meeting of American Bar Association's House of Delegates," *Federal Sentencing Reporter* 26, no. 2 (2013): 75.

96. Ibid.

97. Eric Holder, "Memorandum on Charging Mandatory Minimum Sentences and Recidivist Enhancements in Certain Drug Cases," *Federal Sentencing Reporter* 26, no. 2 (2013): 80.

98. Paul J. Hofer, "Impact Estimates of DOJ Policy Changes and Proposed Legislation Regarding Mandatory Minimums," *Federal Sentencing Reporter* 26, no. 2 (2013): 89.

99. Ibid., 88.

100. Matt Apuzzo, "Holder Endorses Proposal to Reduce Drug Sentences in Latest Sign of Shift," *New York Times*, March 13, 2014, A18.

101. United States Sentencing Commission, *2014 Drug Guidelines Amendment Retroactivity Data Report* (Washington, DC: United States Sentencing Commission, 2016), Table 1.

102. Ibid., Table 7.

103. Margaret Colgate Love, "Reinventing the President's Pardon Power," *Federal Sentencing Reporter* 20, no. 1 (2007): 5–8.

104. Ibid., 5.

105. Mark Osler and Matthew Fass, "The Ford Approach and Real Fairness for Crack Convicts," *Federal Sentencing Reporter* 23, no. 3 (2011): 228.

106. National Association of Criminal Defense Lawyers, News Release: Clemency Project 2014 Surpasses 1,000 Submitted Clemency Petitions, May 16, 2016.

107. Gregory Korte, "Former Administration Pardon Attorney Suggests Broken System in Resignation Letter," *USA Today*, March 28, 2016.

108. S. 1410 (113th Congress).

109. Dick Durbin, Press Release: Durbin and Lee Introduce Smarter Sentencing Act, August 1, 2013.

110. Letter from Chuck Grassley, John Cornyn, and Jeff Sessions, May 12, 2013.

111. Ryan J. Reilly, "Drug Warriors Reject Obama Administration's Call for Softer Sentences," *HuffPost Politics*, February 6, 2014.

112. The letter is quoted in Bill Otis, "Hundreds of Career Prosecutors Revolt against Holder," *Crime and Consequences Blog*, January 30, 2014.

113. Carl Hulse, "Unlikely Cause Unites the Left and the Right: Justice Reform," *New York Times*, February 18, 2015, A1.

114. Lauren Fox, "Chuck Grassley's Closer Than Ever to Giving in on Mandatory-Minimum Reform," *The Atlantic*, July 28, 2015.

115. S. 2123 (114th Congress).

116. Carl Hulse and Jennifer Steinhauer, "Sentencing Overhaul Proposed in Senate with Bipartisan Backing," *New York Times*, October 1, 2015, A1.

117. Lance J. Rogers, "Sentencing Reform Bill Clears Committee," *Bloomberg BNA Criminal Law Reporter*, 98 CrL 94, October 28, 2015.

118. Carl Hulse, "Mitch McConnell Demurs on Prospects of Criminal Justice Overhaul," *New York Times*, December 11, 2015.

119. Ashley Parker, "Donald Trump Tells N.R.A. Hillary Clinton Wants to Let Violent Criminals Go Free," *New York Times*, May 20, 2016, A1.

120. Nick Gass, "Sen. Tom Cotton: U.S. Has 'Under-Incarceration' Problem," *POLITICO*, May 19, 2016, http://www.politico.com/story/2016/05/tom-cotton-under-incarceration-223371.

121. Biller Keller and Tim Golden, "Eric Holder on His Legacy, His Regrets, and His Feelings about the Death Penalty," themarshallproject.org, November 17, 2014.

122. The 2008 figures come from the Bureau of Justice Statistics online tool, Federal Criminal Case Processing Statistics, http://www.bjs.gov/fjsrc/var.cfm?ttype=one_variable&agency=BOP&db_type=Prisoners&saf=STK. The 2016 figures come from the Bureau of Prisons Web site, https://www.bop.gov/about/statistics/statistics_inmate_age.jsp, reflecting data as of April 23, 2016. The weapons category includes explosives and arson offenses. The fraud category includes extortion and bribery. The 2008 fraud category includes racketeering, but it is not clear whether the 2016 figure does. The 2008 sex category comprises sexual abuse, nonviolent sex offenses, and mail/transport of obscene materials.

123. United States Sentencing Commission, *2015 Sourcebook of Federal Sentencing Statistics* (Washington, DC: United States Sentencing Commission, 2016), Table 13.

124. "Race, Violence ... Justice? Looking Back at Jena 6," National Public Radio, August 30, 2011, http://www.npr.org/2011/08/30/140058680/race-violence-justice-looking-back-at-jena-6.

Chapter 6

1. I exclude from this chapter a line of Eighth Amendment cases that deal with the conditions of confinement. That aspect of Eighth Amendment law is touched on in the next chapter.

2. This passivity by the Supreme Court resulted in part from the understanding that the Eighth Amendment applied only to the federal government and did not limit state penal practices. This understanding changed in 1962 with the Court's decision in *Robinson v. California*, discussed later.

3. Trop v. Dulles, 356 U.S. 86, 100-01 (1958) (plurality).

4. 370 U.S. 660, 667 (1962).

5. For instance, to note just one example, the Fifth Amendment declared, "No person shall ... be *deprived of life*, liberty, or property, without due process of law."

6. Evan J. Mandery, *A Wild Justice: The Death and Resurrection of Capital Punishment in America* 63 (New York: W. W. Norton & Co., 2013).

7. Ibid., 64.

8. Ibid., 257–258.

9. Ibid., 257.

10. Ibid., 247.
11. Ibid., 248–249.
12. Ibid., 253.
13. Ibid., 258.
14. Ibid., 236.
15. Ibid.
16. Ibid., 401.
17. Ibid.
18. Ibid., 403.
19. Ibid., 404.
20. 433 U.S. 584, 594, 595–596 (1977) (plurality).
21. 458 U.S. 782, 789–795 (1982).
22. 477 U.S. 399, 408 (1986).
23. 487 U.S. 815, 849 (1988) (O'Connor, J., concurring).
24. Ibid., 852.
25. Ibid., 858–859.
26. Mandery, *A Wild Justice*, 265.
27. Tracy L. Snell, *Capital Punishment, 2013—Statistical Tables* (Washington, DC: Department of Justice, 2014).
28. Jeffrey M. Jones, "U.S. Death Penalty Support Lowest in More Than 40 Years," *Gallup*, October 29, 2013, http://www.deathpenaltyinfo.org/documents/gallup-10-29-13.pdf.
29. Death Penalty Information Center, *Death Sentences by Year since 1976*, http://www.deathpenaltyinfo.org/death-sentences-year-1977-2009; Death Penalty Information Center, *Number of Executions since 1976*, http://www.deathpenaltyinfo.org/executions-year.
30. Linda E. Carter, Ellen S. Kreitzberg, and Scott Howe, *Understanding Capital Punishment Law*, 3rd ed. (New Providence, NJ: Matthew Bender, 2012).
31. Roper v. Simmons, 543 U.S. 551, 565 (2004).
32. Atkins v. Virginia, 536 U.S. 304, 342, 347 (2003) (Scalia, J., dissenting).
33. *Roper*, 543 U.S. at 609, 615 (Scalia, J., dissenting).
34. Kennedy v. Louisiana, 554 U.S. 407, 448 (2008) (Alito, J., dissenting).
35. Callins v. Collins, 510 U.S. 1141 (1994) (Blackmun, J., dissenting).
36. Mandery, *A Wild Justice*, 439–440.
37. Ibid., 438.
38. Williams v. Taylor, 529 U.S. 362, 395–96 (2000).
39. Anthony M. Kennedy, Speech at the American Bar Association Annual Meeting, August 9, 2003, http://www.supremecourt.gov/publicinfo/speeches/sp_08-09-03.html.
40. *Roper*, 543 U.S. at 568 (internal quotation marks and citation omitted).
41. Solem v. Helm, 463 U.S. 277, 283 (1983).
42. Ibid., 303.

43. Harmelin v. Michigan, 501 U.S. 957, 1001 (1991) (Kennedy, J., concurring in part and concurring in the judgment) (emphasis added, internal quotation marks and citations omitted).

44. Ibid., 1002.

45. Ibid., 1004.

46. Ibid., 1005.

47. Ewing v. California, 538 U.S. 11, 18 (2003) (plurality).

48. Ibid., 30.

49. Kennedy, Speech at the American Bar Association Annual Meeting.

50. David Mills and Michael Romano, "The Passage and Implementation of the Three Strikes Reform Act of 2012 (Proposition 36)," *Federal Sentencing Reporter* 25: 265 (2013).

51. Death Penalty Information Center, *Size of Death Row by Year*, http://www.deathpenaltyinfo.org/death-row-inmates-state-and-size-death-row-year#year.

52. Graham v. Florida, 130 S. Ct. 2011, 2018 (2010).

53. Ibid., 2023.

54. Ibid., 2024.

55. Ibid., 2051.

56. Ibid., 2030, 2032–2033.

57. Miller v. Alabama, 132 S. Ct. 2455, 2477 (Roberts, C.J., dissenting).

58. Not until 12 years after *Atkins*, in *Hall v. Florida*, did the Court begin to impose restraints on how states defined what the Court now referred to as "intellectual disability."

59. 337 U.S. 241, 244 (1949).

60. Ibid., 249–250.

61. McMillan v. Pennsylvania, 477 U.S. 79, 85 (1986).

62. Almendarez-Torres v. United States, 523 U.S. 224, 227 (1998).

63. Apprendi v. New Jersey, 530 U.S. 466, 468–469 (2000).

64. Ibid., 518, 520.

65. Harris v. United States, 536 U.S. 545, 570–71 (2002) (Breyer, J., concurring).

66. Kennedy did not write in *Apprendi*, but joined Justice O'Connor's dissent, which emphasized the potential impact of the majority opinion on state and federal sentencing guidelines. *Apprendi*, 530 U.S. at 550–551 (O'Connor, J., dissenting).

67. Kennedy, Speech at the American Bar Association Annual Meeting.

Chapter 7

1. These figures come from the online prisoner data tool of the U.S. Bureau of Justice Statistics, available at http://www.bjs.gov/index.cfm?ty=nps. The numbers are year-end jurisdiction totals, which include state prisoners held under contract in institutions not operated by the state, but

which do not include jail inmates under county jurisdiction. As we will see later in this chapter, these distinctions are important to the California story.

2. "Violent crime rate" refers to reported incidents of violent "index" crimes (nonnegligent homicide, rape, robbery, and aggravated assault), per 100,000 state residents. Data through 2012 come from the FBI's online tool, http://www.ucrdatatool.gov/index.cfm. Figures for 2013 and 2014 come from the FBI's annual *Crime in the United States* reports, which are available at https://ucr.fbi.gov/ucr-publications.

3. E. Ann Carson, *Prisoners in 2014* (Washington, DC: Bureau of Justice Statistics, 2015), 12.

4. Ibid., 8; Jonathan Simon, *Mass Incarceration on Trial: A Remarkable Court Decision and the Future of Prisons in America* (New York: New Press, 2012), 19.

5. Simon, *Mass Incarceration on Trial*, 18.

6. Vanessa Barker, *The Politics of Imprisonment: How the Democratic Process Shapes the Way America Punishes Offenders* (New York: Oxford University Press, 2009), 58.

7. Ibid., 67.

8. Ibid., 68–69.

9. Michael Vitiello et al., "A Proposal for a Wholesale Reform of California's Sentencing Practice and Policy," *Loyola of Los Angeles Law Review* 38, no. 2 (2004): 920.

10. Ibid., 921.

11. Allen Hopper, James Austin, and Jolene Forman, "Shifting the Paradigm or Shifting the Problem? The Politics of California's Criminal Justice Realignment," *Santa Clara Law Review* 54 (2014): 542.

12. Franklin E. Zimring, Gordon Hawkins, and Sam Kamin, *Punishment and Democracy: Three Strikes and You Are Out in California* (New York: Oxford University Press, 2001), 4.

13. Maura Dolan, "Ex-Chief Justice Rose Bird Dies of Cancer at 63," *Los Angeles Times*, December 5, 1999, http://articles.latimes.com/1999/dec/05/news/mn-40743.

14. W. David Ball, "Normative Elements of Parole Risk," *Stanford Law and Policy Review* 22, no. 2 (2011): 395–396.

15. Simon, *Mass Incarceration on Trial*, 19–20.

16. Ibid., 19.

17. Ibid.

18. Hopper, Austin, and Forman, "Shifting the Paradigm," 540, citing government analysts, quoted in Cary J. Rudman and John Berthelsen, *An Analysis of the California Department of Corrections' Planning Process: Strategies to Reduce the Costs of Incarceration State Prisoners* (1991).

19. Ibid.

20. Michael Vitiello, "Reforming California Sentencing Practice and Policy: Are We There Yet?" *McGeorge Law Review* 46 (2014): 695.

21. Paige M. Harrison and Allen J. Beck, *Prisoners in 2005* (Washington, DC: Bureau of Justice Statistics, 2006), 7.

22. Coleman v. Wilson, 912 F. Supp. 1282, 1316 (E.D. Cal.).

23. Ibid., 1306, 1308.

24. Ibid., 1315, 1316.

25. 131 S. Ct. 1910, 1926 (2011).

26. Ibid., 1926–1927.

27. Ibid., 1927.

28. Joshua Page, *The Toughest Beat: Politics, Punishment, and the Prison Officers Union in California* (New York: Oxford University Press, 2011), 133.

29. Ibid., 130.

30. Ibid., 131.

31. Ibid., 121, 132–133.

32. Ibid., 127.

33. Ibid., 130.

34. Little Hoover Commission, *Solving California's Corrections Crisis: Time Is Running Out* (Sacramento, CA: Little Hoover Commission, 2007). The quotation comes from the cover letter accompanying the report, dated January 25, 2007.

35. Ibid., i–ii.

36. Michele Deitch, "The Need for Independent Prison Oversight in a Post-PLRA World," *Federal Sentencing Reporter* 24, no. 4 (2012): 237.

37. Mark Tushnet and Larry Yackle, "Symbolic Statutes and Real Laws: The Pathologies of the Antiterrorism and Effective Death Penalty Act and the Prison Litigation Reform Act," *Duke Law Journal* 47, no. 1 (1997); David C. Fathi, "The Prison Litigation Reform Act: A Threat to Civil Rights," *Federal Sentencing Reporter* 24, no. 4 (2012).

38. Brown v. Plata, 131 S. Ct. 1910, 1929 (2011).

39. Little Hoover Commission, *Solving California's Corrections Crisis*, 1; Donald Specter, "Everything Revolves Around Overcrowding: The State of California's Prisons," *Federal Sentencing Reporter* 22, no. 3 (2010): 195.

40. Barker, *Politics of Imprisonment*, 80.

41. Hopper, Austin, and Forman, "Shifting the Paradigm," 550–551.

42. Page, *Toughest Beat*, 128–129.

43. *Brown*, 131 S. Ct. at 1928.

44. Ibid., 1946.

45. Ibid., 1928, 1947.

46. Ibid., 1937.

47. Ibid., 1942 (quoting former warden and acting secretary of California prison system).

48. Simon, *Mass Incarceration on Trial*, 146.

49. *Brown*, 131 S. Ct. at 1924.

50. Simon, *Mass Incarceration on Trial*, 146.

51. Hadar Aviram, "The Correctional Hunger Games: Understanding Realignment in the Context of the Great Recession," *Annals of the American Academy of Political and Social Science* 664 (2016): 263.

52. Roger K. Warren, "Probation Reform in California: Senate Bill 678," *Federal Sentencing Reporter* 22, no. 3 (2010): 187.

53. Ibid., 187–188.

54. Joan Petersilia, "A Retrospective View of Corrections Reform in the Schwarzenegger Administration," *Federal Sentencing Reporter* 22, no. 3 (2010): 152.

55. Ibid., 150–151.

56. Ibid., 151.

57. Ibid.

58. Ibid.

59. Aviram, "Correctional Hunger Games," 266.

60. Kathryn Jett and Joan Hancock, "Realignment in the Counties," *Federal Sentencing Reporter* 25, no. 4 (2013): 236.

61. Hopper, Austin, and Forman, "Shifting the Paradigm," 555–558.

62. Aaron J. Rappaport, "Realigning California Corrections," *Federal Sentencing Reporter* 25, no. 4 (2013): 211, quoting Franklin Zimring and Gordon Hawkins, *The Scale of Imprisonment* (Chicago: University of Chicago Press, 1991), 211.

63. Ibid., 210. The North Carolina story was included in Chapter 4.

64. Little Hoover Commission, *Solving California's Corrections Crisis*, ii.

65. Rappaport, "Realigning California Corrections," 210.

66. Ibid., 214; Hopper, Austin, and Forman, "Shifting the Paradigm," 581.

67. Magnus Lofstrom and Steven Raphael, "Incarceration and Crime: Evidence from California's Public Safety Realignment Reform," *Annals of the American Academy of Political and Social Science* 664 (2016): 196. Specifically, the Lofstrom-Raphael study found a link between realignment and motor vehicle theft. Another study by the Center on Juvenile and Criminal Justice, making different assumptions, found no causal link between realignment and changes in the rate of motor vehicle theft. Little Hoover Commission, *Sensible Sentencing for a Safer California* (Sacramento: Little Hoover Commission, 2014), 16.

68. Wendy S. Still, "San Francisco Realignment: Raising the Bar for Criminal Justice in California," *Federal Sentencing Reporter* 25, no. 4 (2013): 249.

69. Ibid., 251.

70. Rappaport, "Realigning California Corrections," 211.

71. Leroy D. Baca and Gerald K. Cooper, "Can AB 109 Work in Los Angeles County?" *Federal Sentencing Reporter* 25, no. 4 (2013): 241.

72. Mia Bird and Ryken Grattet, "Realignment and Recidivism," *Annals of the American Academy of Political and Social Science* 664 (2016): 176.

73. Hopper, Austin, and Forman, "Shifting the Paradigm," 582–583.

74. Ibid., 585–586.

75. Ibid., 587–589.

76. California Department of Corrections and Rehabilitation, *An Update to the Future of California Corrections* (Sacramento: California Department of Corrections and Rehabilitation, 2016), 8.

77. "California's Prison Population Is Finally Down, But Will It Last?" Reuters, January 29, 2015.

78. David Mills and Michael Romano, "The Passage and Implementation of the Three Strikes Reform Act of 2012 (Proposition 36)," *Federal Sentencing Reporter* 25, no. 4 (2013): 266.

79. Ibid.

80. Ibid.

81. Ibid., 267.

82. Ibid.

83. Steve Cooley, "Proposition 36: A Brief History," *Federal Sentencing Reporter* 25, no. 4 (2013): 264.

84. The language is reproduced from the arguments for Proposition 36 contained in the official voter guide for November 2012, which is available at http://vig.cdn.sos.ca.gov/2012/general/pdf/36-arg-rebuttals.pdf.

85. Mills and Romano, "Passage and Implementation of the Three Strikes Reform Act," 267.

86. Erik Eckholm, "California Convicts Are Out of Prison after Third Strike, and Staying Out," *New York Times*, February 26, 2015.

87. The arguments for Proposition 47 contained in the official voter guide are available at http://web.archive.org/web/20141010001739/http://www.voterguide.sos.ca.gov/en/propositions/47/arguments-rebuttals.htm.

88. Ibid.

89. California Department of Corrections and Rehabilitation, *An Update to the Future of California Corrections*, 29.

90. Cindy Chang, Marisa Gerber, and Ben Poston, "Unintended Consequences of Prop. 47 Pose Challenge for Criminal Justice System," *Los Angeles Times*, November 6, 2015, http://www.latimes.com/local/crime/la-me-prop47-anniversary-20151106-story.html.

91. MyProp47, *About Proposition 47*, http://myprop47.org/about/ (accessed July 24, 2016).

92. California Proposition 36, Changes in the "Three Strikes" Law, *Ballotpedia: The Encyclopedia of American Politics*, https://ballotpedia.org/California_Proposition_36,_Changes_in_the_%22Three_Strikes%22_Law_(2012).

93. California Proposition 47, Reduced Penalties for Some Crimes Initiative, *Ballotpedia: The Encyclopedia of American Politics*, https://

ballotpedia.org/California_Proposition_47,_Reduced_Penalties_for_Some
_Crimes_Initiative_(2014).

94. Page, *Toughest Beat*, 194–204; Vitiello, "Reforming California Sentencing Practice and Policy," 721–722.

95. Carson, *Prisoners in 2014*, 12. To be more specific, five states exceeded their design capacity by an even greater extent than California's 136.6 percent. Two additional states were above the 130 percent level. Seventeen states did not report design capacity to the Bureau of Justice Statistics, so there may be even more states that were near or above California's overcrowding level.

96. California Department of Corrections and Rehabilitation, *An Update to the Future of California Corrections*, 27.

97. Hopper, Austin, and Forman, "Shifting the Paradigm," 613–614.

98. Vitiello, "Reforming California Sentencing Practice and Policy," 709–711.

99. Ibid., 714–715.

100. These are the two-strikes sentence enhancement and the treatment of simple burglary as a serious felony.

101. California Proposition 34, The End the Death Penalty Initiative, *Ballotpedia: The Encyclopedia of American Politics*, https://ballotpedia.org/California_Proposition_34,_the_End_the_Death_Penalty_Initiative_(2012).

102. California Proposition 62, Repeal of the Death Penalty, *Ballotpedia: The Encyclopedia of American Politics*, https://ballotpedia.org/California_Proposition_62,_Repeal_of_the_Death_Penalty_(2016).

103. Hopper, Austin, and Forman, "Shifting the Paradigm," 566–572.

104. Bird and Grattet, "Realignment and Recidivism," 190.

105. Wendy S. Still, "A Practitioner's Perspective on Realignment: A Giant Win in San Francisco," *Annals of the American Academy of Political and Social Science* 664 (2016): 227.

106. Keith Wattley, "Insight into California's Life Sentences," *Federal Sentencing Reporter* 25, no. 4 (2013): 271–272.

107. Ibid., 272.

108. Chapter 312, Statutes of 2013 (SB 260).

109. Chapter 471, Statutes of 2015 (SB 261).

110. Rob Kuznia, "An Unprecedented Experiment in Mass Forgiveness," *Washington Post*, February 8, 2016, https://www.washingtonpost.com/national/an-unprecedented-experiment-in-mass-forgiveness/2016/02/08/45899f9c-a059-11e5-a3c5-c77f2cc5a43c_story.html.

111. Ibid.

112. California Parole and Juvenile Trial Opportunity Modification Initiative, Proposition 57, *Ballotpedia: The Encyclopedia of American Politics*, https://ballotpedia.org/California_Parole_and_Juvenile_Trial_Opportunity_Modification_Initiative,_Proposition_57_(2016)#cite_note-Supreme-2.

Chapter 8

1. Michael M. O'Hear, "The New Politics of Sentencing," *Federal Sentencing Reporter* 15, no. 1 (2002): 3.

2. E. Ann Carson, *Prisoners in 2014* (Washington, DC: U.S. Department of Justice, Bureau of Justice Statistics, 2015), 16.

3. David Mills and Michael Romano, "The Passage and Implementation of the Three Strikes Reform Act of 2012 (Proposition 36)," *Federal Sentencing Reporter* 25, no. 4 (2013): 267.

4. Mark D. Ramirez, "Punitive Sentiment," *Criminology* 51, no. 2 (2013): 337, 341.

5. *An Overview of Public Opinion and Discourse on Criminal Justice Issues* (New York: Opportunity Agenda, 2014), 20.

6. Ibid., 11.

7. Michael O'Hear, *Wisconsin Sentencing in the Tough-on-Crime Era: How Judges Retained Power and Why Mass Incarceration Happened Anyway* (Madison, WI: University of Wisconsin Press, 2017), Chapter 8.

8. Michael M. O'Hear and Darren Wheelock, "Public Attitudes toward Punishment, Rehabilitation, and Reform: Lessons from the Marquette Law School Poll," *Federal Sentencing Reporter* 29, no. 1 (2016).

9. O'Hear, *Wisconsin Sentencing*, Chapters 4, 8.

10. Probation numbers come from the online correctional statistics analysis tool of the U.S. Bureau of Justice Statistics: http://www.bjs.gov/probation/.

11. Christina Carmichael, *Juvenile Justice and Youth Aids Program* (Madison, WI: Wisconsin Legislative Fiscal Bureau, 2015), 27.

12. Ibid., 45; Art Zimmerman, *Juvenile Justice and Youth Aids Program* (Madison, WI: Wisconsin Legislative Fiscal Bureau, 2003), 44.

13. Avlana K. Eisenberg, "Incarceration Incentives in the Decarceration Era," *Vanderbilt Law Review* 69, no. 1 (2016): 119–139.

14. O'Hear, *Wisconsin Sentencing*, Chapter 8.

15. Kevin O'Leary, "How California's Fiscal Woes Began: A Crisis 30 Years in the Making," *Time*, July 1, 2009, http://content.time.com/time/nation/article/0,8599,1907504,00.html?iid=tsmodule.

16. Ramirez, "Punitive Sentiment," 337; Peter K. Enns, "The Public's Increasing Punitiveness and Its Influence on Mass Incarceration in the United States," *American Journal of Political Science* 58, no. 4 (2014): 862.

17. James D. Unnever and Francis T. Cullen, "The Social Sources of Americans' Punitiveness: A Test of Three Competing Models," *Criminology* 48, no. 1 (2010): 104, 114.

18. National Center for Health Statistics, *Health, United States, 2015* (Hyattsville, Maryland: U.S. Department of Health and Human Services, 2015), 99.

19. Jennifer L. Truman and Lynn Langton, *Criminal Victimization, 2014* (Washington, DC: U.S. Department of Justice, Bureau of Justice Statistics, 2015), 2. This figure is based on the National Crime Victimization Survey and includes both reported crime and crime that was not reported to the police. "Serious violent crime" encompasses rape, robbery, and aggravated assault.

20. National Center for Health Statistics, *Health, United States, 2015*, 166, 170, 200.

21. *An Overview of Public Opinion and Discourse on Criminal Justice Issues*, 12.

22. Marc Mauer, *Race to Incarcerate* (New York: New Press, 2006), 189–190.

23. *An Overview of Public Opinion and Discourse on Criminal Justice Issues*, 18.

24. Julian V. Roberts, Loretta J. Stalans, David Indermaur, and Mike Hough, *Penal Populism and Public Opinion: Lessons from Five Countries* (New York: Oxford University Press, 2003), 175–176.

25. Joshua Rovner, *Declines in Youth Commitments and Facilities in the 21st Century* (Washington, DC: Sentencing Project, 2015).

26. Vincent Schiraldi, Bruce Western, and Kendra Bradner, *Community-Based Responses to Justice-Involved Young Adults* (Washington, DC: U.S. Department of Justice, National Institute of Justice, 2015).

27. Mark R. Fondacaro and Megan J. O'Toole, "American Punitiveness and Mass Incarceration: Psychological Perspectives on Retributive and Consequentialist Responses to Crime," *New Criminal Law Review* 18, no. 4 (2015): 500.

28. Matthew R. Durose, Alexia D. Cooper, and Howard N. Snyder, *Recidivism of Prisoners Released in 30 States in 2005: Patterns from 2005 to 2010* (Washington, DC: Department of Justice, Bureau of Justice Statistics, 2014).

29. Unnever and Cullen, "Social Sources of Americans' Punitiveness," 117.

30. Nazgol Ghandoosh, *Race and Punishment: Racial Perceptions of Crime and Support for Punitive Policies* (Washington, DC: The Sentencing Project, 2014), 13–17.

31. Unnever and Cullen, "Social Sources of Americans' Punitiveness," 106.

32. Hadar Aviram, *Cheap on Crime: Recession-Era Politics and the Transformation of American Punishment* (Oakland, CA: University of California Press, 2015), 156–157.

33. Ibid., 156 (quoting David Greenberg).

34. Fondacaro and O'Toole, "American Punitiveness and Mass Incarceration," 483.

35. Jon Mooallem, "You Just Got Out of Prison. Now What?" *New York Times Magazine*, July 16, 2015.

36. Carolyn Côté-Lussier, "The Functional Relation between Social Inequality, Criminal Stereotypes, and Public Attitudes toward Punishment of Crime," *Psychology, Public Policy, and Law* 22, no. 1 (2016): 52.

37. Saneta deVuono-powell, Chris Schweidler, Alicia Walters, and Azadeh Zohrabi, *Who Pays? The True Cost of Incarceration on Families* (Oakland, CA: Ella Baker Center, Forward Together, Research Action Design, 2015), 7–8.

38. Christopher Uggen and Suzy McElrath, "Parental Incarceration: What We Know and Where We Need to Go," *Journal of Criminal Law and Criminology* 104, no. 3 (2014): 599.

39. Committee on Causes and Consequences of High Rates of Incarceration, *The Growth of Incarceration in the United States: Exploring Causes and Consequences* (Washington, DC: National Academies Press, 2014), 279.

40. Uggen and McElrath, "Parental Incarceration," 600.

41. Bettina Muenster and Jennifer Trone, "Why Is America so Punitive? A Report on the Deliberations of the Interdisciplinary Roundtable on Punitiveness in America," *Federal Sentencing Reporter* 28, no. 5 (2016): 346.

42. David A. Green, "Penal Optimism and Second Chances: The Legacies of American Protestantism and the Prospect for Penal Reform," *Punishment & Society* 15, no. 2 (2013): 125.

43. Ibid.

44. *An Overview of Public Opinion and Discourse on Criminal Justice Issues*, 71.

45. *Felon Disenfranchisement: A Primer* (Washington, DC: Sentencing Project, 2016).

46. Sheryl Gay Stolberg, "Virginia Governor Restores Voting Rights to Felons," *New York Times*, April 22, 2016.

47. Alison Shames and Ram Subramanian, "Doing the Right Thing: The Evolving Role of Human Dignity in American Sentencing and Corrections," *Federal Sentencing Reporter* 27, no. 1 (2014): 13.

Index

About the Author

MICHAEL O'HEAR is a professor of law at Marquette University. He is an editor of the journal *Federal Sentencing Reporter* and has published dozens of articles on sentencing law, criminal procedure, and public opinion about the criminal justice system. He is also the author of *Wisconsin Sentencing in the Tough-on-Crime Era: How Judges Retained Discretion and Why Mass Incarceration Happened Anyway* (University of Wisconsin Press).